Design Standards
for Children's Environments

Linda Cain Ruth, AIA

McGraw-Hill

New York San Francisco Washington, D.C. Auckland Bogotá
Caracas Lisbon London Madrid Mexico City Milan
Montreal New Delhi San Juan Singapore
Sydney Tokyo Toronto

Library of Congress Cataloging-in-Publication Data

Ruth, Linda Cain.
    Design standards for children's environments / Linda Cain Ruth.
        p.   cm.
    Includes index.
    ISBN 0-07-057809-5 (alk. paper)
    1. Architecture and children—United States. 2. Architecture—
Human factors—United States. 3. Play environments—United States.
4. Children's paraphernalia—United States—Purchasing. I. Title.
NA2543.Y6R88   1999
720'.83—dc21
                                                    99-29058
                                                      CIP

McGraw-Hill

*A Division of The **McGraw·Hill** Companies*

1 2 3 4 5 6 7 8 9 0 AGM/AGM 9 0 4 3 2 1 0 9

ISBN 0-07-057809-5

The sponsoring editor for this book was Wendy Lochner, the editing supervisor was Tom Laughman, and the production supervisor was Pamela A. Pelton. It was set in Univers by North Market Street Graphics.

Printed and bound by Quebecor/Martinsburg.

McGraw-Hill books are available at special quantity discounts to use as premiums and sales promotions, or for use in corporate training programs. For more information, please write to the Director of Special Sales, McGraw-Hill, 11 West 19 Street, New York, NY 10011. Or contact your local bookstore.

 This book is printed on recycled, acid-free paper containing a minimum of 50% recycled, de-inked fiber.

To D.K., Alex, and Phillip

Contents

Introduction

In 1988, when I gave birth to my second son, I became a stay-at-home mom. Although I was thrilled to have the opportunity to be with my children full-time, I felt that this decision certainly meant that my practice of architecture would be put on hold for a considerable amount of time. I never dreamed that it would actually be this period of time that would give new meaning and purpose to the direction in which I would eventually reenter the field of design. In fact, in retrospect, the time that I spent at home with my children was not at all a separation from the practice of architecture; instead, it became an intense programming session with a very special user group. It was during these years, in which I participated in the local Mother's Day Out program, sat for extended lengths of time in pediatricians' offices, and spent many afternoons at various parks, that I realized that many spaces that were supposedly designed for children, fall far short of meeting the physical and psychological needs of the child. Even less consideration was afforded to the caregiver.

When it was time to return to my practice of architecture, I decided to focus my work on designing environments for children. It was not too many projects later that I discovered how difficult and time-consuming it was to locate basic design information for children, even though it was readily available for adults. Major design references commonly used in the practice of architecture are based on adult dimensions and only slightly document children, and then usually only from age 5. This wasn't of much help when my pediatrician client said that the majority of his patients were 2 and 3 years old. For the first few projects, trying to find the furniture companies that carry children's furniture meant calling them individually and asking specifically if they carried children's furnishings. I learned that many companies do not include these products in their catalogs because they make up such a low percentage of their overall sales. As I started to accumulate children's design data and product information, I began to wonder what designers, who may design a bank building one day and a shopping mall the next, do when they are faced with the challenge of designing an environment for children in the face of the ever-present project deadline. It was at that point that I decided that the development of a design reference for children would allow me to positively affect the lives of far more children than I ever could by designing only a few projects a year on my own. It became my goal to create a resource that would enable designers to spend more time effectively concentrating on creating enriching environments for children and less time tracking down design support information.

This book is intended for anyone responsible for the design or maintenance of spaces in which children are the primary users: architects, interior designers, landscape architects, as well as facility owners, operators, and managers. It covers commercial as well as residential designs and products.

Part I offers several types of helpful dimensional information. Chapter 1 includes anthropometric data of children from birth to age 18. The need for this information was realized when I found myself measuring my own sons to determine a proper mounting height for a magazine rack that could be reached by a 6-year-old but not a 2-year-old. I wondered what designers who did not have 6-year-olds wandering around their offices did in similar situations. Creating environments that acknowledge the size of the primary user is the first step in allowing the child to feel a sense of control over the environment, thus promoting self-competence and self-esteem.

Chapter 2 offers appropriate dimensions for typical objects within the child's built environment and shows how they, too, change from birth to age 18. For example, supplies such as crayons or paper are often placed in the center of tables for the shared use of the children sitting at the table. Specifying a table size that allows the children to be able to physically reach the crayons from all sides not only promotes a sense of cooperation among the children, but goes a long way in helping a caregiver maintain a productive and calm atmosphere. In addition to dimensions of the built environment, this chapter also highlights the pending Americans with Disabilities Act (ADA) guidelines for building elements in facilities that primarily serve children.

Chapter 3 synthesizes the Consumer Product Safety Commission's (CPSC's) safety guidelines for play areas, the American Society for Testing and Materials (ASTM) standards for the design of play areas and equipment, and the ADA's newly developed guidelines for play areas. It is hoped that combining the information from these documents into one source will prove to be more convenient and informative for the designer.

Chapter 4 consists of dimensions of typical, and sometimes not so typical, products that are often found in children's environments, giving the designer information that is helpful in the layout of spaces for children. The need for this chapter came after I found myself specifying a Little Tikes kitchen play set for an outdoor playhouse. It is almost a certainty that the most comprehensive design library in any design firm will not have the specs on a product such as this anywhere in their myriad of product catalogs.

Part II features the first source list developed for designers that lists products appropriate for use in children's environments. The list combines products from the interior design industry, the child care and preschool industry, the health care industry, and even the toy industry, into a useful source list that gives the designer a more comprehensive overview of the products that are available, as well as allows for comparisons to be made among the products.

Part III consists of two chapters that give additional information that will be useful to the designer. Chapter 8 outlines the development of children's abilities and perceptions in the first stages of life from birth to age 10. This chapter will serve as a reminder to those of us whose children are long past the wonderful toddler and young childhood years when seemingly every day is filled with newfound abilities. How soon we forget such milestones as at what age children can sit alone or walk up and down stairs unassisted. Understanding the capabilities of the users of a space is a basic requirement of proper design. This outline will also be helpful to designers who have not had many opportunities to be around children very much and who are not aware of the timeline of the many developmental changes that occur in the first years of life.

Chapter 9 offers the designer a concise bibliography of the most effective and highly regarded resources in the area of children's design. Organizations that are directly involved in the issues are listed, as well as literature sources that will broaden the designer's understanding of the needs of the children for which he or she is designing. This section is divided into the areas of design for accessibility, child care and preschool, health care, children's museums, outdoor play, and schools. In conjunction with this chapter, a listing of state agencies that are responsible for the licensing of child care facilities throughout the United States are listed in Appendix A. The licensing procedure in each state delineates certain aspects of the physical environment that the designer should be aware of from the start of the design process. In addition, Appendix B includes dimensioned diagrams of areas required for several children's games and athletic playing fields and courts. Activities such as these are often incorporated into the designs of children's facilities or adjacent support facilities.

It is hoped that the information and format of this book will free up some always needed extra time to concentrate on developing designs that touch the spirit of the children who will live, learn, and grow in the spaces that are created.

For future revisions, please send any comments regarding your use of this book, ways in which it can be improved, or items that would make it more comprehensive to:

Linda Cain Ruth, AIA
1104 S. Gay Street
Auburn, AL 36830
Fax: 334-821-8481
E-mail: lcruth@auburn.campuscwix.net

Acknowledgments

Much has been written and said of the importance of providing nurturing environments for children. It is often forgotten how important nurturing environments are for adults as well. I am fortunate that even as an adult, I have been afforded such an environment by my husband, D.K. A gifted architect and teacher, his support of me and his confidence in the value of this project have kept me going long past the point at which I believed my capabilities would certainly end. The writing of this book has allowed me to grow as a designer and develop an even greater appreciation for the uniqueness of children and their needs from the environments that are created for them. This book could not have become a reality without the patience and support of D.K and my two wonderful sons, Alex and Phillip, who were the true inspirations for this book.

I also wish to thank the many people who moved in and out of the role of supporter, as if on cue, throughout the life of this project: John Mouton, who pushed me out of the starting blocks; Everett Smethurst, who provided the road map; my editor, Wendy Lochner, who believed in the potential of the project from the start; Nancy Hosey, who endured countless phone calls of off-the-wall questions about source lists and furnishings; Norbert Lechner, who provided valuable advice and support as an established author; Jennifer Magnolfi and Edzard van Santen for their services as translators, which allowed me to include wonderful products from their homelands of Italy and Germany; and the biggest thanks to Steve Brown, who gave up his last "free" summer to create the numerous computer graphics and to become an adopted big brother to my sons.

I would also like to thank the many manufacturers and distributors of children's products that not only provided product information, specifications, and samples, but also included much-appreciated words of encouragement as well. Special thanks to the interior designers at Godwin & Associates in Atlanta, Georgia, for sharing their resources in the design of pediatric facilities, and to the Montgomery Toys "R" Us for believing we weren't the competition when we showed up to photograph their merchandise. A special thanks to Tom, who has been behind me and this project during its entire development, spending countless hours on the phone and never complaining.

Last, I wish to thank all my neglected friends and long-suffering family members and colleagues, who learned to not ask how the book was coming. You can ask now.

ANTHROPOMETRIC, DIMENSIONAL, AND GUIDELINE INFORMATION FOR DESIGNING ENVIRONMENTS FOR CHILDREN

Anthropometric Measurements of Children

From the day they are born, children start on a wonderful path of development in many dimensions: cognitively, socially, and emotionally. The change that is most obvious, and at times seems almost detectable with the naked eye, is their physical development. Following are charts that delineate several anthropometric measurements of the child's body as it grows from birth to age 18. The designer will find these measurements useful in many ways. For example, they can be used for locating objects in the environment within a child's reach, but they may also be used to position out of the reach of small children any harmful objects or things that are best managed only by older children or adults.

These charts are not to be used as guides for health, but only as guidelines from which to design. Within several of the charts, data from two or three sources were combined in the absence of one complete data set. In addition, extrapolations and interpolations were made in some instances based on the trend of the data. In almost all cases, curves were smoothed for ease of use. If exact numeric precision is required, it is recommended that the reader consult the original sources of data that are listed at the end of Part One.

The data presented is based largely on studies of children from the United States and Great Britain. This must be taken into consideration when designing for populations that may vary in stature from these groups. The data for boys and girls has been combined for all measurements except height and weight, which are shown for boys and girls, separately and together. This is due to the fact that height and weight measurements show the largest degree of disparity between boys and girls, especially during the late-teen years. The differences may impact design if the space or element is intended for use by all girls or all boys.

When available, the 5th, 50th, and 95th percentiles are presented and noted on each chart. This indicates that among all children of any particular age group, 5 percent will fall below and 5 percent will fall above the smallest and largest indicated measurements. The 50 percent indicator represents the average child at that age. In the late-teen years, when the largest disparity between boys and girls appears, the 5 percent is typically representative of the smallest girls, whereas the 95 percent includes most children, including the largest boys.

Height (Including Infant Length)—Boys and Girls

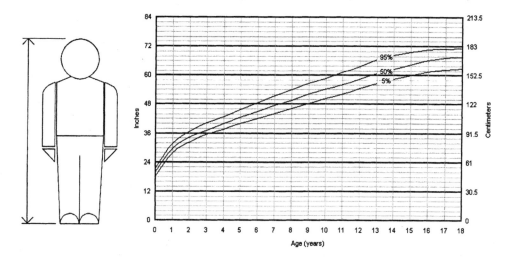

This chart may also be used to determine the height of a high shelf, because these are typically mounted at approximately the same height as the top of the head.

Height (Including Infant Length)—Boys

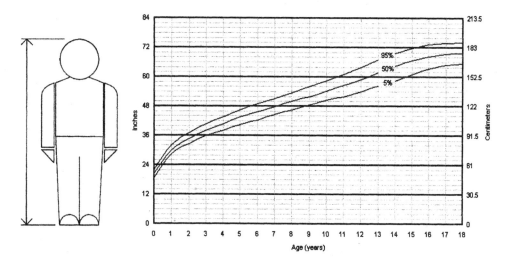

Height (Including Infant Length)—Girls

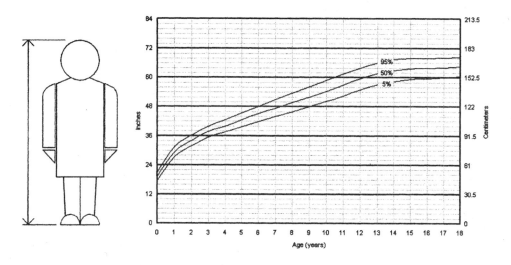

Weight—Boys and Girls

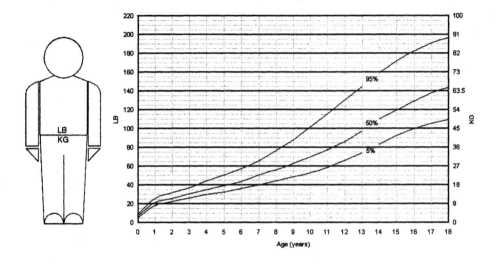

Weight—Boys

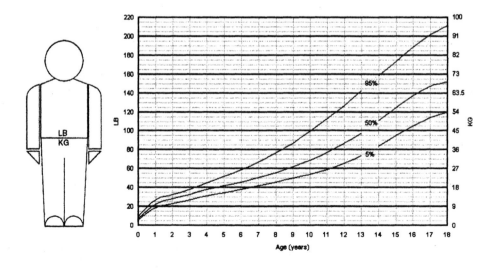

Weight—Girls

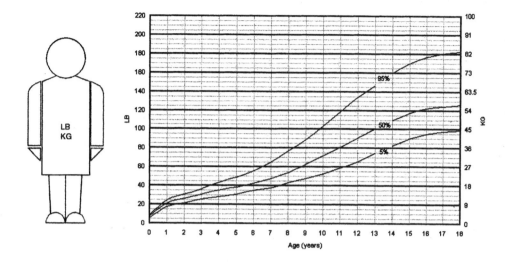

Standing Eye Level

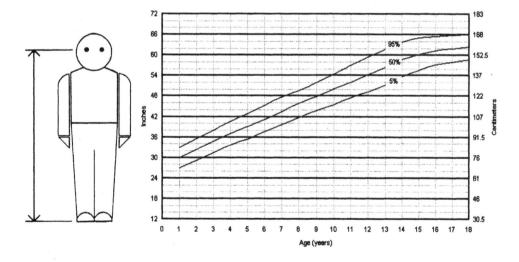

This chart may also be used to determine the mounting height for clothes hooks and rods, because these items are typically mounted approximately at eye level.

Shoulder Width

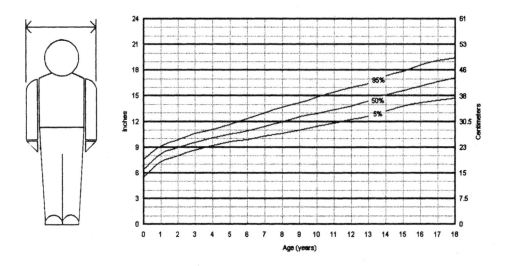

Crotch Height

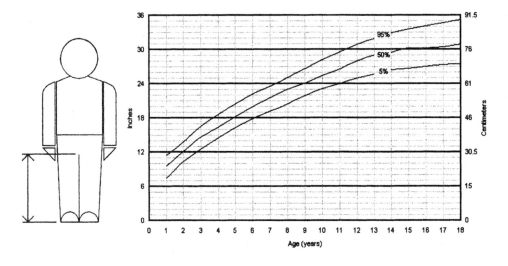

Standing Center of Gravity

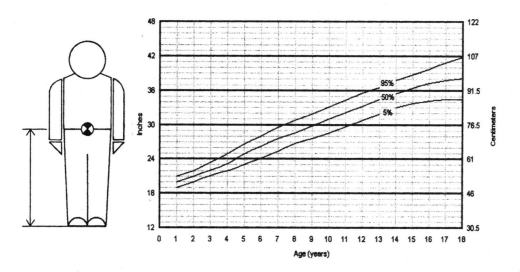

Vertical Reach to Grip

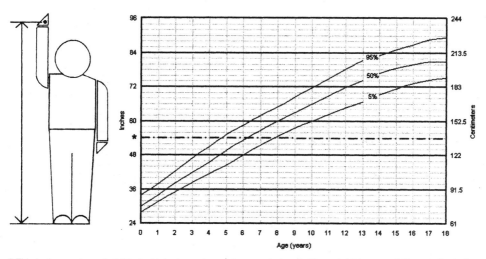

* This is the maximum height at which elements may be mounted and still meet ADA accessibility standards for adults.

Accessible High and Low Reach to Grip—Forward and Side

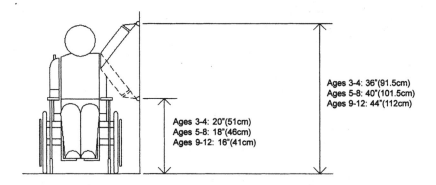

Ages 3-4: 36"(91.5cm)
Ages 5-8: 40"(101.5cm)
Ages 9-12: 44"(112cm)

Ages 3-4: 20"(51cm)
Ages 5-8: 18"(46cm)
Ages 9-12: 16"(41cm)

The entire range of 16 to 44 inches (41 to 91.5 cm) is considered accessible. The age divisions are additional suggestions included in the Americans with Disabilities Act Accessibility Guidelines' (ADAAG's) *Building Elements Designed for Children's Use.*

Span

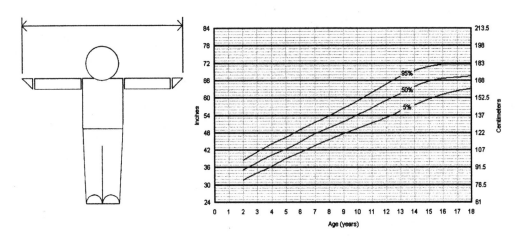

Seated Height

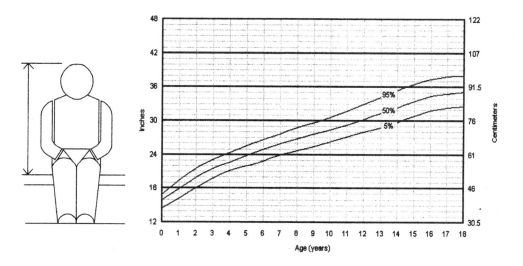

Seated Eye Level

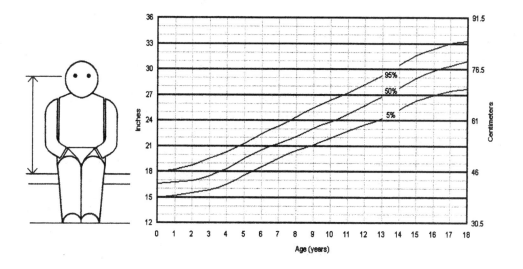

Seated Back-to-Knee Length

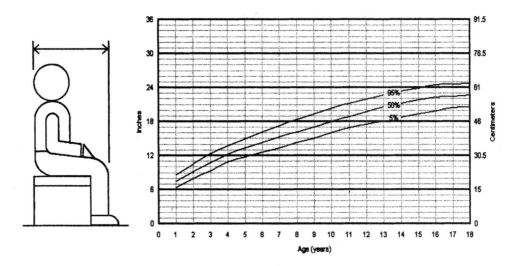

Seated Back-to-Sole Length

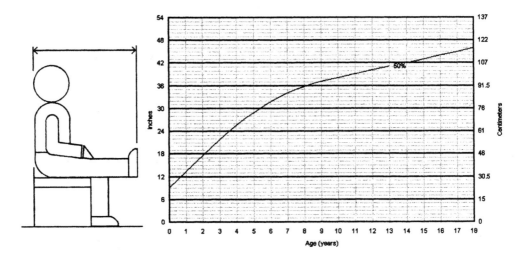

Seated Knee Height

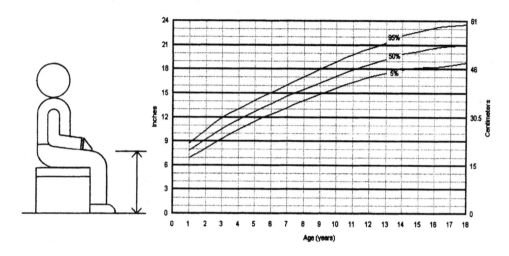

Head Width

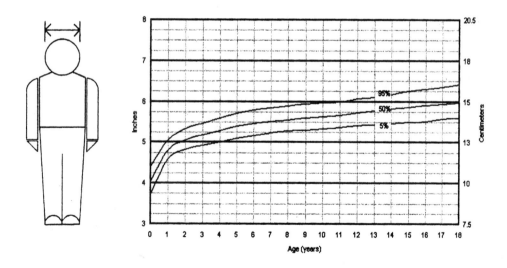

Head Depth

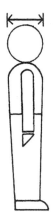

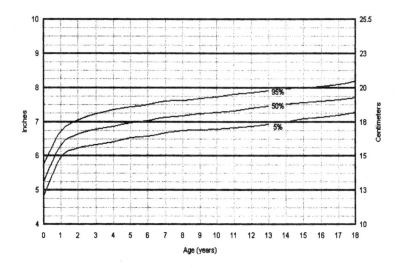

Hand Width

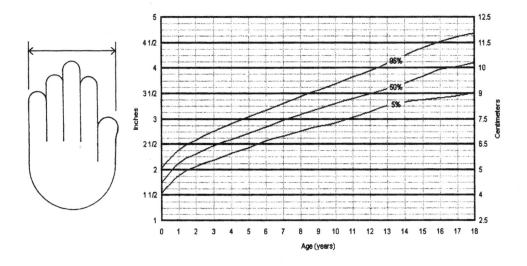

Hand Length

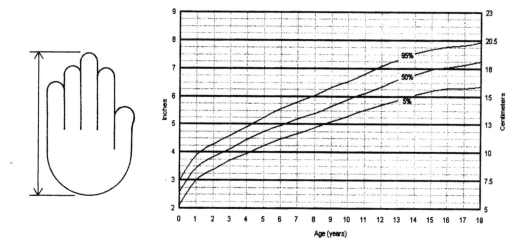

Diameter of Minimum Hand Clearance

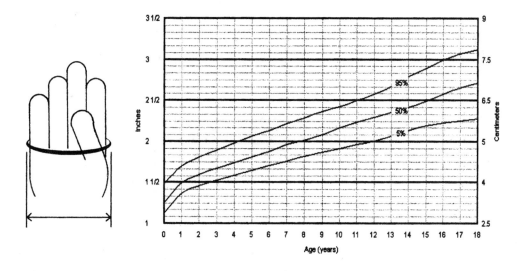

Foot Width

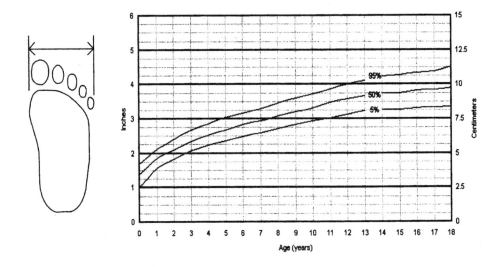

Foot Length

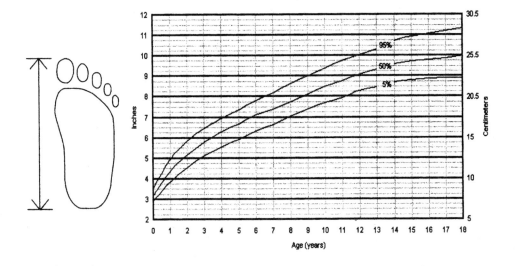

CHAPTER **2**

Standard Dimensions of Children's Built Environments

Children are active participants in learning about the world around them. They begin to understand size by whether they can hold something in their hands or wrap their arms around it. They learn that things can be soft or hard, smooth or bumpy by touching them, and as infants and toddlers, even placing them in their mouths. To accommodate this active learning process, it is beneficial for the environment to reflect the size of the child and facilitate the child's ability to see and reach objects and feel comfortable within his surroundings. A space that is reflective of the child's physical size and abilities heightens their sense of confidence in their ability to perform simple tasks more independently. Appropriate sizes and heights for elements such as windows, countertops, and stair rails make a child's space more inviting and enjoyable for the child and will prolong the child's interest and participation in constructive activities.

Following are charts and diagrams of typical objects that require special consideration when being designed for use by children. As in the previous chapter, when possible, the 5th, 50th, and 95th percentiles are indicated to offer the designer a range of sizes as opposed to an absolute. The designer will need to determine which is appropriate for the situation under consideration. The charts are based on anthropometric studies of children in the United States and Great Britain. Special situations or populations of dissimilar stature may require some adaptation of the information presented.

Most of the accessibility standards and recommendations that are presented are from the Final Rule of the Architectural and Transportation Barriers Compliance Board's ADA Accessibility Guidelines for Buildings and Facilities; Building Elements Designed for Children's Use, which was published in the *Federal Register* on January 13, 1998. These guidelines, when adopted by the Department of Justice, will affect building elements designed specifically for use by children ages 12 and younger. The rule covers all newly constructed and altered facilities covered by Titles II and III of the Americans with Disabilities Act (ADA) of 1990. For convenience, this document will be referred to as the ADAAG for Children, and its information is presented based on the assumption of imminent approval by the Department of Justice of the Final Rule. It may be assumed that issues that are not addressed are not changed from the standard ADAAG requirements. The ADAAG for Children may be viewed in its entirety from the Access Board's web site at www.access-board.gov/rules/child.htm. Hard copies of the publication may be ordered by calling the Access Board's automated publications order line at 800-872-2253 or 202-272-5434 and requesting publication S-30. In addition to the standards and recommendations included in the ADAAG for Children, several of the recommendations made by the Center for Accessible Housing (CAH) at North Carolina State University that were not incorporated into the Final Rule as requirements are also presented in this chapter. Much of the research that formed the basis for the ADAAG for Children was developed by the CAH.

When considering a young child that is standing and a child in a wheelchair, the differences in many dimensional aspects are not as great as for adults. Therefore, the recommendations for such things as accessible mounting heights often place elements in a location that is comfortable for all children, not only those with special needs. Although they are not required, when possible, the incorporation of CAH recommendations into the design of spaces can prove to be beneficial in creating environments that are sensitive to the smaller size of all children, as well as the needs of disabled children.

A copy of the Executive Summary of the CAH report is available from the Access Board or from the Center for Accessible Housing by contacting either of the following:

**U.S. Architectural and Transportation Barriers
  Compliance Board (Access Board)**
1331 F Street, NW, Suite 1000
Washington, D.C. 20004-1111
800-872-2253, Ext. 27, or 202-272-5434,
  Ext. 27
800-993-2822 or 202-272-5449 (TTY)

The Center for Accessible Housing
School of Design
North Carolina State University
P.O. Box 8613
Raleigh, NC 27695-8613
919-515-3082
Fax: 919-515-3023

Minimum Clear Widths for Accessible Passageways and Routes

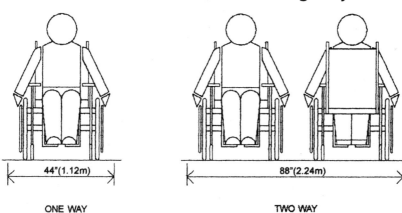

ONE WAY   TWO WAY

In environments for adults, the minimum clear width of passageways and accessible routes for a single wheelchair is 36 in (91 cm) and 60 in (1.5 m) in passageways where wheelchairs may pass each other. Although not required by the ADA, the CAH study recommends that, in environments for children, the minimum clear width for single wheelchair passage be increased to 44 in (112 cm) and to 88 in (2.2 m) where two children in wheelchairs may pass each other. These widths are also recommended for ramps that are to be used by children. It is felt that this added width accommodates age- and disability-related differences between the skill levels of children and adults.

Accessible Ramps

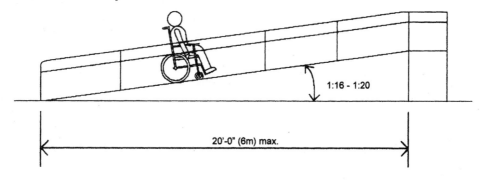

The ADAAG for Children does not alter the design requirements for ramps used primarily by children for accessibility. However, the CAH report states that many children, especially those using manual wheelchairs who have limited strength and stamina, experienced difficulty ascending ramps at the maximum-allowed 1 : 12 slope. The study recommends that ramps that are to be used mainly by children have a slope between 1 : 16 and 1 : 20, with the latter being preferred. The study also recommends that the maximum horizontal run for any slope not be greater than 20 ft (6 m). See the sections regarding widths of accessible passageways and handrails for additional CAH recommendations concerning ramps.

Handrail Height (Secondary Handrails)

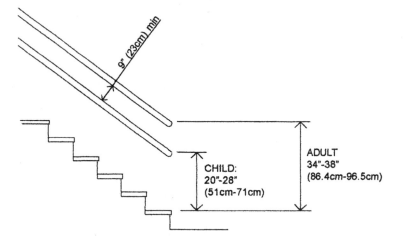

Although not a requirement, the ADAAG for Children recommends that a secondary handrail be mounted below the standard handrail at ramps and stairs within buildings where children are the principal users. The typical mounting height of handrails to be used by adults is 34 to 38 in (86 to 96.5 cm). For children, it is recommended that an accessible handrail be mounted 20 to 28 in (51 to 71 cm) from the surface of the ramp or from the stair nosing to the top of the handrail. The Consumer Product Safety Commission (CPSC) also addresses the height of handrails, and although made in the context of play environments, the recommendations may be useful in the design of standard interior circulation areas, as well. The CPSC recommends that handrails for children of ages 2 to 5 be 22 to 26 in (56 to 66 cm) above the stair or ramp surface. Notice that this range is included in the ADAAG's range of accessibility by children. The CPSC recommends a handrail height of 22 to 38 in (56 to 96.5 cm) for children ages 6 to 12. Between 28 and 34 in (71 and 86 cm), a handrail is not considered accessible by ADA for either children or adults. The distance between the two handrails should be at least 9 in (23 cm) to reduce the risk of entrapment.

Handrail Diameter

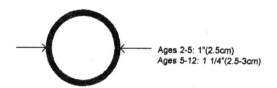

Ages 2-5: 1"(2.5cm)
Ages 5-12: 1 1/4"(2.5-3cm)

Because the use of a secondary handrail for children is not required by the ADAAG for Children, an appropriate diameter for children's handrails is not addressed. However, the CAH study recommends railing diameters of 1 in (25 mm) for children under 5 years of age and from 1 to 1¼ in (25 to 32 mm) for children ages 5 to 12. This is further supported by the ADAAG for Play Areas, which requires an outside diameter of 0.95 to 1.55 in (24 to 39 mm) for handrails within play areas, with 1¼ in (32 mm) being preferred. It is important to note that these smaller diameters are not allowable as grab bars. The ADAAG's requirements for the diameters of grab bars remain at 1¼ to 1½ in (32 to 38 mm).

Platform Heights

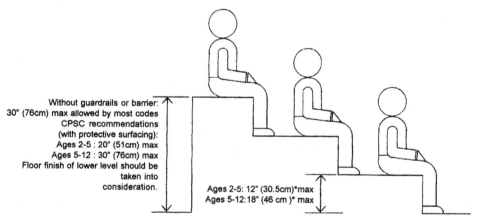

Without guardrails or barrier:
30" (76cm) max allowed by most codes
CPSC recommendations
(with protective surfacing):
Ages 2-5 : 20" (51cm) max
Ages 5-12 : 30" (76cm) max
Floor finish of lower level should be
taken into
consideration.

Ages 2-5: 12" (30.5cm)*max
Ages 5-12:18" (46 cm)* max

* If left open, any spaces between stepped platforms should be less than 3½ in (9 cm) or greater than 9 in (23 cm) to reduce the potential of entrapment.

Elevated platforms are often used in children's spaces to help define activity or indoor play areas and to provide seating that allows a second or third row of children to see over the heads of children sitting in front of them for leader-directed group activities, such as reading and discussion. Although the design of these platforms is not directly addressed, most building codes do allow raised floor surfaces up to 30 in (76 cm) without guardrails.

The CPSC's *Handbook for Public Playground Safety* addresses stepped platforms in relation to their use in playground settings above a protective safety surfacing. On such tiered platforms, a child's fall may either be onto the surfacing below or onto a lower platform. The CPSC's handbook recommends that platforms for children of ages 2 to 5 should not be over 20 in (51 cm) above a protective surfacing without a handrail. For children of ages 6 and older, this distance is increased to 30 in (76 cm). If used in interior situations, both of these heights are allowed by most codes, even without the presence of a safety surface. However, the designer is strongly advised to consider the potential for accidental falls and the finish of the lower level when determining the platform height and the need for a guardrail.

The CPSC handbook further suggests that the maximum difference in height between stepped platforms should be 12 in (30.5 cm) for preschool-age children and 18 in (46 cm) for school-age children. These dimensions are designed for platforms that are being used for play activities. For risers that are to be used primarily as a group seating area, the designer should refer to the data included under "Seat Height" to determine an appropriate change in platform height that will allow for comfortable seating. Guardrails are often required when the change in platform heights exceeds 18 in (46 cm).

Door Hardware Height

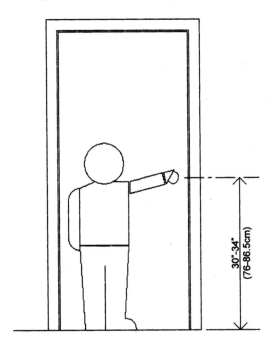

30"-34" (76-86.5cm)

Standard mounting height of door hardware for use by adults is between 36 and 42 in (91 and 106.5 cm). For accessible door hardware that will be used mainly by children, the CAH study recommends that door hardware be mounted between 30 and 34 in (76 and 86 cm) above the floor. This is in compliance with the ADAAG for adult requirement that accessible door hardware be located below 48 in (122 cm).

Signage

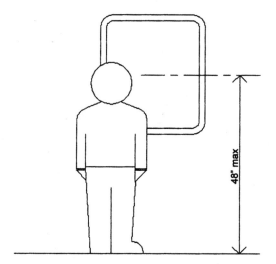

48" max

Most children learn very simple and common words by approximately age 6 or 7. For young children, it may be more beneficial to design visual "landmarks" into the environment or use pictograms for wayfinding.

The CAH study recommends that signage to be used by children should be mounted at a height no higher than 48 in (122 cm) above the finished floor to the centerline of the sign.

Standing Worktop Heights

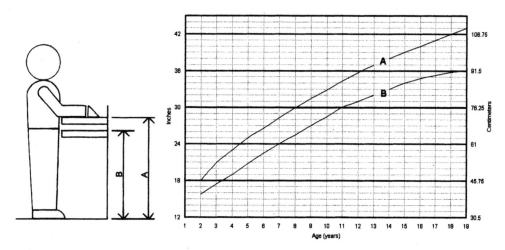

A High counter height: Elbow height—requires little to no bending

B Low counter height: Requires a small degree of bending—same proportion as the height of a standard kitchen counter height to an average adult

Standing Worktop Depth

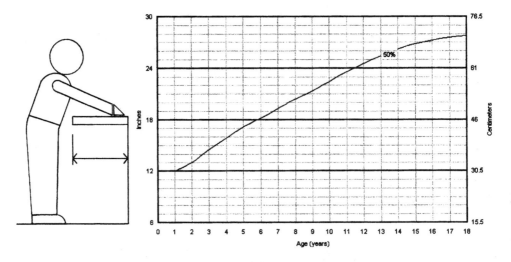

The standing worktop depth that allows for a comfortable reach will be affected by the overall height of the worktop. The lower the worktop, the greater the depth can be due to a greater ability to bend and extend the reach. The data presented on the following chart is based on a low counter height that would be proportional to a standard kitchen counter height for an adult of average height.

Seated Worktop Height

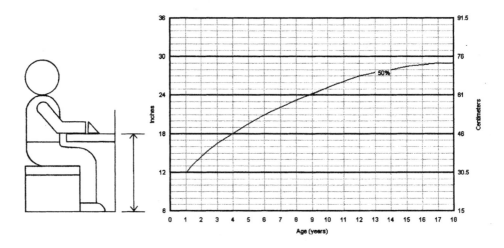

Seated Worktop Depth

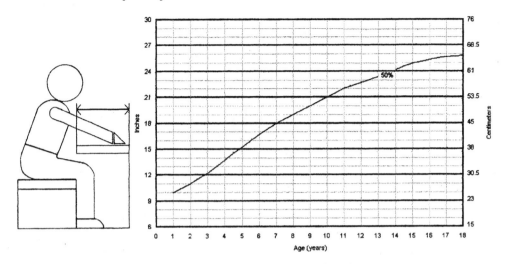

This chart may be used to determine an appropriate size for large rectangular or circular tables that seat more than one child. Often, in these situations, children must share supplies that are placed in the center of the table. In this situation, doubling the distance that a child can reach from one direction can provide a guide for the diameter or overall width required for a large table at which two children may be seated across from one another.

Accessible Tables

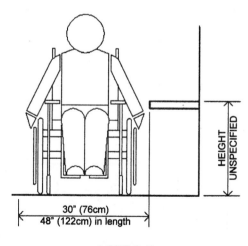

AGES 0–5

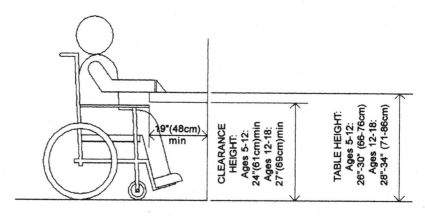

AGES 5–12 and 12–18

The ADAAG for Children makes distinctions between the requirements for accessible tables that are used by children of ages 5 and younger and tables used by children between 5 and 12 years of age. For tables that will be used by children of ages 5 and younger, the height of the table is not specified and a knee space clearance is not required. However, a 30-by-48-in (76-by-122-cm) clear floor space situated parallel to the table or counter is required so that a child in a wheelchair can make a parallel approach to the side of the worktop.

For tables that are to be used by children between ages 5 and 12, the ADAAG for Children requires a knee space at least 24 in (61 cm) high, 30 in (76 cm) wide, and 19 in (48 cm) deep. The tops of accessible worktops for children over 5 years of age are required to be 26 to 30 in (66 to 76 cm) above the finished floor. For children over age 12, the standard ADAAG requirements are in effect, which increases the required minimum knee space clearance height to 27 in (69 cm) and the allowable table heights to between 28 and 34 in (71 and 86 cm) above the finished floor

Seat Width

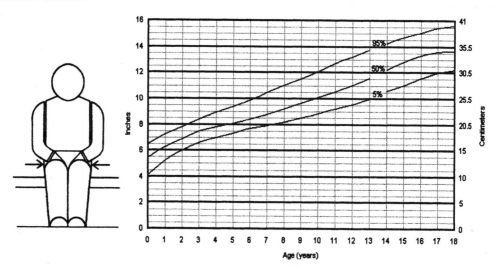

The data in the chart is the width of the child's lower body in the seated position. It may be desirable to design seats or chairs that are slightly wider for comfort. Allowances for the arms must be made when determining the overall width of a seated child. For this dimension, see "Shoulder Width" in Chapter 1.

Seat Height

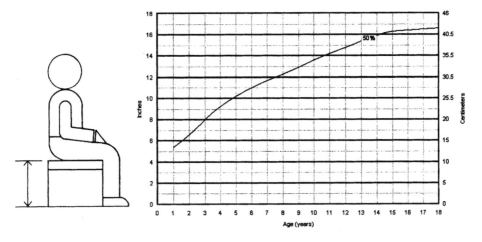

Seat Depth

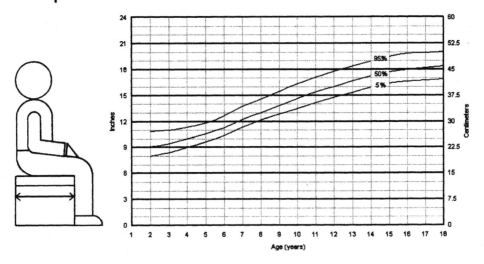

Storage

STANDING SHELF HEIGHT

High shelves should be mounted approximately level with the top of the head. Therefore, the "Height" charts in Chapter 1 can be used as guides for the appropriate height to mount high shelves.

CLOTHES HOOKS AND RODS

Clothes hooks and rods should be mounted at approximately eye level. The information found in the "Standing Eye Level" chart (Chapter 1) can be used.

ACCESSIBLE STORAGE

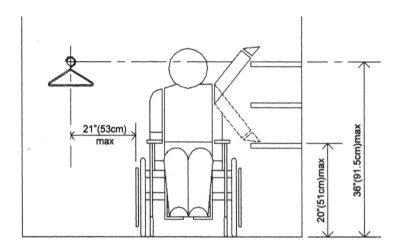

Guidelines for accessible storage are given in the ADAAG for Children as a function of the side and front reach range, which is given in Chapter 1, and is between 16 and 44 in (41 and 112 cm). Recommendations as to the division of this range by age groups are also given.

However, the CAH study recommends a slightly narrower range of 20 in (51 cm) minimum and 36 in (91 cm) maximum above the floor for storage shelves and clothes hooks and rods. A further CAH recommendation places the centerline of a clothes rod at a maximum of 21 in (53 cm) from the side of the user's wheelchair. Storage elements that are adjustable in height are also recommended.

ACCESSIBLE LOCKERS

The CAH study recommends that accessible lockers used by children be a minimum of 15 in (38 cm) wide. Shelves and hooks should be between 36 and 42 in (91 and 107 cm) above the floor. This issue is not addressed by the ADAAG for Children.

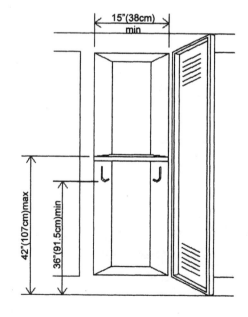

Bathrooms

SINK HEIGHT

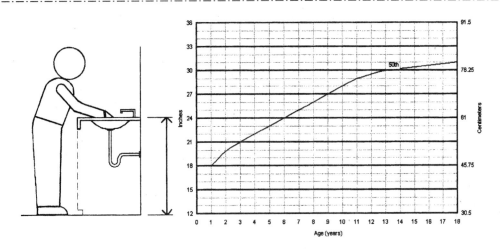

Clearances necessary for plumbing may make the lower lavatory heights unachievable. For guidelines on an appropriate depth of the countertop, refer to the data in the section "Standing Worktop Depth" in this chapter.

ACCESSIBLE SINK HEIGHT

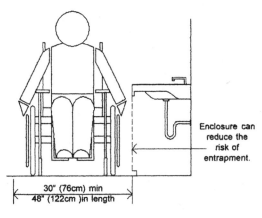

Enclosure can reduce the risk of entrapment.

30" (76cm) min
48" (122cm)in length

AGES 0–5

For accessible sinks that will be used primarily by children ages 5 and younger, the ADAAG for Children does not require the customary knee space clearances. Instead, a 30-by-48-in (76-by-122-cm) clear floor space, parallel to the sink, must be provided to allow for a parallel approach.

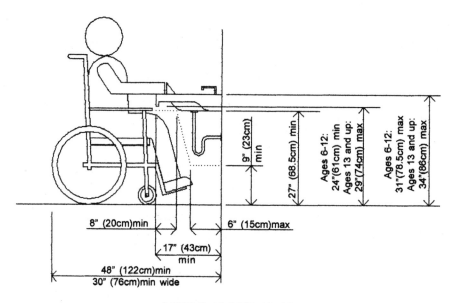

AGES 6–12 AND 13–18

For accessible sinks that will be used by children over 12 years of age, the standard ADAAG requirements apply. These requirements are shown in the following diagram. A 30-by-48 in (76-by-122-cm) clear floor space must be provided with 17 to 19 in (43 to 48 cm) of the clear floor space located beneath the fixture. For accessible sinks that will be used primarily by children ages 6 through 12, the ADAAG for Children reduces the allowable apron clearance to 24 in (61 cm) minimum and the allowable rim or counter surface height to 31 in (79 cm).

ACCESSIBLE FAUCETS

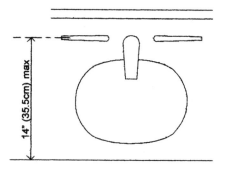

The CAH recommends that faucets mounted on the rim or counter surface of sinks be no farther than 14 in (36 cm) back from the front edge of the apron, especially when the sink is to be used primarily by children ages 2 through 4. In some cases, this may be achieved by mounting the faucets to the side of the sink. Auto sensors have also been used successfully.

TOILETS

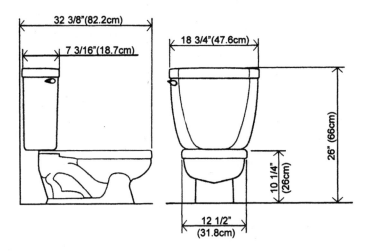

TANK MODEL

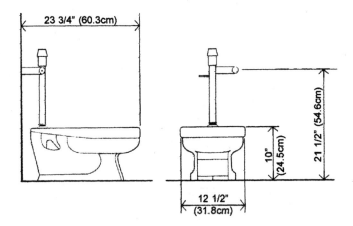

FLUSH VALVE MODEL

The diagrams are of American Standard's Baby Devoro tank and flush-valve models. They may be used as guides for general design work, as they are fairly representative of similar products that are available. A list of children's toilet manufacturers may be found in the "Source List" in Chapter 6.

ACCESSIBLE TOILETS, FLUSH CONTROLS, GRAB BARS, AND TOILET PAPER DISPENSERS

The ADAAG for Children provides exceptions to some of the requirements for toilets and restroom furnishings when they are to be used primarily by children ages 12 and younger. Exceptions are made to the requirements of the clear floor space and the height of toilets, grab bars, flush controls, and toilet paper dispensers. For each of these elements, specifications are given that are acceptable alternatives to the adult requirements of ADAAG. Choosing to use the alternative specifications for children is optional. However, once one of the exceptions has been adopted in a design, it must be followed in all categories.

The ADAAG for Children provides further assistance by suggesting age divisions within the ranges of dimensions for the various elements. These divisions are for three age groups: (1) ages 3 and 4, (2) ages 5 through 8, and (3) ages 9 through 12. The acceptable alternatives for children are shown in the following table along with the suggested age group divisions. The specifications of one age group should be applied consistently to the installation of the toilet and related elements. For children above the age of 12, the requirements for accessibility are the same as for adults.

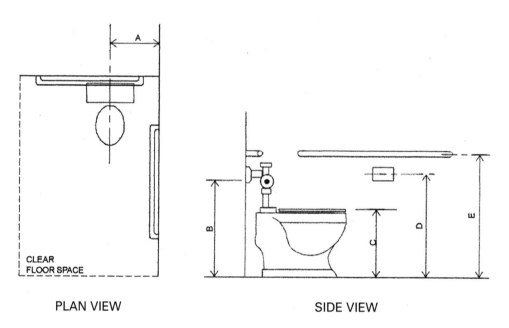

PLAN VIEW   SIDE VIEW

A Distance from centerline of toilet to side wall or partition on which the side grab bar and toilet paper dispenser are located. All other requirements of ADAAG's Section 4.16.7(1)—Clear Floor Space remain in effect. See www.access-board.gov/bfdg/fig28.html.

B Maximum height allowed for flush controls. Controls must be mounted on the open side of the toilet and must be hand operated or automatic.

C Height of toilet seat above floor. Seats that are equipped to spring back to a lifted position are prohibited.

D Mounting height of toilet paper dispenser measured from the floor to the centerline of the dispenser.

E Mounting height of grab bars located to back and side of toilet. See the following section "Grab Bars" for additional specifications.

	Ages 3–4	Ages 5–8	Ages 9–12	Ages 12+
A	12 in (30.5 cm)	12–15 in (30.5–38 cm)	15–18 in (38–45.5 cm)	18 in (45.5 cm)
B	36 in (91.5 cm)	36 in (91.5 cm)	36 in (91.5 cm)	44 in (112 cm)
C	11–12 in (28–30.5 cm)	12–15 in (30.5–38 cm)	15–17 in (38–43 cm)	17–19 in (43–48 cm)
D	14 in (35.5 cm)	14–17 in (35.5–43 cm)	17–19 in (43–48.5 cm)	19 in (48.5 cm)
E	18–20 in (45.5–51 cm)	20–25 in (51–63.5 cm)	25–27 in (63.5–68.5 cm)	33–36 in (84–91.5 cm)

Adapted from: Architectural and Transportation Barriers Compliance Board, *Americans with Disabilities Act (ADA) Guidelines for Buildings and Facilities; Building Elements Designed for Children's Use,* 1998.

GRAB BARS

Grab bars are required on the back and side wall of all accessible toilets. The acceptable mounting heights are listed in the preceding table. In addition, the ADA requires that the rear grab bar be at least 36 in (91 cm) long. Because of the lower mounting height of rear grab bars for young children, conflicts may occur between their placement and building or plumbing code requirements for flush controls. The conflicts may interfere with the child's free hand movement along the bar. In these situations, the final rule of the ADAAG for Children allows for the rear grab bar to be split or to be shifted to the open side.

Also, due to the exception that allows toilets used by children to be located closer to the side wall, splitting the rear grab bar may not always be practical or possible. In these situations in which the centerline of the toilet is less than 15 in (38 cm) from the side wall, a rear grab bar with a minimum length of 24 in (61 cm), mounted on the open side of the toilet, is acceptable.

The diameter of the grab bars remains the same as for adults, 1 to 1¼ in (25 to 31 mm). Although not addressed in or required by the Final Rule of the ADAAG for Children, comments received in its development supported the use of textured or rubber-covered surfaces on grab bars for children.

ACCESSIBLE TOILET STALLS

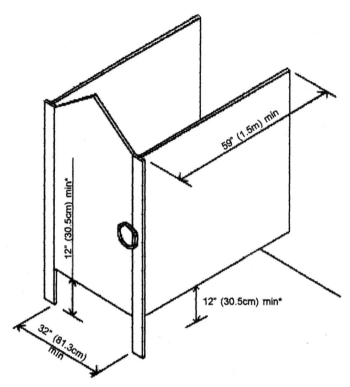

* Only one side partition is required to be at least 12 in (30.5 cm) above the floor.

The ADAAG for Children allows for exceptions in the design of accessible toilet stalls that will be used primarily by children ages 12 and younger. The allowable exceptions for the distance from the centerline of the toilet to the side wall, as well as the exceptions for flush controls and the heights of toilet seats, grab bars, and toilet paper dispensers are the same as those shown in the preceding table. Additional exceptions for the depth of the toilet stall, and the height of the front and one side partition are provided in the ADAAG for Children. Apart from these elements, the requirements for a child's toilet stall remain the same as those for adult toilet stalls, including the width of the door, which must provide a minimum 32-in (81-cm) clear opening.

   Accessible children's toilet stalls must be at least 59 in (1.5 m) deep, whether a floor-mounted or wall-mounted toilet is used. This is different from the adult ADAAG, which allows a 56-in- (14.2-m-) deep toilet stall if a wall-mounted toilet is used. The 3-in "credit" is also not available when using the alternate stalls in cases of alteration work in which the standard toilet stall is not feasible. These stalls must be at least 69 in (17.5 m) deep.

   An additional requirement of accessible toilet stalls for children is that the front partition and at least one side partition must be at least 12 in (30.5 cm) above the floor to provide toe clearance. This is 3 in (76 mm) higher than the minimum required for adults because children's footrests are generally higher than those of adults.

Adopting the aforementioned exceptions for the design of children's toilet stalls is optional. However, the designer may not adopt single exceptions. The exceptions as a whole must be adopted to comply with the ADAAG regulations for accessible children's toilet stalls.

ACCESSIBLE URINALS

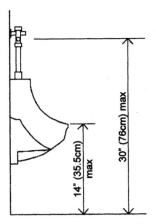

The CAH study recommends that accessible urinals used by children should be stall type or wall hung with an elongated rim at a maximum of 14 in (35.5 cm) above the floor. The study further recommends that the flush controls be mounted no more than 30 in (76 cm) above the floor. Both of these recommendations are in compliance with standard ADA regulations, which require a maximum rim height of 17 in (43 cm) and flush controls at a maximum of 44 in (112 cm) above the floor.

Mirrors

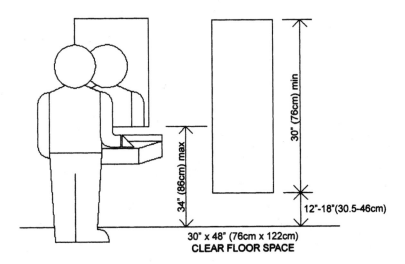

For standard mounting heights of mirrors to be used by children, the "Height" and "Standing Eye Level" charts in Chapter 1 can serve as guidelines.

There are no special regulations or alternatives regarding accessible mirrors for children. However, ADAAG does recommend the use of full-length mirrors along with the provision of a 30-by-48-in (76-by-122-cm) clear floor space directly in front of the mirror. This space allows a forward approach by a child in a wheelchair. The CAH study further recommends that the bottom edge of a full-length mirror be a maximum of 18 in (46 cm) above the floor. A minimum of 12 in (30.5 cm) above the floor will place the mirror safely above the footrest of a child's wheelchair. The CAH study also recommends that the mirror itself be no less than 30 in (76 cm) in length. For mirrors located above lavatories that are to be used by children, ADAAG recommends that the bottom of the mirror be mounted as low as the plumbing fixtures and related elements will allow. This dimension should not exceed 34 in (86.5 cm) above the floor.

Accessible Equipment and Controls

ACCESSIBLE WATER FOUNTAINS

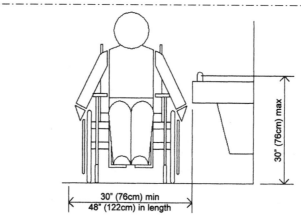

PARALLEL APPROACH

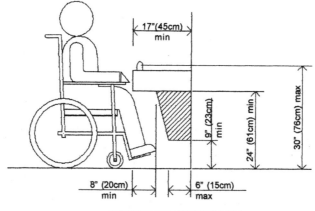

FORWARD APPROACH

Requirements for accessible water fountains for adults are based on knee and toe clearances that allow for a forward approach. However, the availability of products that can meet these same requirements when installed at a height of accessibility for children is questionable. Therefore, the ADAAG for Children makes an exception for accessible water fountains that are to be used primarily by children ages 12 and younger. In lieu of knee and toe clearances, there must be a clear floor space of 30 by 48 in (76 by 122 cm) parallel to the water fountain. This will allow a wheelchair to approach the water fountain from a parallel position. In addition, the spout must be no higher than 30 in (76 cm) from the ground or floor.

Clearances for a more comfortable forward approach by the child to the water fountain are highly desirable. The CAH study recommends a knee space that is 24 in (61 cm) high from the floor or ground to the bottom of the apron and at least 17 in (43 cm) deep and 36 in (91.5 cm) wide. Additional clearances are shown in the accompanying diagram that delineate an area beneath the water fountain in which refrigeration equipment may be located and still permit a forward approach.

PUBLIC TELEPHONES

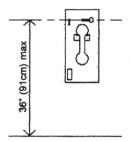

The CAH study recommends that public telephones, intended for use by children, be mounted so that the highest operable part of the telephone, typically the coin slot, is 36 in (91.5 cm) above the floor. A 30-by-48-in (76-by-122-cm) clear floor space directly in front of the telephone should be provided to allow a child in a wheelchair to make a forward approach to the phone.

ELEVATORS

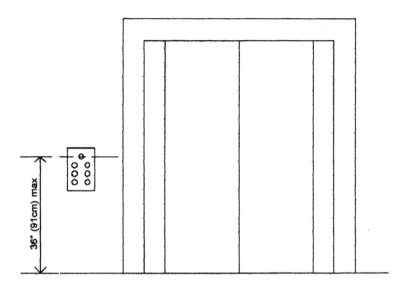

36" (91cm) max

The CAH study recommends that all controls for an elevator, including the call buttons on each floor and the car controls and emergency communication system within the elevator cab, be mounted so that the highest control is 36 in (91.5 cm) maximum above the floor. Inside the cab, it is additionally recommended that the emergency controls, including the emergency alarm and emergency stop, be grouped together at the bottom of the panel and have their centerlines no less than 24 to 30 in (61 to 76 cm) above the floor.

Because many disabled children have limited hand and finger control, it is further recommended that the call buttons be a minimum of 1½ to 2 in (38 to 51 mm) in diameter and a minimum of 1 in (25 mm) apart.

Design Guidelines
for Children's Play Environments

A child's desire—in fact, need—to play serves as an integral part of the child's physical and social development. Through play, the child learns new skills and enhances existing motor and social skills. In fact, when designing for children, the play environment is as important as those areas used for sleeping, eating, and learning. Designing the play environment to meet these needs in a way that is safe, challenging, and fun is the formidable task that is presented to the designer.

Much of the information contained in this chapter addresses the issue of safety and is based on the safety guidelines that have been published by the Consumer Product Safety Commission (CPSC) in their 1997 publication, *Handbook for Public Playground Safety*. Creating fun and challenging play environments around these safety guidelines will help ensure positive and safe play experiences for both the child and those responsible for their safety while playing. Although these guidelines have been developed with the assumption that the equipment is located outdoors and above some type of protective safety surfacing, many of the dimensions and design recommendations may have applications for indoor elements, such as lofts and indoor play structures.

The information presented is that which is used most often in the design process. The original document should be referred to for more detailed information. Copies of the document are available free of charge by sending a postcard with a return address and request for Publication No. 325 to:

Publication Request
Office of Information and Public Affairs
U.S. Consumer Product Safety Commission
Washington, D.C. 20207

The document may also be viewed on the CPSC web site at www.cpsc.gov/cpscpub /pubs/playbk97.pdf. Much of the information in the CPSC publication reflects the information contained in the American Society for Testing and Material (ASTM) document F 1487-95, *Standard Consumer Safety Performance Specification for Playground Equipment for Public Use*. The ASTM document contains detailed information about the construction and performance requirements of playground equipment, as well as layout, accessibility, installation, and maintenance recommendations. Copies of the ASTM publication may be purchased by contacting ASTM at 610-832-9585 or through their web site at www.astm.org.

The Architectural and Transportation Barriers Compliance Board has recently issued a notice of proposed rule making with regard to the *Americans with Disabilities Act Accessibility Guidelines; Play Areas.* This document, when adopted by the Department of Justice, will amend ADAAG by adding a special section that will ensure that newly constructed and altered play areas are accessible and usable by children with disabilities. The requirements of the pending ADAAG for play areas are included in the following information and are referenced as though they have already been adopted. For the current status of the adoption of this document, contact the Architectural and Transportation Barriers Compliance Board at www.access-board.gov. For convenience, this document will be referred to as the ADAAG for Play Areas. The ADAAG for Play Areas may be accessed within the web site of the Architectural and Transportation Barriers Compliance Board at www.access-board.gov/rules/playfac.htm.

Although a portion of the following chapter specifically addresses the general provisions covered by the ADAAG for Play Areas, specific accessibility requirements are located within the description of each type of play equipment. Design modifications for equipment to be used by children ages 2 to 5 that are required or suggested by either the CPSC or the ADAAG are also highlighted. It is hoped that conveniently locating this information alongside the recommendations for standard equipment will assist the designer in creating play environments that successfully integrate the special needs of children of all ages into the design of playgrounds and play structures.

Although many facets of designing residential play areas parallel those that are discussed in regard to public playgrounds, there are several differences of which the designer needs to be aware. In addition to standards for public parks, both the CPSC and the ASTM have issued similar documents regarding safety tips for residential playgrounds. *Home Playground Safety Tips,* developed by the CPSC, may be viewed within the Commission's web site at www.cpsc.gov:70/00/CPSC_Pubs/Rec_Sfy/323.txt. Hard copies of this document are available free of charge by sending a postcard with a return address and request for Fact Sheet No. 323 to:

Publication Request
Office of Information and Public Affairs
U.S. Consumer Product Safety Commission
Washington, D.C. 20207

ASTM's *Standard Consumer Safety Performance Specification for Home Playground Equipment* offers a thorough description of the safety standards for the manufacture, installation, and maintenance of home playground equipment. Copies of the ASTM document, F 1148-97a, may be obtained through the organization's web site at www.astm.org or by contacting the ASTM at 610-832-9585.

The last portion of this chapter includes a list of nontoxic and toxic plant materials. This list was originally published in Steen B. Esbensen's book, *An Outdoor Classroom.* Young children often learn about their world by placing unfamiliar objects in their mouth. This innate method of exploration coupled with a child's fascination with the beauty and uniqueness of plants and trees can have serious consequences. It is hoped that the list will be useful in the selection of plant materials for use in outdoor areas that will be used by very young children.

Use Zones

A use zone is the area of ground or surface that is directly below and around a piece of play equipment. Along with the area directly below the piece of equipment, the use zone typically extends a minimum of 6 ft (1.5 m) from the perimeter of the equipment. For playgrounds that may experience occasional overcrowding, it may be desirable to increase the use zone beyond the standard 6 ft (1.8 m). It is within this area that protective safety surfacing should be located. Use zones should be free from any obstructions, including other pieces of play equipment. Within the following information, the use zone recommended by the CPSC for a piece of play equipment is conveniently given at the start of the discussion of that equipment. This will allow the designer to know how much unobstructed area around a piece of equipment must be provided when selecting it for use on a playground.

Some pieces of equipment, such as slides and swings, require larger use zones. Some pieces of equipment are also allowed to overlap use zones of other pieces of play equipment. These situations are also noted with the description of the individual pieces of equipment.

Selection of a Protective Surface

The surfacing under and around playground equipment is the most important contributor or detractor of a playground's safety. Because falls from playground equipment will happen regardless of the quality and safety of the play equipment, providing a safe surface for the child to land on will go far in reducing the extent of injury. The following steps may be used in the process of selecting a playground surface if manufactured playground equipment is being used. If the playground structure will be custom designed and built, Steps 1 and 2 may occur simultaneously.

Step 1: Determine the maximum *fall height* either of a single piece of play equipment or for an entire playground. See the section entitled "Fall Heights," which follows.

Step 2: Determine the types of surfaces and the appropriate depths that have a *critical height* that is equal to or greater than the maximum fall height that is present on the playground. See the section entitled "Critical Heights," which follows.

Step 3: Analyze the advantages and disadvantages of each type of surfacing identified in Step 2 to decide which protective surfacing best meets the needs of the project under consideration. See the section entitled "Characteristics of Surfaces," which follows.

FALL HEIGHTS

The fall height is the distance from the ground to the highest point of a piece of play equipment from which a child may fall. The first step in determining the proper surfacing for a playground is to determine the highest fall height that is present on the playground. The pieces of equipment may be independent of each other or combined into one larger play structure. Listed in the following table are the locations that are recommended in the CPSC's *Handbook for Public Playground Safety* as the fall heights for common pieces of playground equipment. If a particular piece of equipment is not listed, it may be assumed that the fall height is the highest point attainable by a child using the equipment.

Fall Heights of Common Playground Equipment

Equipment		Fall Height
Climbers and horizontal ladders		Maximum height of the structure
Elevated platforms (including slide platforms)		Height of the platform
Merry-go-rounds		Height of any part at the perimeter on which a child may sit or stand
Seesaws		Maximum height attainable by any part of the seesaw
Spring rockers		Maximum height of the seat or play surface
Swings		Height of the pivot point (the point at which the swing's suspending elements connect to the supporting structure)

CRITICAL HEIGHTS

The critical height of a surfacing material is the height below which a life-threatening head injury from a fall would not be expected to occur. Each playground surface material has been tested at a variety of depths to determine its critical height for that depth. The critical height of the protective surface material should be greater than the fall height of the equipment that was determined in Step 1. Using this criterion, one or more surface materials at certain depths can be identified from the following table. The table lists the CPSC's report of the critical heights of the most common loose-fill and unitary playground surfacing materials. For loose-fill products, whether the material is compressed affects the critical height; therefore, it is desirable to have a margin of safety by selecting a material and depth with a critical height that is greater than the fall height. Unitary materials include rubber mats and shock-absorbing compositions of rubberlike materials and binders that are poured in place at the playground site.

Critical Heights of Common Surfacing Materials

| Material | Uncompressed depth | | | Compressed depth |
	6 in (15 cm)	9 in (23 cm)	12 in (30.5 cm)	9 in (23 cm)
Wood chips	7 ft (2.1 m)	10 ft (3 m)	11 ft (3.4 m)	10 ft (3 m)
Double-shredded bark mulch	6 ft (1.8 m)	10 ft (3 m)	11 ft (3.4 m)	7 ft (2.1 m)
Engineered wood fibers	6 ft (1.8 m)	7 ft (2.1 m)	>12 ft (3.6 m)	6 ft (1.8 m)
Fine sand (play sand)	5 ft (1.5 m)	5 ft (1.5 m)	9 ft (2.3 m)	5 ft (1.5 m)
Coarse sand	5 ft (1.5 m)	5 ft (1.5 m)	6 ft (1.8 m)	4 ft (1.2 m)
Fine gravel	6 ft (1.8 m)	7 ft (2.1 m)	10 ft (3 m)	6 ft (1.8 m)
Medium gravel	5 ft (1.5 m)	5 ft (1.5 m)	6 ft (1.8 m)	5 ft (1.5 m)
Shredded tires	10–12 ft (3–3.6 m)	See supplier test data	See supplier test data	See supplier test data
Unitary materials	See supplier test data	See supplier test data	See supplier test data	Not applicable

Adapted from: U.S. Consumer Product Safety Commission, *Handbook for Public Playground Safety*, 1997.

GUIDELINE. The fall height of play equipment should be less than the critical height of surfacing material.

CHARACTERISTICS OF SURFACES

To help select a surface, the CPSC has included in the appendix of the *Handbook for Public Playground Safety* a listing of the characteristics, advantages, and disadvantages of both loose-fill and unitary (rubber mats and poured-in-place compositions) playground surfacing materials. They are listed in the following table. This information will help to determine the optimum playground surfacing material based on the needs of a particular project or site.

Characteristics of Typical Playground Surfacing Materials

Material	Fall-Absorbing Characteristics	Installation/ Maintenance	Advantages	Disadvantages
Wood chips, bark mulch, engineered wood fibers	Cushioning effect depends on air trapped within and between individual particles, and presupposes an adequate depth of material. See the table "Critical Heights of Common Surfacing Materials" for performance data.	• Should not be installed over existing hard surfaces (e.g., asphalt, concrete). • Requires a method of containment (e.g., retaining barrier, excavated pit). • Requires good drainage underneath material. • Requires periodic renewal or replacement and continuous maintenance (e.g., leveling, grading, sifting, raking) to maintain appropriate depth and remove foreign matter.	• Low initial cost • Ease of installation • Good drainage • Less abrasive than sand • Less attractive to cats and dogs (compared with sand) • Attractive appearance • Readily available	The following conditions may reduce cushioning potential: • Rainy weather, high humidity, freezing temperatures. • Over time, decomposes, is pulverized, and compacts, requiring replenishment. • Depth may be reduced by displacement due to children's activities or by material being blown by wind. • Can be blown or thrown into children's eyes. • Subject to microbial growth when wet. • Conceals animal excrement and trash (e.g., broken glass, nails, pencils, and other sharp objects that can cause cut and puncture wounds). • Spreads easily outside of containment area. • Can be flammable. • Subject to theft by neighborhood residents for use as mulch.
Sand, gravel	See the table "Critical Heights of Common Surfacing Materials" for performance data.	• Should not be installed over existing hard surfaces (e.g., asphalt, concrete). • Requires a method of containment (e.g., retaining barrier, excavated pit). • Requires good drainage underneath material. • Requires periodic renewal or replacement and continuous maintenance (e.g., leveling, grading, sifting, raking) to maintain appropriate depth and remove foreign matter.	• Low initial cost • Ease of installation • Does not pulverize • Not ideal for microbial growth • Nonflammable • Readily available • Not susceptible to vandalism except by contamination • Gravel less attractive to animals than sand	The following conditions may reduce cushioning potential: • Rainy weather, high humidity, freezing temperatures. • With normal use, combines with dirt and other foreign materials. • Depth may be reduced due to displacement by children's activities and sand may be blown by wind. • May be blown or thrown into children's eyes. • May be swallowed.

Characteristics of Typical Playground Surfacing Materials (*Continued*)

Material	Fall-Absorbing Characteristics	Installation/ Maintenance	Advantages	Disadvantages
Sand, gravel (*cont.*)		• Requires that compacted sand should periodically be turned over, loosened, and cleaned. • Requires that gravel be periodically broken up and hard pan be removed.		• Conceals animal excrement and trash (e.g., broken glass, nails, pencils, and other sharp objects that can cause cut and puncture wounds). Sand • Spreads easily outside of containment area. • Small particles bind together and become less cushioning when wet; when thoroughly wet, sand reacts as a rigid material. • May be tracked out of play area on shoes; abrasive to floor surfaces when tracked indoors; abrasive to plastic materials. • Adheres to clothing. • Susceptible to fouling by animals. Gravel • Difficult to walk on. • If displaced onto nearby hard surface pathways, could present a fall hazard. • Hard pan may form under heavily traveled areas.
Shredded tires	Manufacturer should be contacted for information on critical height of materials when tested according to ASTM F1292. See the table "Critical Heights of Common Surfacing Materials" for performance data.	• Should not be installed over existing hard surfaces (e.g., asphalt, concrete). • Requires a method of containment (e.g., retaining barrier, excavated pit). • Requires good drainage underneath material. • Requires continuous maintenance (e.g., leveling, grading, sifting, raking) to maintain appropriate depth and remove foreign matter.	• Ease of installation • Has superior shock-absorbing capability • Is not abrasive • Less likely to compact than other loose-fill materials • Not ideal for microbial growth • Does not deteriorate over time	• Is flammable. • Unless treated, may cause soiling of clothing. • May contain steel wires from belted tires. Note: Some manufacturers provide a wire-free guarantee. • Depth may be reduced due to displacement by children's activities. • May be swallowed.

Characteristics of Typical Playground Surfacing Materials (*Continued*)

Material	Fall-Absorbing Characteristics	Installation/ Maintenance	Advantages	Disadvantages
Rubber or rubber-over-foam mats or tiles, poured-in-place urethane and rubber compositions	Manufacturer should be contacted for information on critical height of materials when tested according to ASTM F1292.	Some unitary materials can be laid directly on hard surfaces, such as asphalt or concrete. Others may require expert undersurface preparation and installation by the manufacturer or a local contractor. Materials generally require no additional means of containment. Once installed, the materials require minimal maintenance.	• Low maintenance • Easy to clean • Consistent shock absorbency • Material not displaced by children during play activities • Generally low life cycle costs • Good footing (depends on surface texture) • Harbors few foreign objects • Generally no retaining edges needed • Is accessible to the handicapped	• Initial cost relatively high. • Undersurfacing may be critical for thinner materials. • Often must be used on almost level uniform surfaces. • May be flammable. • Subject to vandalism (e.g., ignited, defaced, cut). • Full rubber tiles may curl up and cause tripping. • Some designs susceptible to frost damage.

ADA Accessibility Guidelines for Play Areas

In 1998, the Architectural and Transportation Barriers Compliance Board issued a notice of proposed rule making for the *Americans with Disabilities Act Accessibility Guidelines for Play Areas.* When adopted, newly constructed and altered play areas will be required to comply with the ruling's specifications.

Following is a brief summary of some of the provisions of the document. The summary is meant to give designers an initial understanding of the intentions of the ruling and a means to do a cursory analysis of the compliance of the design of a new or renovated playground or structure for children ages 2 and up.

A complete copy and current status of the ruling may be obtained by contacting the Architectural and Transportation Barriers Compliance Board through their web site at www.access-board.gov/rules/playfac.htm or through the Board's automated publications order line by calling 202-272-5434, press 1, then 1 again, and request publication S-35. Persons using a TTY should call 202-272-5449 and record a name, address, telephone number, and request publication S-35.

DEFINITIONS

The following definitions may be helpful in understanding the playground elements that are discussed in later sections of this chapter, particularly, as they relate to the ADAAG for Play Areas.

- *Clear space:* Unobstructed space for a stationary wheelchair or mobility device. Clear space is 30 by 48 in (76 by 122 cm) with a slope that is not steeper than 1 : 48 in any direction. When not specifically stated, the appropriate orientation and location of clear spaces is at the designer's discretion.

- *Composite play structure:* Two or more play components attached or functionally linked to create an integrated unit that provides more than one play activity.
- *Elevated play component:* A play component that is part of a composite play structure and approached above or below grade.
- *Ground-level play component:* A play component that is approached and exited at the ground level. Examples include swings, climbers, manipulative panels, and spring rockers.
- *Maneuvering space:* Unobstructed space that allows a child to make turns and negotiate within a play area. A maneuvering space may be either 60 in (1.5 m) in diameter (A) or a T-shaped space that is 36 in (91 cm) wide at the top and stem within a 60-by-60-in (1.5-by-1.5-m) square (B). The slope may be no steeper than 1 : 48 in all directions.

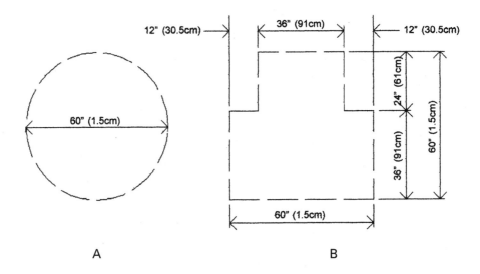

A   B

- *Play area:* A portion of a site containing play components designed and constructed for children in a specified age range.
- *Play component:* An element intended to generate specific opportunities for play, socialization, or learning.
- *Soft contained play equipment:* A play structure made up of one or more components in which the user enters a fully enclosed play environment that uses pliable materials.

ALTERING EXISTING PLAY AREAS

- Many play areas are altered to create safer separations between various pieces of play equipment. If the existing play area is changed or extended more than one

use zone, the play area must be brought into compliance with the current requirements of the ADAAG for Play Areas.

ACCESSIBLE ROUTES

- At least one accessible route must be provided within the boundary of a play
  area. The accessible route must connect accessible play components, including entry and exit points. Example: An accessible slide requires an accessible route, with accessible surfacing, serving the entry and exit points of the
  slide.

- The accessible route must be a minimum of 60 in (1.5 m) wide and be clear of
  protrusions at or below 80 in (2 m) above the surface (A). However, if a play area
  is less than 1,000 ft², this width may be reduced to a minimum of 44 in (112 cm)
  wide, provided that maneuvering space is provided if the route exceeds 30 ft
  (9.14 m) in length (B). Another exception is made allowing an accessible route to
  be a width of 36 in (91 cm) for a maximum distance of 60 in (1.5 m). If more
  than one segment of the accessible route is 36 in (91 cm) wide, they must be
  connected by segments that are 60 in (1.5 m) wide and at least 60 in (1.5 m) in
  length (C).

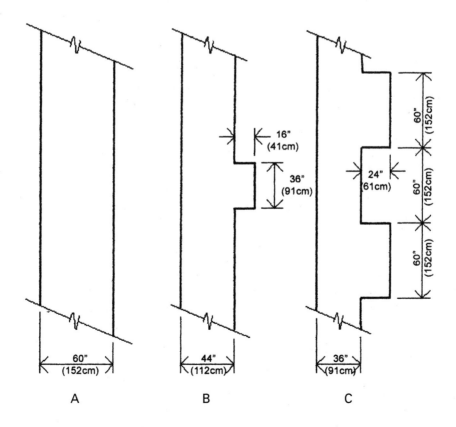

A   B   C

- For elevated accessible routes, including ramps, the permitted width is a minimum of 36 in (91 cm). The width of the elevated route may be reduced to 32 in (81 cm) for a distance of 24 in (61 cm).
- ADAAG requires that elements may not project more than 4 in (10.2 cm) into a circulation path if the leading edge is above 27 in (68 cm) and below 80 in (2 m). The ADAAG for Play Areas requires that at least one accessible route in a play area be free of such protruding objects.
- Wheelchair lifts may be used as part of an accessible route.

SURFACING

- Accessible surfaces must be firm, stable, and slip resistant.
- Accessible surfaces within the use zone must be impact attenuating and comply with ASTM F 1292.

TRANSFER SYSTEMS

Transfer systems are a method of reaching play equipment. Children with disabilities, who are able, use them to move from their wheelchairs or mobility devices onto the play equipment or structure. The transfer system consists of two components: a transfer platform and transfer step(s). The transfer platform serves as an entry platform and is provided at a height that allows wheelchair users to transfer from wheelchairs. Transfer steps are designed to facilitate movement above or below the platform to accessible play components.

- Transfer platforms and transfer steps must have a level surface that provides a clear space 14 in (35.6 cm) minimum in depth and 24 in (61 cm) minimum in width.
- The transfer platform must be 11 in (28 cm) minimum to 18 in (46 cm) maximum above the ground or surface.
- Transfer steps may be a maximum of 8 in (46 cm) high.
- A level and clear space of 30 by 48 in (76 by 123 cm) must be provided alongside the 24-in- (61-cm-) minimum side of the transfer platform. Neither clear space nor maneuvering space is required on elevated structures with transfer access only.
- A means of support for transferring must be provided at both transfer platforms and transfer steps. Such means may consist of a grip on the edge of the platform or step or some other element that provides a means of support.

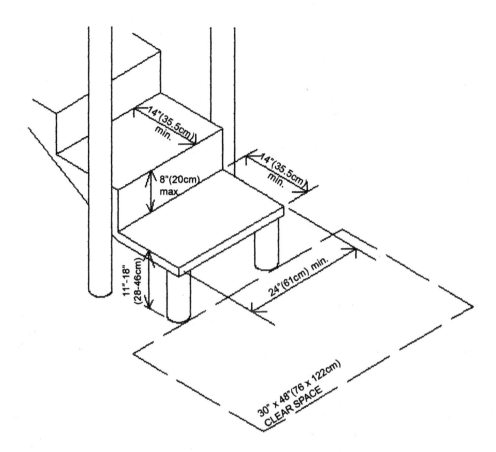

ACCESSIBLE PLAY COMPONENTS

Play components are considered accessible if they provide the following features:

- Clear space adjacent to the play component that is 30 in (76 cm) minimum by 48 in (122 cm) minimum; slope of 1 : 48 maximum in all directions.

- Maneuvering space on the same level as the play component. See *maneuvering space* in the section "Definitions" in this chapter for diagrams of minimal dimensions of maneuvering spaces. Maneuvering space and clear space may overlap.

- Manipulative and interactive features within the reach range of children with disabilities. These ranges are 36 in (91 cm) high and 20 in (51 cm) low for ages 2 to 5 and 40 in (102 cm) high and 18 in (46 cm) low for ages 5 to 12.

- Entry point or seat at an appropriate height for transfer, which is 11 in (28 cm) minimum and 24 in (61 cm) maximum. Transfer supports must also be provided.

GROUND-LEVEL PLAY COMPONENTS

- One of each type of ground-level component must be accessible. Accessibility requires clear floor or ground space and, for such elements as manipulative panels, mounting within the allowable reach range. See the section entitled "Interactive and Manipulative Panels" following in this chapter.
- The number of accessible ground-level play components must be at least equal to 50 percent of the total number of elevated play components, unless the elevated play components are accessible by a ramp.
- Accessible ground-level play components must be integrated into the play area and not grouped into one area.

ELEVATED PLAY COMPONENTS

- At least 50 percent of all elevated play components must be accessible.

  Example: An elevated composite structure with 10 play components may include 2 slides, 4 climbers, and 4 activity panels. At least 5 of these components must be accessible.
- If fewer than 20 elevated play components are provided (accessible and nonaccessible), transfer systems may be used to connect accessible elevated components instead of ramps.

  Example: A play structure with 18 elevated play components is required to provide at least 9 accessible elevated components. These accessible elevated components may be connected by a transfer system.
- If a play structure has 20 or more elevated play components, no more than 50 percent of the accessible elevated play components may be connected by a transfer system.

  Example: A play structure with 24 elevated play components is required to have at least 12 accessible elevated play components. Only 6 of the accessible components may be connected by a transfer system. The other 6 play components must be connected by ramps.

SOFT CONTAINED PLAY STRUCTURES

- When three or fewer entry points are provided for each structure, a minimum of one entry point must be on an accessible route.
- When four or more entry points are provided, an accessible route is required to at least two entry points.
- A transfer system may be used as a part of the accessible route connecting entry points.
- Wheelchair lifts may be used as part of an accessible route.

General Hazards in Playground Design

Below is a brief summary of recommendations offered by the CPSC in the *Handbook of Public Playground Safety* regarding some of the more common hazards encountered in the design of play areas. The original report should be consulted for a complete discussion on each of these issues.

SHARP POINTS, CORNERS, AND EDGES

- The exposed open ends of all tubing not resting on the ground or otherwise covered should be covered by caps or plugs that cannot be removed without the use of tools.
- Wood parts should be smooth and free from splinters.
- Round all corners on both metal and wood.
- All metal edges should be rolled or have rounded capping.

PROTRUSIONS AND PROJECTIONS

- Protrusions and projections should comply with the testing methods outlined in ASTM F 1438-95.
- The diameter of a protrusion should not increase in the direction away from the surrounding surface toward the exposed end.

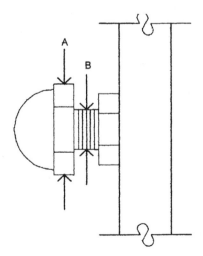

Unacceptable protrusion because
diameter of A is greater than diameter of B

ENTRAPMENT

- The interior opposing surfaces of any openings should not be more than 3½ in (8.9 cm) or less than 9 in (23 cm) to reduce the potential of entrapment. This applies to all completely bounded openings, except where the ground serves as an opening's lower boundary.

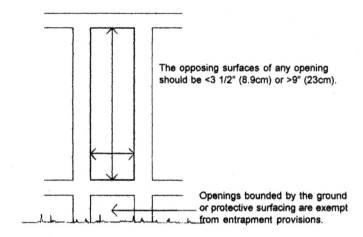

The opposing surfaces of any opening should be <3 1/2" (8.9cm) or >9" (23cm).

Openings bounded by the ground or protective surfacing are exempt from entrapment provisions.

- As shown, angles running horizontally that are created by adjacent components should be greater than 55° (A), unless the lower leg is horizontal or slopes downward (B). For angles less than 55°, an insert that is of sufficient size to prevent a 9-in- (23-cm-) diameter template from touching both sides of the angle components at the same time should be installed within the angle (C).

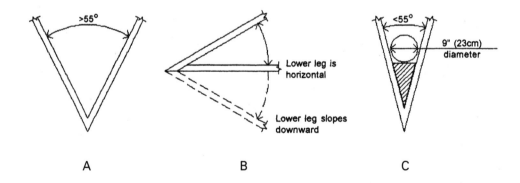

>55°

Lower leg is horizontal

Lower leg slopes downward

<55°

9" (23cm) diameter

A   B   C

TRIPPING

- All anchoring devices for playground equipment, such as concrete footings or horizontal bars at the bottom of flexible climbers, should be installed below ground level, beneath the base of the protective surfacing material, to eliminate the hazard of tripping.

- Retaining walls should be highly visible and any change of elevation should be obvious.

SUSPENDED ELEMENTS

- Cables, wires, ropes, or similar flexible components suspended below 7 ft (1.8 m) and between play units or from the ground to a play unit within 45° of horizontal should not be located in areas of high traffic. They should also be brightly colored or contrast with surrounding equipment to add to their visibility.

Playgrounds for Two- to Five-Year-Olds

It is strongly recommended that within the playground, children between the ages of 2 and 5 have separate play areas from older children. In addition, several types of equipment are not recommended for use on playgrounds for the younger children, whereas other types of equipment may be used with modifications that take into account the reduced ranges of motion of children this age and their less-developed skill levels. Following is a list of those pieces of play equipment that are not recommended for use in play areas intended for children ages 2 to 5. Throughout the remainder of the chapter, the recommendations for playground design and design modifications for equipment meant for children in this age range will be highlighted.

The CPSC does not recommend the use of the following pieces of equipment or play events in play areas intended for preschool children ages 2 to 5:

- Chain or cable walks
- Free-standing arch climbers
- Free-standing climbing events with flexible components
- Fulcrum seesaws
- Log rolls
- Long spiral slides (more than one turn—360°)
- Overhead rings
- Parallel bars
- Swinging gates
- Track rides
- Vertical sliding poles

Accessory Elements for Play Environments

FENCE HEIGHT (NONSECURITY)

The following describes fences that do not perform the function of security for adults and are not regulated by building codes. Security fences should remain at the standard or required height with special attention being given to whether gate hardware should be operable by children and if so, of what age.

Fences that are to be used to direct pedestrian circulation, define activity areas, or discourage physical access while providing visual access are often used in children's outdoor play areas. The following chart suggests heights for such fences. The heights given place the top of the fence midway between a child's navel and collarbone. It is important to design fences that are above the center of gravity of the oldest and tallest anticipated child that will be playing in the area. The information on the following chart may be verified for appropriateness with the "Center of Gravity" chart in Chapter 1.

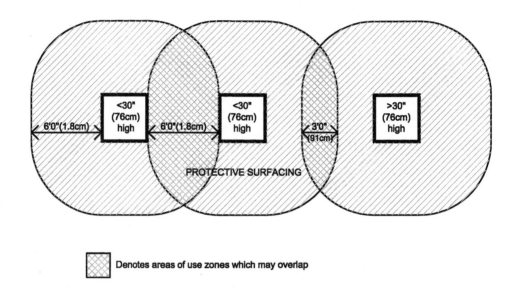

Denotes areas of use zones which may overlap

The use of horizontal members in the design of a fence often encourages climbing. If this is desirable, attention should be given to the surface beneath the fence. A fall height should be calculated from the highest location above the ground that is attainable by the child and appropriate surfacing provided. See "Fall Height" previously discussed in this chapter. All openings in fences within children's areas should be less than 3½ in (89 mm) or greater than 9 in (23 cm) between any two opposing sides to reduce the possibility of entrapment.

STATIONARY EQUIPMENT (EXCLUDING SLIDES)

Use zone: Stationary equipment is defined as any play structure that does not move or does not have components that move during its intended use. The use zone of stationary equipment, excluding slides, is a minimum of 6 ft (1.8 m) in all directions from the perimeter of the equipment. The use zones of stationary pieces of playground equipment may overlap if none of the play surfaces of the equipment is more than 30 in (76 cm) above the playground surfacing. If one of the play surfaces is over 30 in (76 cm) above the playground surfacing, it may only overlap another use zone by 3 ft (91 cm).

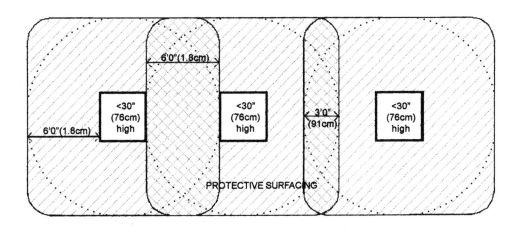

Denotes areas of use zones which may overlap

INTERACTIVE AND MANIPULATIVE PANELS

Use zone: Interactive panels are considered stationary equipment. The use zone is a minimum of 6 ft (1.8 m) from the perimeter of the equipment. See the preceding section entitled "Stationary Equipment" for information regarding possible overlapping with other use zones.

Interactive and manipulative panels come in a wide variety of designs and offer children more sedentary play opportunities within the playground. These panels may be freestanding but are often attached to playstructures. Depending on the design, they may be operated by one, or more than one child. The panels should be mounted at a height that makes them easily reached by the youngest anticipated user. The appropriate mounting height for these panels may be determined using the anthropometric data given in Chapter 1.

Modifications for Accessibility

Refer to "Accessibility Requirements" earlier in this chapter regarding the number of interactive and manipulative panels that must be provided.

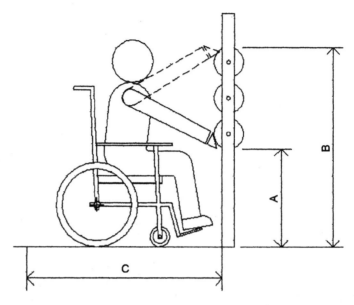

A–B For accessibility by children of ages 2 to 5, the features of the manipulative and interactive play components should be mounted so that the bottom edge of the features is not less than 20 in (51 cm) above the ground and the upper edge of the features is not more than 36 in (91.5 cm) above the ground.

For children over the age of 5, the features of the play components should be mounted so that the bottom edge of the features is not less than 18 in (45.5 cm) above the ground and the upper edge of the features is not more than 40 in (101.5 cm) above the ground. This range is appropriate for both forward and side approaches to the panel.

C Unless elevated and accessible by means of a transfer system, a 30-in- (76-cm-) minimum by 48-in- (123-cm-) minimum clear space must be provided to allow for the approach to the play panel. To provide for a forward approach, the 48-in (123-cm) dimension should be perpendicular to the panel. For a side approach, the 30-in (76-cm) dimension should be perpendicular to the panel.

HANDRAILS (FOR PLAY AREAS)

The handrails described are for use with stairs and ramps of play structures of which children are the primary users. They are not to be used in situations that are governed by building codes and accessibility requirements. Refer to the section entitled "Handrail Height" in Chapter 2 for those situations.

Handrails should be provided on both sides of all stairways and stepladders that have more than one tread. They should begin with the first step and extend continuously the full length of the stairway or stepladder.

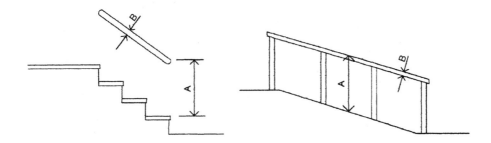

A The vertical distance between the top surface of the handrail and the top front edge of a step (tread nosing) or ramp surface should be between 22 and 38 in (56 and 96.5 cm).

B The diameter or maximum cross-sectional dimension of a handrail is recommended to be between 0.95 and 1.55 in (24 and 39 mm), with a diameter of 1¼ in (32 mm) being preferred.

MODIFICATIONS

Modification for ages 2 to 5:
A The vertical distance between the top surface of the handrail and the top front edge of a step (tread nosing) or ramp surface should be between 22 and 26 in (56 and 66 cm).

Requirements for Accessibility:
Accessible ramps that lead from the ground level onto the play structure and are located within the use zone of the structure are not required to have handrails. However, ramps connecting elevated play events are required to have handrails. These handrails should be 20 in (51 cm) minimum to 28 in (71 cm) maximum above the ramp surface. The diameter or width of the handrails should be 0.95 in (24 mm) minimum to 1.55 in (39 mm) maximum. An additional handrail for adults is not required.

PLATFORMS, GUARDRAILS, AND PROTECTIVE BARRIERS

Stepped platforms are typically found on composite structures. The platforms are layered or tiered so that a child may fall onto a lower platform rather than the protective surfacing.

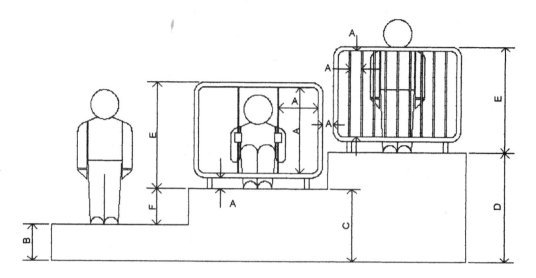

A Platforms, guardrails, and protective barriers should not have openings with dimensions greater than 3½ in (89 mm) or less than 9 in (229 mm), to reduce the hazard of entrapment. They should also not create openings within this range with adjacent platforms or elements.

B Platforms that are less than 30 in (76 cm) above the protective surfacing do not necessarily require a guardrail or protective barrier.

C Guardrails should be used for platforms that are 30 to 48 in (76 to 122 cm) above the protective surfacing. A guardrail protects a child from an unintentional fall, but allows a child to climb through the openings. See E regarding design.

D Protective barriers should be used for platforms that are more than 48 in (122 cm) above the protective surfacing. A protective barrier protects a child from an unintentional fall, and also prevents the child from climbing through or over the barrier. See E regarding design.

E Guardrails and protective barriers should have a minimum height of 38 in (96.5 cm) above the platform. Horizontal elements should not be used in the infill area of either guardrails or protective barriers, because they provide a means for climbing. Solid panels are also not recommended as infill, because they make supervision difficult.

F The maximum difference in height between stepped platforms should be 18 in (46 cm), unless there is an alternate means to move from platform to platform (stairs, ramp, ladder, etc.). Openings between platforms that do not conform to the entrapment provisions (item A) should be closed.

Modifications for ages 2 to 5:
B Platforms that are less than 20 in (51 cm) above the protective surfacing do not necessarily require a guardrail or protective barrier.

C Guardrails should be used for platforms that are 20 to 30 in (51 to 76 cm) above the protective surfacing.

D Protective barriers should be used for platforms that are more than 30″ (76 cm) above the protective surfacing.

E Guardrails and protective barriers should have a minimum height of 29 in (74 cm) above the platform.

F The maximum difference in height between stepped platforms should be 12 in (30.5 cm), unless there is an alternate means to move from platform to platform (stairs, ramp, ladder, etc.). Entrapment provisions apply (see item **A**).

Play Equipment for Play Environments

COMPOSITE PLAY STRUCTURES

Many playgrounds contain composite play structures that offer a variety of play events that are attached to create one integral unit. The use zone for these types of structures is typically 6 ft (1.8 m) minimum from the perimeter of the equipment, except where slides occur at which point the use zone requirements at the exit points for slides must be observed and may increase the use zone (see section on Slides). On residential play areas, swings will also increase the use zone of a composite play structure beyond the standard 6 ft (1.8 m) guideline (see section on Residential Playgrounds). However, it is not recommended to attach swings to composite play structures on public playgrounds.

GOING UP AND DOWN

Stairs

The following describes stairs that are play elements that provide access to and/or egress from play equipment and are not meant for use in situations that are governed by life safety codes or accessibility requirements.

Use zone: Because stairs are stationary equipment, the use zone is a minimum of 6 ft (1.8 m) from the perimeter of the equipment. See the section entitled "Stationary Equipment" earlier in this chapter for information regarding possible overlapping with other use zones.

Handrails should be provided at all stairs that have more than one tread. The section entitled "Handrails (for Play Areas)" in this chapter provides handrail design information when only one handrail is to be provided and intended for use primarily by children in play areas. In Chapter 2, the sections entitled "Handrail Height" and "Handrail Diameter" provide information on handrails for children that are provided as a secondary handrail to one intended for use by adults, in which the latter is governed by building and accessibility standards.

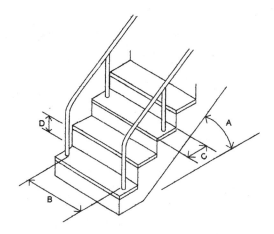

A The maximum angle of slope created by the ground and the stairs should be 35°.

B The clear width of the stairs should be a minimum of 16 in (41 cm) for use by one child at a time and a minimum of 36 in (91.5 cm) for situations in which two children side by side may be using the stairs.

C Each tread should be a minimum of 8 in (203 mm) deep, whether the risers are open or closed.

D The maximum recommended riser height is 12 in (30.5 cm). The steps should be evenly spaced, including the spacing between the top step and the surface of the platform. To reduce the risk of entrapment, no open space within the design of the steps should have a dimension that is greater than 3½ in (89 mm) and less than 9 in (229 mm).

MODIFICATIONS

Modifications for ages 2 to 5:
B The clear width of the stairs should be 12 in (30.5 cm) minimum for one-way use and 30 in (76 cm) minimum for two-way use.
C Each tread should be a minimum of 7 in (18 cm) deep, whether the risers are open or closed.
D The maximum recommended riser height is 9 in (23 cm). The provisions to reduce the risk of entrapment still apply.

Stepladders

Use zone: Because stepladders are stationary equipment, the use zone is a minimum of 6 ft (1.8 m) from the perimeter of the equipment. See the section entitled "Stationary Equipment" earlier in this chapter for information regarding possible overlapping with other use zones.

Handrails are recommended at all stepladders that have more than one tread. The section entitled "Handrails (for Play Areas)" in this chapter provides handrail design information when one handrail is to be provided and is intended for use primarily by children in play areas.

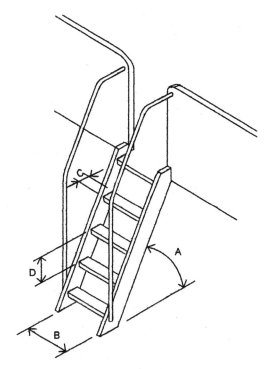

A The angle of slope created by the ground and the ladder should be between 50° and 75°.

B The clear width of the ladder should be a minimum of 16 in (41 cm) for use by one child at a time and a minimum of 36 in (91.5 cm) for situations in which two children may be using the ladder side by side.

C Each tread should be a minimum of 3 in (76 mm) deep if the risers are open and a minimum of 6 in (152 mm) deep if the risers are closed.

D The maximum recommended tread-to-tread distance is 12 in (30.5 cm). The steps should be evenly spaced, including the spacing between the top step and the surface of the platform. To reduce the risk of entrapment, no open space within the design of the steps should have a dimension that is greater than 3½ in (89 mm) and less than 9 in (229 mm).

Modifications for ages 2 to 5:
B The clear width of the ladder should be between 12 and 21 in (30.5 and 53 cm) and is intended for use by one child at a time. Ladders that allow for two children side by side are not recommended for children in this age group.
C Each tread should be a minimum of 7 in (18 cm) deep, whether the risers are open or closed.
D The maximum recommended tread-to-tread distance is 9 in (23 cm). The provisions to reduce the risk of entrapment apply.

Ramps

Following are guidelines for ramps that are not necessarily designed to provide wheelchair access to play equipment. For ramps that provide wheelchair access, see the sidebar on accessibility modifications in this section.

Use zone: Because ramps are stationary equipment, the use zone is a minimum of 6 ft (1.8 m) from the perimeter of the equipment. See the section entitled "Stationary Equipment" earlier in this chapter for information regarding possible overlapping with other use zones.

To reduce the risk of entrapment, no open space within the design of a ramp should have a dimension that is greater than 3½ in (89 mm) and less than 9 in (229 mm).

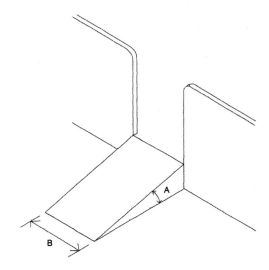

A The maximum recommended slope is 1 : 8.

B The recommended clear width is 16 in (41 cm) minimum for one-way use and 36 in (91 cm) minimum for two-way use.

MODIFICATION

Modification for ages 2 to 5:
B The recommended clear width is 12 in (30.5 cm) minimum for one-way use and 30 in (76 cm) minimum for two-way use.

Modifications for accessibility:
The requirements for accessible ramps within a play area are shown on the following diagram. The maximum slope for accessible ramps within a play area is 1 : 16, and they may not rise more than 12 in (30.5 cm) without a landing. They must also provide a clear width of 36 in (91 cm).

For handrail requirements, see the sidebar on accessibility requirements in the section entitled "Handrails (for Play Areas)" earlier in this chapter.

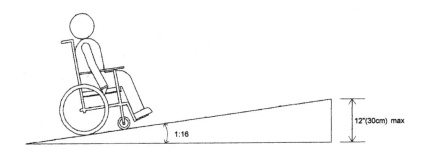

12"(30cm) max

1:16

Climbers

Use zone: Because climbers are stationary equipment, the use zone is a minimum of 6 ft (1.8 m) from the perimeter of the equipment. See the section entitled "Stationary Equipment" earlier in this chapter for information regarding possible overlapping with other use zones.

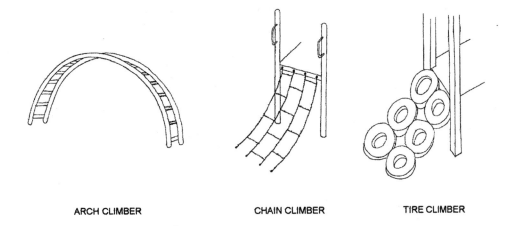

ARCH CLIMBER   CHAIN CLIMBER   TIRE CLIMBER

Climbing equipment comes in a wide variety of designs. The most common element among them is the use of bars as handgrips to climb from one location to another. Bars used for climbing should have a diameter or maximum cross-sectional dimension between 0.95 and 1.55 in (24 and 39 mm), with 1¼ in (32 mm) being preferred.

Climbers should not have climbing bars or other structural components in the interior of the structure onto which a child may fall from a height of greater than 18 in (46 cm). Following are recommendations for specific types of climbers.

- For arch climbers, the maximum recommended distance between rungs is 12 in (30.5 cm).
- Climbing grids made from ropes, chains, and tires should be securely anchored at both ends. When connected to the ground, the anchoring devices should be

installed below ground level, beneath the base of the protective surfacing material. Connections within the grid should be securely fixed, and spaces between the grid components should satisfy entrapment criteria. See the section entitled "Entrapment" earlier in this chapter.

MODIFICATIONS

Modifications for ages 2 to 5:

Because children in this age group have not yet developed some of the physical skills necessary for certain climbing activities (including balance, coordination, and upper-body strength), they may have difficulty using upper-body devices.

Where climbers are used, an alternate means of descent should be provided that is less challenging (i.e., stairs, slide, etc.). The ability of young children to ascend climbing components develops earlier than their ability to descend the same components. For this reason, freestanding arch climbers are not recommended.

In addition, flexible climbing grids made from ropes, chains, and tires should not be the only means of access to play equipment for this age group, because they require more advanced balancing ability than children this age have typically developed.

Rung Ladders

Use zone: Because rung ladders are stationary equipment, the use zone is a minimum of 6 ft (1.8 m) from the perimeter of the equipment. See the section entitled "Stationary Equipment" earlier in this chapter for information regarding possible overlapping with other use zones.

Because the rungs serve as handgrips, rung ladders do not require handrails. However, some form of support should be provided at the transition between the top of the ladder and the platform. This may be accomplished with the use of vertical handrails to the sides of the opening or loop handgrips extending over the top of the access.

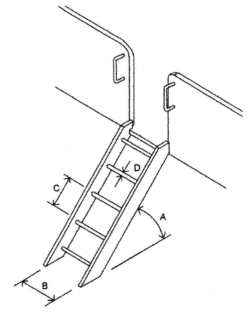

A The angle of slope created by the ground and the ladder should be between 75° and 90°.

B The clear width of the ladder should be a minimum of 16 in (41 cm).

C The rungs of a rung ladder should be evenly spaced, including the spacing between the top rung and the surface of the platform. The maximum distance between rungs should be 12 in (30.5 cm). To reduce the risk of entrapment, the rungs should not be less than 9 in (23 cm) apart.

D The diameter of the rungs should be between 0.95 and 1.55 in (24 and 39 mm) with 1¼ in (32 mm) preferred.

Modification for ages 2 to 5:
B The clear width of the ladder should be a minimum of 12 in (30.5 cm).

Climbing Ropes

Use zone: The use zone is a minimum of 6 ft (1.8 m) from the perimeter of the equipment. See the section "Stationary Equipment" earlier in this chapter for information regarding possible overlapping with other use zones.

A climbing rope should be secured at both ends and should not be capable of being looped back on itself, creating a loop with an inside perimeter greater than 5 in (12.7 cm). Refer to the following figure.

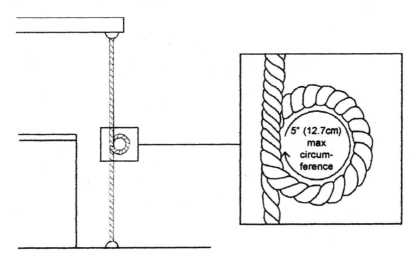

Seesaws

Use zone: The use zone of a seesaw is a minimum of 6 ft (1.8 m) from the perimeter of the equipment. See the section "Stationary Equipment" earlier in this chapter for information regarding possible overlapping with other use zones. It must be noted that although the use zone remains constant at 6 ft (1.8 m) from the perimeter, the length of the seesaw will affect the depth of surfacing. The longer the seesaw, the greater the fall height (maximum obtainable height by the child) will be. The critical height of the surfacing material beneath the seesaw should be greater than the fall height. See the section entitled "Selection of a Protective Surface" earlier in this chapter.

Although they are highly recommended for preschool children, the spring-centered seesaws discussed in the "Modifications for ages 2 to 5" sidebar may also be desirable for playgrounds used by older children due to their increased safety.

If traditional fulcrum seesaws are used, they should be constructed so that the maximum angle between the seesaw board and the ground is 25°. The fulcrum should not present a pinch or crush hazard. Partial car tires or some other shock-absorbing material should be embedded in the ground underneath the seats of fulcrum seesaws, or secured on the underside of the seats.

Handholds should be provided at each seating position and should not extend beyond the sides of the seat. Footrests should not be provided on fulcrum seesaws.

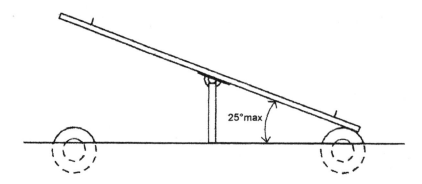

MODIFICATION

Modification for ages 2 to 5:

Fulcrum seesaws are not recommended for children in this age group because of the potential of one child dismounting without the foresight that it will cause the other child to abruptly hit the ground. However, seesaws that are designed with spring centering devices prevent this from occurring and are considered acceptable. Footrests may also be used on spring-centered seesaws.

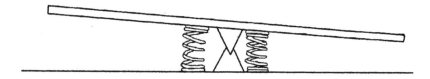

SEESAW WITH SPRING CENTERING

Slides

Use zone: The use zone to the sides of a slide should be a minimum of 6 ft (1.8 m) from the perimeter of the equipment. In the front of the exit from the slide, the use zone should be a minimum of $H + 4$ ft, measured from the point on the slide chute at which the slope becomes less than 5° from horizontal. H is the vertical distance from the playground surfacing at the exit to the highest point of the chute. Regardless of the height of the highest point of the chute, the use zone in front of the exit must be at least 6 ft (1.8 m) from the end of the slide, but it does not need to exceed 14 ft (4.3 m). The use zone for slides may not overlap the use zone of another piece of equipment.

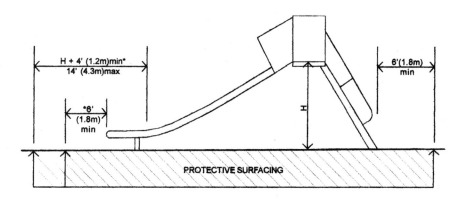

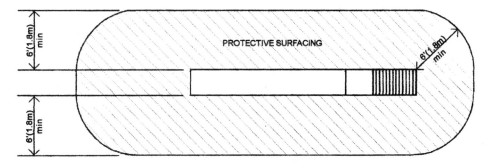

Slide Entries and Exits: The following recommendations concerning the design of entry and exit areas are for all slides. Following these recommendations are additional design guidelines for straight, embankment, spiral, tube, and roller slides.

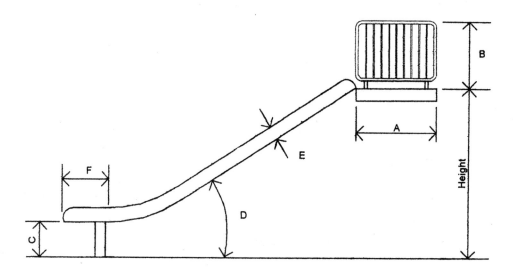

A All slides should be provided with a platform or area that is a minimum depth of 22 in to allow for the transition from standing to sitting at the top of the inclined sliding surface. This area should be horizontal and be at least as wide as the slide itself. There should not be any spaces or gaps between the platform and the start of the slide chute. Handholds should be provided at the entrance to the slide to aid in the transition from standing to sitting and to decrease the risk of falls. The incorporation of an element that will channel a user into a sitting position, such as a guardrail or hood, without encouraging climbing is also recommended.

B See "Platforms, Guardrails, and Protective Barriers" earlier in this chapter for guidelines on the design of the enclosure of the platform.

C For slides that are less than 4 ft (1.2 m) in height (from the highest point of the chute to the protective surfacing), the height of the exit region should be no more than 11 in (28 cm) from the protective surfacing. For slides that are over 4 ft (1.2 m) in height, the exit region should be between 7 and 15 in (18 and 38 cm) above the protective surfacing.

Straight Slides: The following guidelines are to be used in addition to the preceding recommendations for the design of the slide entry and exit areas.

D The average incline of a slide chute should be no more than 30 degrees, with no single portion of the slope being greater than 50 degrees.

E Sides of straight slides with flat open chutes should be 4 in (10 cm) minimum in height. The sides should continue along both sides of the chute for the entire length of the inclined sliding surface. Except for roller slides, the sides should be an integral part of the chute without any gaps between the sides and the sliding surface. Refer to the following diagrams for allowances in side heights for slide chutes that are circular, semicircular, or curved in cross section.

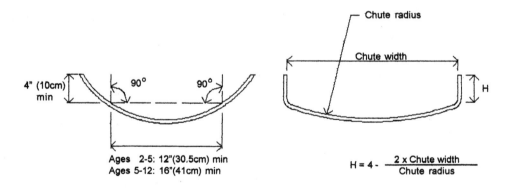

CIRCULAR CROSS SECTION   CURVED CROSS SECTION

F The exit region should be essentially horizontal, parallel to the ground and have a minimum length of 11 in (28 cm).

Embankment Slides: In addition to the preceding recommendations for the design of the slide entry and exit areas (**A**, **B**, and **C**), the slide chute of an embankment slide should be a maximum of 12 in (30.5 cm) above the ground. Some means should be provided at the slide chute entrance to minimize the use of the slide by children on skates, skateboards, or bicycles.

Spiral Slides: The following guidelines are to be used in addition to the preceding recommendations for the design of the slide entry and exit areas.

Modification for ages 2 to 5:
Due to a reduced lack of ability to maintain balance and control, only short spiral slides of one turn (360°) or less are recommended for children of this age.

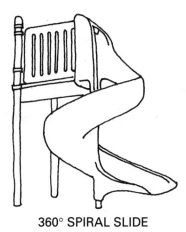

360° SPIRAL SLIDE

Tube Slides: In addition to the preceding recommendations for the design of the slide entry and exit areas (**A**, **B**, and **C**), the minimum internal diameter of a tube slide should not be less than 23 in (58.4 cm). Barriers should be provided or surfaces textured to prevent sliding on the top (outside) of the tube. Extra supervision and/or transparent tube sections should be considered to allow for supervision of the interior of the slide.

Roller Slides: In addition to the preceding recommendations for the design of the slide entry and exit areas (**A**, **B**, and **C**), the space between adjacent rollers and between the ends of the rollers and the stationary structure should be less than ³⁄₁₆ in (5 mm).

Sliding Poles

Use zone: The use zone for sliding poles is a minimum of 6 ft (1.8 m) from the perimeter of the equipment, including the pole and the entry platform. See "Stationary Equipment" earlier in this chapter for information regarding possible overlapping with other use zones.

A The horizontal distance between a sliding pole and the edge of the structure used for access should be 18 in (46 cm) minimum and 20 in (51 cm) maximum.

B The pole should extend at least 60 in (1.52 m) above the level of the platform or other structure used for access to the sliding pole.

C The diameter of the sliding pole should be no greater than 1.9 in (48 mm).

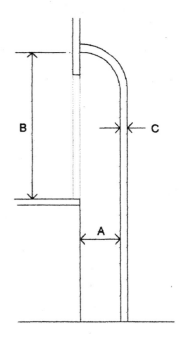

MODIFICATION

Modification for ages 2 to 5:
　　Because of their low level of upper-body strength and coordination, sliding poles are not recommended for children in this age range.

Trampolines

Trampolines are not recommended for use on public playgrounds.

GOING ACROSS

Balance Beams

Use zone: The use zone for balance beams is a minimum of 6 ft (1.8 m) from the perimeter of the equipment. See the section entitled "Stationary Equipment" earlier in this chapter for information regarding possible overlapping with other use zones.

A The maximum recommended height of balance beams is 16 in (41 cm).

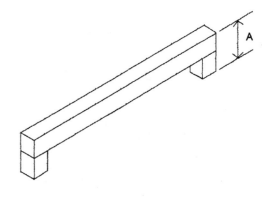

MODIFICATION

Modification for ages 2 to 5:

A The maximum recommended height of balance beams is 12 in (30.5 cm).

Horizontal Rung and Ring Ladders

Use zone: The use zone for horizontal rung and ring ladders is a minimum of 6 ft (1.8 m) from the perimeter of the equipment. See "Stationary Equipment" earlier in this chapter for information regarding possible overlapping with other use zones.

The first handhold on either end of upper-body equipment should not be placed directly above the platform or climbing rung used for mount or dismount to reduce the risk of children falling onto them.

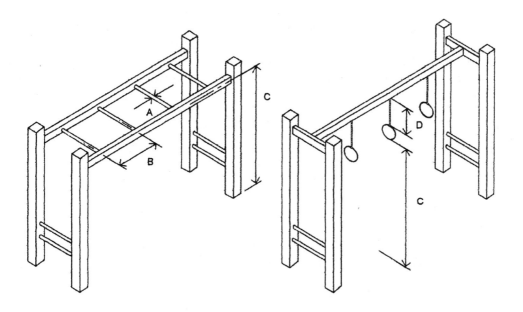

A Rungs should have a diameter between 0.95 and 1.55 in (24 and 39 mm), with 1¼ in (32 mm) being preferred.

B The center-to-center spacing of horizontal ladder rungs should be greater than 9 in (23 cm) to reduce the risk of entrapment, but no more than 15 in (38 cm).

C The maximum distance from the center of the grasping device (rung or ring) to the protective surfacing should be 84 in (2.13 m).

D The maximum length of chain used to suspend overhead swing rings should be 12 in (30.5 cm).

MODIFICATIONS

Modifications for ages 2 to 5:

Most young children are not able to use upper-body equipment, such as the horizontal ladders, until they are 4 years old; therefore, this equipment is not recommended for toddler play areas for children between ages 2 and 3. In addition, because children in this age group have not yet developed some of the physical skills necessary for certain climbing activities (including balance, coordination, and upper-body strength), they may have difficulty using upper-body devices, such as overhead rings and track rides.

B The center-to-center spacing of horizontal ladder rungs should be greater than 9 in (23 cm) to reduce the risk of entrapment, but no more than 12 in (30.5 cm). The rungs should be parallel to one another and evenly spaced.

C The maximum distance from the center of the rung to the protective surfacing should be 60 in (1.52 m). Rings are not recommended.

GOING AROUND

Merry-Go-Rounds (Including All Rotating Equipment)

Use zone: The use zone for merry-go-rounds extends a minimum of 6 ft (1.8 m) from the perimeter of the platform or equipment. The use zone for a merry-go-round cannot overlap the use zone of another piece of play equipment.

The rotating platform of a merry-go-round should be continuous with no openings that would permit a ⁵⁄₁₆-in-diameter rod to penetrate completely through the surface. The platform should also be approximately circular and should not have an up-and-down movement. No components, including handgrips, should extend beyond the perimeter of the platform.

A Handgrips should have a diameter between 0.95 and 1.55 in (24 and 39 mm), with 1¼ in (32 mm) being preferred.

B The underside of the platform at the perimeter should be a minimum of 9 in (23 cm) above the protective surfacing.

C–D For noncircular platforms, the difference between the maximum radius from the axis of rotation and the minimum radius from the axis of rotation should not exceed 2 in (51 mm): $C - D \leq 2$ in (51 mm).

E The speed of rotation at the periphery should be limited to a maximum of 13 ft (4 m)/s.

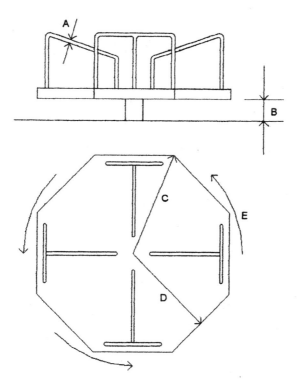

Modification for ages 2 to 5:

Merry-go-rounds should not be used in situations in which a child this age may be playing without close supervision. Preschool-age children have little or no control over this type of equipment once it is in motion.

GOING BACK AND FORTH

Spring Rockers

Use zone: The use zone for spring rockers is a minimum of 6 ft (1.8 m) from the at-rest perimeter of the equipment. For spring rockers on which the user sits, the rocker's use zone may overlap that of adjacent spring rockers, if the seats of both are 30 in (76 cm) or less above the protective surfacing. For spring rockers on which the user stands, the use zone may not overlap with the use zone of another play structure.

The design of the seat of a spring rocker should not allow the rocker to be used by more than the intended number of users. Each seating position should be equipped with handgrips and footrests. The diameter of handgrips should be between 0.95 and 1.55 in (24 and 39 mm), with 1¼ in (32 mm) being the preferred diameter. Care should be taken to minimize the possibility of children pinching their hands or feet between coils or between the spring and a part of the rocker.

Modification for accessibility:

If spring rockers are provided on the playground, at least one must be accessible. Spring rockers on which the user is seated require transfer. Therefore, the entry point or seat must be located between 11 in (28 cm) minimum and 24 in (61 cm) maximum above the ground.

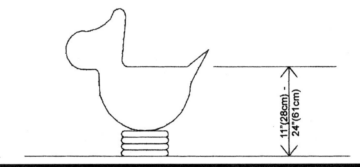

Swings

The following recommendations are for swings that are suspended in such a way as to only allow movement along one axis. Recommendations for swings that allow movement along more than one axis, such as tire swings, follow immediately.

Use zone: The use zone of a single-axis swing extends perpendicularly in both directions from the support beam a minimum distance of twice the height (*H*) from the pivot point to the protective surfacing directly below. This area may not overlap with the use zone of other play structures. The use zones to the sides of the swing extend 6 ft (1.8 m) from the perimeter of the swing structure. These side zones may overlap with the use zones of adjacent swing structures.

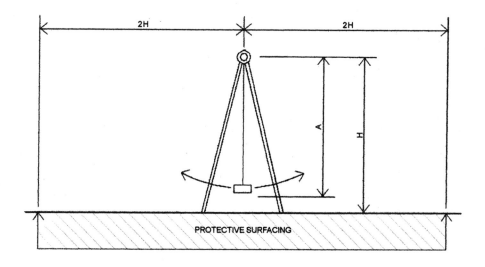

PROTECTIVE SURFACING

2H   2H

A   H

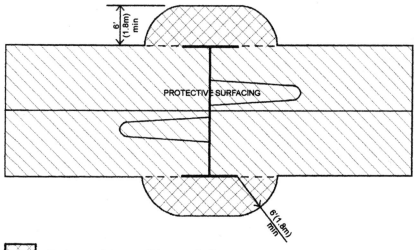

PROTECTIVE SURFACING

6' (1.8m) min

6'(1.8m) min

Denotes area of use zone which may overlap the use zones of adjacent swing structures

MODIFICATION

Modification for ages 2 to 5:

A The use zone for swings intended for use primarily by this age group should extend perpendicularly in both directions a minimum distance of twice the height from the pivot point to the lowest point on a swing seat surface below, when the seat is occupied (**A**).

Swings should be located away from other play equipment or activities to prevent young children from accidentally running into the path of a moving swing. For this same reason, it is not recommended that swings be attached to composite play structures in public play areas. To eliminate climbing, support structures should not have horizontal stabilizing crossbars.

Although no more than two swings should be hung in each bay of a support structure, the number of bays is not limited. Hardware used to secure the suspending elements to the swing seat and to the supporting structure should not be removable without the use of tools. S-hooks should be pinched closed to a maximum gap width of 0.04 in [1 mm (the thickness of a dime)].

Wood or metal swing seats are not recommended. Lightweight rubber or plastic swing seats are preferred. Swing seats should be designed to accommodate no more than one user at a time. Fiber ropes are not recommended for the suspension of swings.

Following is a list of swing types that are not recommended and reasons why they are not recommended for use on public playgrounds.

- *Animal figure swings:* The heavy framework presents an impact injury risk.
- *Multiple-occupancy swings (tire swings excluded):* The greater mass presents the potential for greater impact injury.
- *Rope swings:* These present a strangulation hazard.
- *Trapeze bar/exercise rings combinations:* These are intended for athletic training, not for play areas.

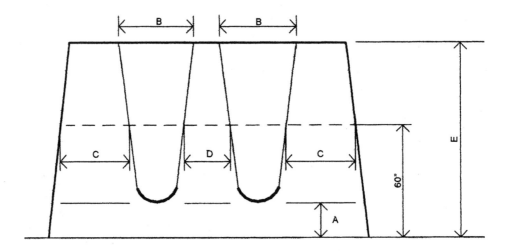

A The distance from the underside of an occupied swing seat to the protective surfacing should be no less than 16 in (41 cm).

B Swing hangers should be spaced no less than 20 in (51 cm) apart.

C At a point 60 in (1.5 m) above the protective surfacing, the distance from the swing support structure and the swing seat suspension member should be a minimum of 30 in (76 cm).

D At a point 60 in (1.5 m) above the protective surfacing, the distance between two swing seat suspension members should be a minimum of 24 in (61 cm).

MODIFICATIONS

Modifications for ages 3 to 5:
A The distance from the underside of an occupied swing seat to the protective surfacing should be no less than 12 in (30.5 cm).

Modifications for toddlers (ages 1 to 2):
Full-bucket swing seats are recommended to provide support on all sides of the young child. It is also recommended that these tot swings be suspended from structures that are separate from other swings for older children.
A For tot swings that are intended to be used with adult assistance, the distance from the underside of an occupied swing seat to the protective surfacing should be no less than 24 in (61 cm) minimum to minimize the likelihood that unsupervised young children may become stuck in the seat.
E It is recommended that the pivot points for swings to be used by this age group be no greater than 8 ft (2.4 m) above the protective surfacing.

Modifications for accessibility:
If swings are provided on the playground, at least one must be accessible. Maneuvering space must be provided at accessible swings. Diagrams of acceptable configurations for maneuvering space are shown earlier in this chapter.
A Swings require transfer; therefore, the swing seat must be located between 11 in (28 cm) minimum and 24 in (61 cm) maximum above the ground.

Tire Swings

Use zone: The use zone of a tire swing extends in all directions from a point on the surface directly below the pivot point for a minimum distance of 6 ft (1.8 m) plus the vertical length (*L*) measured from the pivot point to a point directly below that is at the same height above the ground as the seating surface. This zone should not overlap the use zone of any other equipment. The use zone should also extend a minimum of 6 ft (1.8 m) from the perimeter of the supporting structure. These zones may overlap the use zone of adjacent swing structures or other pieces of play equipment.

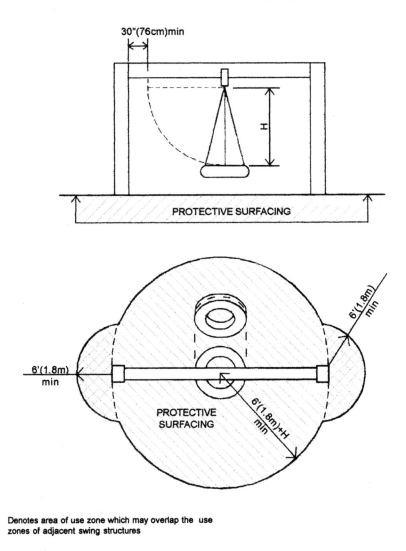

30"(76cm)min

H

PROTECTIVE SURFACING

6'(1.8m) min

6'(1.8m) min

6'(1.8m)+H min

PROTECTIVE SURFACING

Denotes area of use zone which may overlap the use zones of adjacent swing structures

As shown, the minimum clearance between the seating surface of a tire swing and the uprights of the supporting structure should be 30 in (76 cm) when the tire is in a position closest to the support structure. A tire swing should not be suspended within the same support bay as other swings and should not be attached to composite (multicomponent) structures. The hanger mechanisms should not have any accessible pinch points. The use of heavy truck tires should be avoided. Careful inspection is required if steel-belted radials are used to ensure that there are no exposed steel belts. Drainage holes should be provided in the underside of the tire to allow for drainage.

Estimated Costs of Public Playground Construction

As reported in the Architectural and Transportation Compliance Board's ADAAG for Play Areas, rule-of-thumb estimates of the costs of playground construction may be calculated as follows:

Cost of playground equipment (x)

+ Cost of installation (.30x)

+ Cost of surfacing (.12x)

+ Cost of design fees, grading, landscaping, and other expenses (.10x)

= Total project cost or budget

Therefore, if the total budget for a project is known, the costs of equipment, installation, surfacing, design fees, and site work may be calculated using the following formulas:

Cost of playground equipment = Total project cost or budget/1.52

Cost of installation = Cost of equipment $\times$ 0.30

Cost of surfacing = Cost of equipment $\times$ 0.12

Cost of design fees, grading, landscaping,

and other expenses = Cost of equipment $\times$ 0.10

Residential Playgrounds

Issues such as use zones, surfacing, and hazards are discussed in previous sections in relation to the design of public playgrounds. The guidelines presented in those sections are equally applicable to the design of residential playgrounds and play structures.

GENERAL HAZARDS

See the section entitled "General Hazards in Playground Design" earlier in this chapter for additional information.

- Openings that are bound on all sides should not have a dimension that is greater than 3½ in (89 mm) and less than 9 in (23 cm), to reduce the potential of entrapment.
- S-hooks should be closed as tightly as possible.
- Protrusions or catch points that may entangle children's clothing and cause strangulation should be eliminated.
- There should be no exposed moving parts that may present a pinching or crushing hazard.

USE ZONES

As with public playgrounds, use zones should be provided for in the layout of a residential playground as well. Except for swings and slides, this zone will typically be a minimum of 6 ft (1.5 m), extending from the periphery of the equipment in all directions. It is to this limit that protective surfacing should be installed. See earlier in this chapter to determine the use zone for swings and the use zone for slides.

Protective surfacing should be placed under and around all playground equipment. Playground equipment should never be placed on asphalt or concrete. Grass and turf lose their ability to absorb shock through wear and environmental conditions. Refer to the section entitled "Selection of a Protective Surface" in this chapter to determine the optimum surfacing material for home playgrounds.

GUARDRAILS AND PROTECTIVE BARRIERS

The use of guardrails and protective barriers in the design of residential playstructures parallels that on public playgrounds (see earlier in this chapter) with the following exceptions: The height for protective barriers on platforms that are higher than 48 in (1.2 m) above the protective surfacing, but not more than 72 in (1.8 m), should not be less than 27 in (69 cm). The height for protective barriers on platforms that are higher than 72 in (1.8 m) above the protective surfaces should not be less than 33 in (84 cm).

HANDRAILS

Handrails and gripping bars should not exceed 1.6 in (41 mm) in diameter or in the maximum cross-sectional dimension.

SLIDES

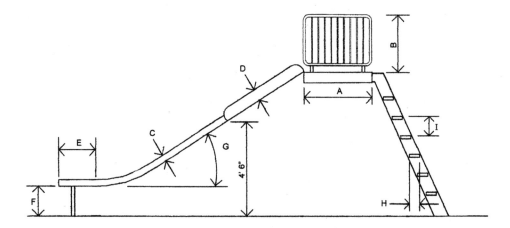

A The transition platform at the top of the slide should be a minimum of 10 in (25 cm) deep and should be at least as wide as the sliding surface.

B A handrail or barrier should be provided on all sides of the transition platform except those of the entrance and exit to and from the platform. See "Guardrails and Protective Barriers" for the recommended heights of the barriers.

C Below a point that is 4 ft 6 in (1.4 m) above the protective surfacing, the slide should have side rails that project perpendicularly from the sliding surface a minimum of 1 in (25 mm).

D Above 4 ft 6 in (1.4 m) to the top platform, side rails should project perpendicularly from the sliding surface a minimum of 2½ in (64 mm).

E The slide bed at the exit from the slide should be a minimum of 6 in (15 cm) in length.

F The end of the slide should not be more than 12 in (30.5 cm) above the protective surfacing.

G The slope of the slide may be a minimum of 18 degrees and a maximum of 48 degrees.

H Ladders with the sole purpose of providing access to slides should have steps that are at least 10 in (25 cm) wide and are at least 1 in (25 mm) deep.

I The steps of the slide ladder should be evenly spaced at a maximum of 11 in (28 cm) when measured vertically.

SWINGS

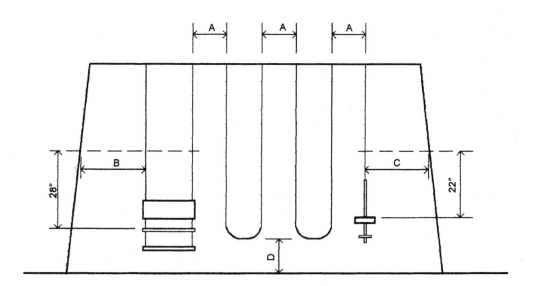

A A minimum distance of 8 in (20 cm) should be provided between adjacent swing elements that are capable of limited lateral motion (i.e., where two or more chains, ropes, or poles are used for suspension). Swing elements that are capable of unlimited lateral motion (i.e., suspended by a single rope or pole) should be separated a minimum of 15 in (38 cm) from adjacent swing elements.

B For swing elements that place supports on both sides of the user (i.e., single-seat swings, multi-occupant swings), a minimum distance of 7 in (18 cm) should be provided between a swing support frame and the swing element when measured at a height 28 in (71 cm) above the seating surface.

C For swing elements that place the support in line with the user (i.e., pendulum seesaws), the minimum distance between the support frame and the swing element should be a minimum of 16 in (41 cm) when measured 22 in (56 cm) above the seating surface.

D The distance from the protective surfacing to the underside of a swing seat should be a minimum of 8 in (20 cm).

Vegetation

The following information is from *An Outdoor Classroom* by Steen B. Esbensen. It includes a list of common nontoxic and toxic vegetable and landscape materials in North America. Depending on where a project is located, other plants in both categories will exist. Special care should be taken to avoid placing toxic plants in areas where very young children, ages 0 to 5, will be among the primary users.

NONTOXIC GARDEN PLANTS

Aster (*Callistephus*)
Begonia
Fuchsia
Forget-me-not (*Myosotis*)
Geranium (*Pelargonium*)
Gloxinia (*Sinningia speciosa*)
Hollyhock (*Althaea*)
Impatiens
Lily—Easter (*Lilium longiflorum*)
Lily—Tiger (*Lilium tigrina*)
Petunia
Phlox
Rose
Snapdragon (*Antirrhinum*)

NONTOXIC HEDGES AND BUSHES

False spirea (*Astilbe*)
Hawthorne/haws (*Crataegus*)
Honeysuckle (*Lonicera*)—all species
Lilac (*Syringa*)
Mock orange (*Philadelphus, pittosporum tobira*)
Spirea (*Spirea japonica*)

TOXIC GARDEN PLANTS

Anemone—all species
Autumn crocus (*Colchicum autumnale*)
Azalea (*Rhododendron*)—all species
Bleeding heart (*Dicentra*)
Bluebell/squill (*Scilla nonscripta, peruviana*)
Buttercup (*Ranunculus*)—all species
Calla lily (*Zantedeschia aethiopica*)
Carnation (*Dianthus caryophyllus*)
Castor-oil, or castor bean, plant (*Ricinus communis*)
Chinese or Japanese lantern (*Physalis*)
Chrysanthemum (*Chrysanthemum*)
Clematis (*Clematis*)
Coneflower (*Rudbeckia hortensis Bailey*)
Daffodil (*Narcissus*)
Dahlia
Delphinium (*Delphinium*)
Foxglove (*Digitalis purpurea*)
Gladiola (*Gladiolus*)—bulb
Hyacinth (*Hyacinthus orientalis*)
Iris
Jonquil (*Narcissus*)
Larkspur (*Delphinium*)—all species

Lily of the valley (*Convallaria*)
Lupine (*Lupinus*)—all species
Morning glory (*Ipomoea tricolor*)
Narcissus (*Narcissus*)
Pansy (*Viola tricolor*)—seeds
Peony (*Paeonia officinalis*)—root
Primrose (*Primula*)
Sweet pea (*Lathyrus odoratus*)—child would have to eat a very large number of seeds before feeling ill
Sweet william (*Dianthus barbatus*)

TOXIC VEGETABLE PLANTS

Avocado leaves
Potato—green patches on tubers and above-ground part
Tomato greens
Rhubarb leaves

TOXIC HEDGES, BUSHES, TREES, AND VINES

Beech—all, but particularly European beech (*Fagus,* all species, particularly *sylvatica*)
Box/boxwood (*Buxus sempervirens*)
Buckthorn (*Rhamnus cathartica*)
Burning bush/spindle tree (*Euonymous alata*)
Caragana
Cherry laurel (*Laurocerasus officinalis*)
Cherry (*Prunus*)—leaves and twigs
Clematis (*Clematis*)
Cotoneaster (*Cotoneaster*)

Daphne (*Daphne mezereum*)
Elderberry (*Sambucus*)—not berries
English ivy (*Hedera helix*)
Holly (*Ilex*)—all species
Horse chestnut (*Aesculus hippocastanum*)
Hydrangea (*Hydrangea*)—all species
Jet bead/jet berry bush (*Rhodotypos tetrapetala Makino*)
Kentucky coffee tree (*Gymnocladus dioica*)
Laburnum/goldenchain tree (*Laburnum anagyroides*)
Lantana (*Lantana camara*)
Leucothoe (*Leucothoe*)
Mountain laurel (*Kalmia latifolia*)
Oak (*Quercus*)—all species
Oleander (*Nerium oleander*)
Periwinkle (*Vinca minor*)
Pieris/lily-of-the-valley bush (*Pieris japonica*)
Privet (*Ligustrum vulgare*)
Red mulberry (*Morus rubra*)
Rhododendron (*Rhododendron*)—all species
Snowberry/waxberry (*Symphoricarpos*)—all species
Strawberry bush (*Euonymus*)
Sumac (Staghorn) (*Rhus typhina*)
Virginia creeper (*Parthenocissus quinquefolia*)
Wisteria (*Wisteria sinensis*)
Yew (*Taxus*)—all species

TOXIC WILD MUSHROOMS

All species—should be considered toxic until identified by a mycologist

CHAPTER 4

Dimensions of Products That Are Common to Children's Environments

The following pages indicate the measurements of furnishings and equipment that are often located in spaces used by children. These dimensions will be useful to the designer in laying out spaces and planning for such functions as storage and dramatic play. Some of the measurements are of products of a particular brand and model. Even if the exact same product is not used, the measurements of the illustrated product can be used as a guideline or approximation of the amount of space that will be needed for a similar product. Other measurements are generic in nature and represent industry-wide norms. The accompanying sketches may also be helpful in acquainting the designer with some of the products that are on the market in a variety of categories. Many of the companies whose products are shown are listed in the company source list in the following section.

Seating

HIGH CHAIRS AND BOOSTER SEATS

Booster chair by Central Specialties
Width: 12 in (30.5 cm)
Depth: 12 in (30.5 cm)
Height: 11 in (27.9 cm)

Central Specialties high chair
Width: 19 in (48.3 cm)
Depth: 20 in (50.8 cm)
Height: 27½ in (69.9 cm)
Seat height: 19 in (48.3 cm)

Graco high chair
Width: 24 in (61 cm)
Depth: 24 in (61 cm)
Height: 39 in (99 cm)

LOUNGERS

Foam lounger
Width: 15 in (38.1 cm)
Length: 42 in (106.7 cm)
Height: 24 in (61 cm)

Bouloum lounger by Arconas
Width: 26 in (66 cm)
Length: 57 in (144.8 cm)
Height: 24 in (61 cm)

ROCKING CHAIRS

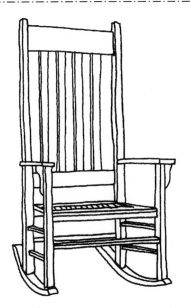

Adult rocker
Width: 24 in (61 cm)
Length: 33½ in (85.1 cm)
Overall height: 48 in (121.9 cm)
Seat height: 16¼ in (41.3 cm)

Child's rocking chair by Community Playthings
Width: 14½ (36.8 cm)
Depth: 18 in (45.7 cm)
Overall height: 24 in (61 cm)
Seat height: 10½ in (26.7 cm)

Wonderland by Design America
Width: 14 in (35.6 cm)
Depth: 21 in (53.3 cm)
Overall height: 22½ in (57.2 cm)
Seat height: 12 in (30.5 cm)

Toddle Rock by Joseph Company
Width: 17½ in (44.5 cm)
Depth: 16 in (40.6 cm)
Overall height: 18 in (45.7 cm)
Seat height: 7¼ in (18.4 cm)

**Little Maverick rocker by National Upholstery
    Company**
Width: 22½ in (57.2 cm)
Depth: 21 in (53.3 cm)
Overall height: 23½ in (59.7 cm)
Seat height: 10 in (25.4 cm)

SOFT (UPHOLSTERED) SEATING

Bean bags
32 in (81.3 cm) diameter

Chair 1 by Lee Industries
Width: 27 in (68.6 cm)
Depth: 26 in (66 cm)
Overall height: 26 in (66 cm)
Seat height: 14 in (35.6 cm)
Ottoman
Width: 21 in (53.3 cm)
Depth: 15 in (38.1 cm)
Height: 12 in (30.5 cm)

JR/672 chair by Nemschoff
Width: 21 in (53 cm)
Depth: 24½ (62.2 cm)
Overall height: 25½ in (64.8 cm)
Seat height: 14 in (35.6 cm)

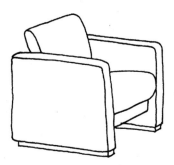

JR/626 chair by Nemschoff
Width: 25 in (63.5 cm)
Depth: 24 in (61 cm)
Overall height: 25 in (63.5 cm)
Seat height: 14¼ (36.2 cm)

Chair 3 by Lee Industries
Width: 23 in (58.4 cm)
Depth: 22 in (55.9 cm)
Seat height: 14 in (35.6 cm)
Overall height: 26 in (66 cm)

Chair 5 by Lee Industries
Width: 27 in (68.6 cm)
Depth: 22 in (55.9 cm)
Overall height: 27 in (68.6 cm)
Seat height: 13 in (33 cm)

Queen Anne wing chair
Width: 35 in (88.9 cm)
Depth: 25½ in (64.8 cm)
Overall height: 24 in (61 cm)
Seat height: 14 in (35.6 cm)

Chair 6 by Lee Industries
Width: 23 in (58.4 cm)
Depth: 23 in (58.4 cm)
Overall height: 34 in (86.4 cm)
Seat height: 15 in (38.1 cm)

Wing slipper chair by Classic Gallery
Width: 26 in (66 cm)
Depth: 29 in (73.7 cm)
Overall height: 28 in (71.1 cm)
Seat height: 15 in (38.1 cm)

Chippendale wing chair by Classic Gallery
Width: 21 in (53.3 cm)
Depth: 20½ in (52.1 cm)
Overall height: 28½ in (72.4 cm)
Seat height: 12 in (30.5 cm)

Loveseat 2 by Lee Industries
Width: 43 in (109.2 cm)
Depth: 28 in (71.1 cm)
Overall height: 26 in (66 cm)
Seat height: 14 in (35.6 cm)

Loveseat 4 by Lee Industries
Width: 40 in (101.6 cm)
Depth: 26 in (66 cm)
Overall height: 26 in (66 cm)
Seat height: 15 in (38.1 cm)

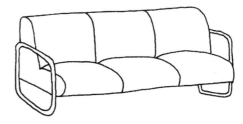

JR/672 sofa by Nemschoff
Width: 57 in (144.8 cm)
Depth: 24½ in (62.2 cm)
Overall height: 25½ in (64.8 cm)
Seat height: 14 in (35.6 cm)

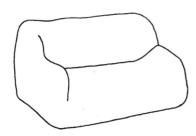

R & R by August, Inc.
Width: 40 in (101.6 cm)
Depth: 23 in (58.4 cm)
Overall height: 22 in (55.9 cm)
Seat height: 12½ in (31.8 cm)

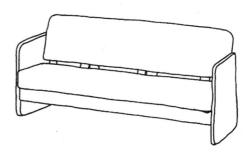

JR/616 sofa by Nemschoff
Width: 56½ in (143.5 cm)
Depth: 24 in (61 cm)
Overall height: 25 in (63.5 cm)
Seat height: 14¼ in (36.2 cm)

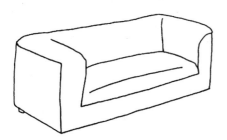

Loveseat by Classic Gallery
Width: 44 in (111.8 cm)
Depth: 29 in (73.7 cm)
Overall height: 28 in (71 cm)
Seat height: 15 in (38.1 cm)

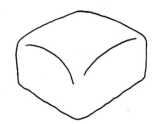

Linn Jr. modular seating group by August Inc.
Seat height: 13½ in (34.3 cm)
Overall height: 22 in (55.9 cm)
Straight section
Width: 20 in (50.8 cm)
Depth: 23½ in (59.7 cm)

Curved section
Diameter of front curve: 9 ft (2.74 m)
Wedge: 30°

Bench
Width: 20 in (50.8 cm)
Depth: 23½ (59.7 cm)
Height: 13½ in (34.3 cm)

NONWOOD CHAIRS

9000 chair by Virco Manufacturing Co.
Width: 19 in (48.3 cm)
Depth: 21½ (54.6 cm)
Overall height: 30 in (76.2 cm)
Seat height: 18 in (45.7 cm)

Lower seat heights available.
Bucket seat stacking chair by Childcraft

Seat height	10 in (25.4 cm)	12 in (30.5 cm)	14 in (35.6 cm)	16 in (40.6 cm)
Width	17 in (43.2 cm)	17 in (43.2 cm)	18 in (45.7 cm)	17 in (43.2 cm)
Depth	16 in (40.6 cm)	17 in (43.2 cm)	18 in (45.7 cm)	18 in (45.7 cm)

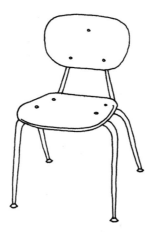

Overall height	23 in (58.4 cm)	23 in (58.4 cm)	26 in (66 cm)	28 in (71.1 cm)
Contemporary chair by Childcraft				
Seat height	10 in (25.4 cm)	12 in (30.5 cm)	14 in (35.6 cm)	16 in (40.6 cm)
Width	17 in (43.2 cm)	17 in (43.2 cm)	17 in (43.2 cm)	17 in (43.2 cm)
Depth	16 in (40.6 cm)	16 in (40.6 cm)	17 in (43.2 cm)	18 in (45.7 cm)
Overall height	22 in (55.9 cm)	23 in (58.4 cm)	25 in (63.5 cm)	27 in (68.6 cm)

All-purpose chair by Capitol

Seat height					
(adjustable)	12½ in (31.8 cm)	13½ in (34.3 cm)	14½ in (36.8 cm)	15½ in (39.4 cm)	16½ in (41.9 cm)
Width	15 in (38.1 cm)	15¼ in (38.7 cm)	15½ in (39.4 cm)	15¾ in (40 cm)	16¼ in (41.3 cm)
Depth	16½ in (41.9 cm)	17 in (43.2 cm)	17½ in (44.5 cm)	17¾ in (45.1 cm)	
Overall height	25¼ in (64.1 cm)	26¼ in (66.7 cm)	27¼ in (69.2 cm)	28¼ in (71.8 cm)	29¼ in (74.3 cm)

200-Series folding chair by KI

Seat height	12½ in (31.8 cm)	15¼ in (38.7 cm)
Width	14¼ in (36.2 cm)	16¼ in (41.3 cm)
Depth	14½ in (36.8 cm)	17¾ in (45.1 cm)
Overall height	22¾ in (57.8 cm)	28¼ in (71.8 cm)

Rainbow chair by The Little Tikes Company

Width: 12½ in (31.8 cm)
Depth: 11¾ in (29.8 cm)
Overall height: 16¼ in (41.3 cm)
Seat height: 10½ in (26.7 cm)

Versa Junior by KI

Seat height	10½ in (26.7 cm)	13 in (33 cm)	14½ in (36.8 cm)
Width	13 in (33 cm)	13 in (33 cm)	17¼ in (43.8 cm)
Depth	13 in (33 cm)	13 in (33 cm)	17¼ in (43.8 cm)
Overall height	21½ in (54.6 cm)	24 in (61 cm)	29 in (73.6 cm)

Bola Jr. by Fixtures Furniture

Seat height	10 in (25.4 cm)	13 in (33 cm)
Width	18 in (45.7 cm)	18 in (45.7 cm)
Depth	17 in (43 cm)	20 in (50.8 cm)
Overall height	21 in (53.3 cm)	24 in (61 cm)

Baseline by Angeles

Seat height	7 in (17.8 cm)	9 in (22.9 cm)	11 in (27.9 cm)	13 in (33 cm)	15 in (38.1 cm)
Width	13 in (33 cm)	13 in (33 cm)	13 in (33 cm)	13 in (33 cm)	13 in (33 cm)
Depth	11 in (28 cm)	11 in (28 cm)	11 in (28 cm)	11 in (28 cm)	13 in (33 cm)
Overall height	18 in (45.7 cm)	20 in (50.8 cm)	23 in (58.4 cm)	26 in (66 cm)	29 in (73.7 cm)

Scamps by Haworth
Width: 15¾ in (40 cm)
Depth: 19 in (48.3 cm)
Overall height: 25 in (63.5 cm)
Seat height: 14 in (35.6 cm)

Shape chair by The Children's Furniture Corp.
Width: 15 in (38.1 cm)
Depth: 16 in (40.6 cm)
Overall height: 25 in (63.5 cm)
Seat height: 14 in (35.6 cm)
Circle and triangle backs also available.

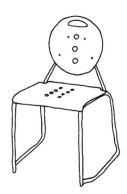

Charlie/Kids by Loewenstein
Width: 16½ in (41.9 cm)
Depth: 17 in (43.2 cm)
Overall height: 25 in (63.5 cm)
Seat height: 14 in (35.6 cm)

Fast/Kids by Loewenstein
Width: 15½ in (39.4 cm)
Depth: 15 in (38.1 cm)
Overall height: 23 in (58.4 cm)
Seat height: 13½ in (34.3 cm)

WOOD CHAIRS

Kinderlink by Skools, Inc.
Width: 21 in (53.3 cm)
Depth: 18 in (45.7 cm)—9 ft 4 in (2.84 m) diameter
    inside curve
Height: 12 in (30.5 cm)

Me-Do-It chairs by Community Playthings

Seat height	5 in (12.7 cm)	6½ in (16.5 cm)
Width	11 in (27.9 cm)	11 in (27.9 cm)
Depth	12 in (30.5 cm)	12½ in (31.8 cm)
Overall height	12¾ in (32.4 cm)	14¼ in (36.2 cm)

Armchairs by Childcraft

Seat height	6½ in (16.5 cm)	9 in (23 cm)	12 in (30.5 cm)
Width	10½ in (26.7 cm)	10½ in (26.7 cm)	11½ in (29.2 cm)
Depth	8½ in (21.6 cm)	8½ in (21.6 cm)	8½ in (21.6 cm)
Overall height	14¾ in (37.5 cm)	17¼ in (43.8 cm)	20¼ in (51.4 cm)

Classroom Series by Don P. Smith Chair Company

Seat height	10½ in (26.7 cm)	12½ in (31.8 cm)	14½ in (36.8 cm)	16½ in (41.9 cm)	18½ in (47 cm)
Width	13¼ in (33.7 cm)	13¼ in (33.7 cm)	13¼ in (33.7 cm)	15½ in (39.4 cm)	17¾ in (45.1 cm)
Depth	13¼ in (33.7 cm)	13½ in (34.3 cm)	14 in (35.6 cm)	17 in (43.2 cm)	18¾ in (47.6 cm)
Overall height	20½ in (52.1 cm)	22¼ in (56.5 cm)	25½ in (64.8 cm)	29½ in (74.9 cm)	33½ in (85.1 cm)

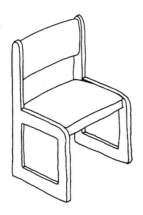

JR/111 sleigh chair by Nemschoff
Width: 15 in (38.1 cm)
Depth: 14 in (35.6 cm)
Overall height: 23 in (58.4 cm)
Seat height: 13 in (33 cm)

Windsor by Kinderworks
Width: 14 in (35.6 cm)
Depth: 13 in (33 cm)
Overall height: 28 in (71.1 cm)
Seat height: 13 in (33 cm)

Children's and junior adult chairs by BBT Group

Seat height	11½ in (29.2 cm)	13½ in (34.3 cm)	15½ in (39.4 cm)	17½ in (44.5 cm)
Width	16 in (40.6 cm)	16 in (40.6 cm)	20 in (50.8 cm)	20 in (50.8 cm)
Depth	13 in (33 cm)	13 in (33 cm)	15 in (38.1 cm)	15 in (38.1 cm)
Overall height	24 in (61 cm)	26 in (66 cm)	31 in (78.7 cm)	33 in (83.8 cm)

Bright Kids chair by The Malnight Company

Seat height	12 in (30.5 cm)	14 in (35.6 cm)	16 in (40.6 cm)	18 in (45.7 cm)
Width	13 in (33 cm)	13 in (33 cm)	16 in (40.6 cm)	16 in (40.6 cm)
Depth	13 in (33 cm)	13 in (33 cm)	16 in (40.6 cm)	16 in (40.6 cm)
Overall height	27 in (68.6 cm)	29 in (73.7 cm)	36 in (91.4 cm)	38 in (96.5 cm)

JR/200 chair by Nemschoff
Width: 14½ in (36.8 cm)
Depth: 15 in (38.1 cm)
Overall height: 24 in (61 cm)
Seat height: 13½ in (34.3 cm)

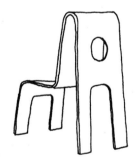

Padova II/Kids by Loewenstein
Width: 13½ in (34.3 cm)
Depth: 14 in (35.6 cm)
Overall height: 24 in (61 cm)
Seat height: 13 in (33 cm)

Stacking chair by Skools Inc.

Seat

height	12 in (30.5 cm)	14 in (35.6 cm)
Width	12 in (30.5 cm)	12 in (30.5 cm)
Depth	20 in (50.8 cm)	20 in (50.8 cm)

Overall

height	26 in (66 cm)	28 in (71 cm)

Childform chair by Danko
Width: 19 in (48.3 cm)
Depth: 18 in (45.7 cm)
Overall height: 27 in (68.6 cm)
Seat height: 14½ in (36.8 cm)

Kidz by Sauder Manufacturing Company

Seat height	10½ in (26.7 cm)	11½ in (29.2 cm)	12¾ in (32.4 cm)	14½ in (36.8 cm)
Width	11¼ in (28.6 cm)	12¼ in (31.1 cm)	13½ in (34.3 cm)	15¼ in (38.7 cm)
Depth	11 in (27.9 cm)	12½ in (31.8 cm)	14¼ in (36.2 cm)	16 in (40.6 cm)
Overall height	16¼ in (41.3 cm)	19 in (48.3 cm)	22½ in (57 cm)	25½ in (64.8 cm)

Wonderland by Design America
Width: 13 in (33 cm)
Depth: 13 in (33 cm)
Overall height: 23½ in (60 cm)
Seat height: 12 in (30.5 cm)

Series B by Thonet

Seat height	13 in (33 cm)	15 in (38.1 cm)	18 in (45.7 cm)
Width	15 in (38.1 cm)	15 in (38.1 cm)	16 in (40.6 cm)
Depth	16 in (40.6 cm)	16 in (40.6 cm)	21 in (53.3 cm)
Overall height	22 in (55.9 cm)	25 in (63.5 cm)	32¼ in (81.9 cm)

Additional seat back shapes available.

Ellipse by The Children's Furniture Company

Seat height	10 in (25.4 cm)	12 in (30.5 cm)	14 in (35.6 cm)
Width	13½ in (34.3 cm)	13½ in (34.3 cm)	13½ in (34.3 cm)
Depth	14½ in (36.8 cm)	14½ in (36.8 cm)	14½ in (36.8 cm)
Overall height	20 in (50.8 cm)	22 in (55.9 cm)	23 in (58.4 cm)

Cloverleaf chair by The Children's Furniture Company

Seat height	10 in (25.4 cm)	12 in (30.5 cm)	14 in (35.6 cm)
Width	14 in (35.6 cm)	14 in (35.6 cm)	14 in (35.6 cm)
Depth	15 in (38.1 cm)	15 in (38.1 cm)	15 in (38.1 cm)
Overall height	20 in (50.8 cm)	22 in (55.9 cm)	24 in (61 cm)

Additional back shapes available.

Child's chair by Ardley Hall
Width: 16½ in (41.9 cm)
Depth: 15 in (38.1 cm)
Overall height: 24 in (61 cm)
Seat height: 13 in (33 cm)

Horseshoe chair by Ardley Hall
Width: 17 in (43.2 cm)
Depth: 14 in (35.6 cm)
Overall Height: 26 in (66 cm)
Seat height: 13 in (33 cm)

Glenham Junior by Barlow Tyrie
Width: 16 in (40.6 cm)
Depth: 17 in (43.2 cm)
Overall height: 25 in (63.5 cm)
Seat height: 12 in (30.5 cm)

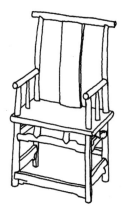

Hat chair by Ardley Hall
Width: 15 in (38.1 cm)
Depth: 12 in (30.5 cm)
Overall height: 27 in (68.6 cm)
Seat height: 13 in (33 cm)

Child's chair by Rustic Twig Furniture
Width: 25 in (63.5 cm)
Depth: 18 in (45.7 cm)
Overall height: 35 in (88.9 cm)
Seat height: 11 in (27.9 cm)

Tables and Desks

NONWOOD TABLES

Standard Shapes and Sizes of Nonwood Tables

Standard heights: 16 in (40.6 cm), 18 in (45.7 cm), 20 in (50.8 cm), 22 in (55.9 cm), 24 in (61 cm); adjustable heights 13 to 30 in (33 to 76.2 cm)

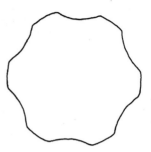

Flower table
Diameter: 60 in (152.4 cm)

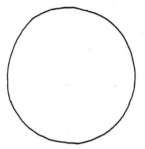

Round table
Diameter: 24 in (61 cm), 36 in (91.4 cm), 42 in (106.7 cm), 48 in (121.9 cm), 60 in (152.4 cm)

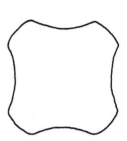

Clover table
Width: 48 in (121.9 cm)
Length: 48 in (121.9 cm)

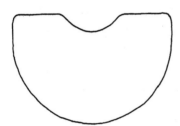

Kidney table
Width: 48 in (121.9 cm)
Length: 72 in (182.9 cm)

Trapezoid table

Width	24 in (61 cm)	30 in (76.2 cm)
Length	48 in (121.9 cm)	60 in (152.4 cm)

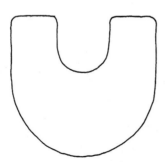

Horseshoe table
Width: 60 in (152.4 cm)
Length: 66 in (167.6 cm)

Square table
Width/length: 30 in (76.2 cm) and 36 in (91.4 cm)

Rectangular table

Width	24 in	24 in	30 in	30 in	30 in	30 in	36 in	36 in	36 in
	(61 cm)	(61 cm)	(76.2 cm)	(76.2 cm)	(76.2 cm)	(76.2 cm)	(91.4 cm)	(91.4 cm)	(91.4 cm)
Length	48 in	54 in	48 in	60 in	72 in	96 in	60 in	72 in	96 in
	(121.9 cm)	(137.2 cm)	(121.9 cm)	(152.4 cm)	(182.9 cm)	(243.8 cm)	(152.4 cm)	(182.9 cm)	(243.8 cm)

Baseline table by Angeles
Height: 14 to 24 in (35.6 to 61 cm) in 2-in (5.1-cm) increments
Round table
Diameter: 42 in (106.7 cm), 48 in (121.9 cm)
Square table
Width/length: 30 in (76.2 cm)
Rectangular table

Width	30 in (76.2 cm)	30 in (76.2 cm)	30 in (76.2 cm)	30 in (76.2 cm)
Length	36 in (91.4 cm)	48 in (121.9 cm)	60 in (152.4 cm)	72 in (182.9 cm)

Bola by Fixtures Furniture
Height: 21 in (53.3 cm)
Round table
Diameter: 30 in (76.2 cm), 36 in (91.4 cm), 42 in (106.7 cm), 48 in (121.9 cm), 54 in (137.2 cm)
Square table
Width/length: 24 in (61 cm), 30 in (76.2 cm), 36 in (91.4 cm), 42 in (106.7 cm), 48 in (121.9 cm)
Rectangular table

Width	24 in (61 cm)	30 in (76.2 cm)	36 in (91.4 cm)	36 in (91.4 cm)
Length	42 in (106.7 cm)	42 in (106.7 cm)	48 in (121.9 cm)	60 in (152.4 cm)

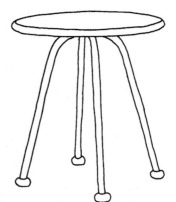

Scamps by Haworth
Height: 24 in (61 cm)
Round table
Diameter: 24 in (61 cm)
Rectangular table
Width: 24 in (61 cm)
Length: 48 in (121.9 cm)

WOOD TABLES

Standard Shapes and Sizes
of Wood Tables

Standard heights: 12 in (30.5 cm), 14 in (35.6 cm), 16 in (40.6 cm), 18 in (45.7 cm), 20 in (50.8 cm), 22 in (55.9 cm), 23 in (58.4 cm), 30 in (76.2 cm)

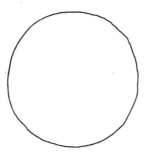

Round table
Diameter: 24 in (61 cm), 30 in (76.2 cm), 36 in (91.4 cm), 42 in (106.7 cm), 48 in (121.9 cm)

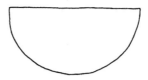

Half-round table

Width	30 in (76.2 cm)	36 in (91.4 cm)	48 in (121.9 cm)	60 in (152.4 cm)
Depth	15 in (38.1 cm)	18 in (45.7 cm)	24 in (61 cm)	30 in (76.2 cm)

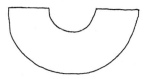

Half-round table with teacher seat cutout

Width	60 in (152.4 cm)	72 in (182.9 cm)	84 in (213.4 cm)
Depth	30 in (76.2 cm)	36 in (91.4 cm)	42 in (106.7 cm)

Trapezoid table
Width: 60 in (152.4 cm)
Depth: 26 in (66 cm)
Short sides are 30 in (76.2 cm) each.

Square table
Width/length: 30 in (76.2 cm), 36 in (91.4 cm), 42 in (106.7 cm), 48 in (121.9 cm)

Rectangular table

Width	24 in (61 cm)	24 in (61 cm)	24 in (61 cm)	30 in (76.2 cm)	30 in (76.2 cm)
Length	30 in (76.2 cm)	36 in (91.4 cm)	48 in (121.9 cm)	48 in (121.9 cm)	60 in (152.4 cm)

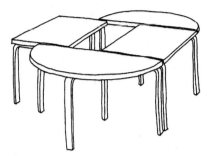

Aalto table by ICF Group
Height: 23¾ in (60.3 cm)
Rectangular table
Width: 23¾ in (60.3 cm)
Length: 39½ in (100.3 cm)
Half-round table
Width: 23¾ in (60.3 cm)
Length: 47¼ in (120 cm)

Bright Kids Collection by Malnight
Width/length: 30 in (76.2 cm) and 36 in (91.4 cm)
Heights: 26 in (66 cm) and 29 in (73.7 cm)

The Wonderland table by Design America
Length: 28 in (71.1 cm)
Width: 20 in (50.8 cm)
Height: 20 in (50.8 cm)

DESKS

Open-front desk by KI
Width: 24 in (61 cm)
Depth: 18 in (45.7 cm)
Height: 22 to 30 in (55.9 to 76.2 cm) in 1-in
    (2.5-cm) increments

Computer table by Childcraft
Width: 28 in (71.12 cm)
Length: 36 in (91.4 cm)
Height: 20¼ to 28¾ in (51.4 to 73 cm)

Lift-lid desk by KI
Width: 24 in (61 cm)
Depth: 18 in (45.7 cm)
Height: 22 to 30 in (55.9 to 76.2 cm) in 1-in
    (2.5-cm) increments

ACTIVITY TOP TABLES

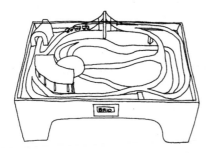

Railway table by Brio
Width: 33¼ in (84.5 cm)
Length: 49½ in (125.7 cm)
Height: 17½ in (44.5 cm)

Lego Building Block table by Lego Dacta
Width/length: 27 in (68.6 cm)
Height: 20 in (50.8 cm)

Sand/water table by Kinderworks
Width: 24 in (61 cm)
Length: 48 in (121.9 cm)
Height: 24 in (61 cm)

PEDIATRIC EXAM TABLES

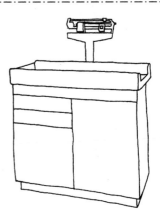

Hausmann Industries
Width: 24 in (61 cm)
Length: 43 in (109.2 cm)
Height: 36 in (91.4 cm) does not include height of
    scale

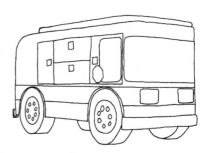

School bus by Goodtime Pediatrics
Width: 28 in (71 cm)
Length: 68 in (172.7 cm)
Height: 35 in (88.9 cm)

Zoopals elephant by Pediatric Designs, Inc.
Width: 34 in (86.4 cm)
Length: 69 in (175.3 cm)
Height: 37 in (94 cm)

PICNIC TABLES

Adirondack Designs
Length: 47½ in (120.6 cm)
Width: 22½ in (57.1 cm)
Height: 24 in (61 cm)

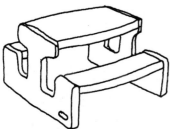

Fusion Coatings, Inc.
Table top: 46 in (121.9 cm) square
Overall width/depth: 78½ in (199.4 cm)

The Little Tikes Company
Length: 39½ in (100.3 cm)
Width: 36½ in (92.7 cm)
Height: 21½ in (54.6 cm)

Nursery and Public Restroom Furnishings and Equipment

CHANGING TABLES

Length: 34 in (86.4 cm)
Depth: 20 in (50.8 cm)
Height: 39 in (99.1 cm)

DIAPER DISPOSAL UNITS

POTTY-CHAIRS

Diaper Dumper by American Infant Care Products
Width: 16¼ in (41.3 cm)
Depth: 16 in (40.1 cm)
Height: 17¼ in (43.8 cm)

Width: 12 in (30.5 cm)
Depth: 14 in (35.6 cm)
Height: 9½ in (24.1 cm) with lid closed

Width: 11¼ in (28.6 cm)
Depth: 13½ in (34.3 cm)
Height: 9 in (22.9 cm)

Diaper Genie by Mondial
Width: 11 in (27.9 cm)
Depth: 12 in (30.5 cm)
Height: 20 in (50.8 cm)

Jumbo Diaper Genie by Mondial
Width: 11½ in (29.2 cm)
Depth: 16½ in (41.9 cm)
Height: 29½ in (74.9 cm)

PUBLIC RESTROOM EQUIPMENT

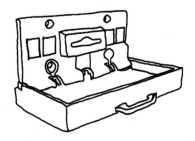

Diaper Deck by American Infant Care Products
Length: 32 in (81.3 cm)
Depth: 18½ in (47 cm)—4½ in (11.4 cm) when
   closed
Height: 14½ in (36.8 cm)

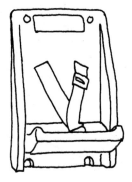

Child protection seat by Koala Corporation
Width: 12 in (30.5 cm)
Depth: 12¼ in (31.1 cm)—6" (15.2 cm) when
   closed
Height: 19 in (48.3 cm)

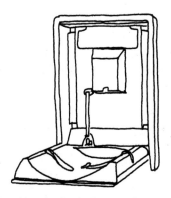

Koala Bear Kare by Koala Corporation
Width: 22 in (55.9 cm)
Depth: 35 in (88.9 cm)—5¼ in (13.3 cm) when
   closed
Height: 36 in (91.4 cm)
Lengthwise-mounted model also available.

Furnishings for Resting and Sleeping

STANDARD MATTRESS SIZES

	Width	Length
Bassinet	18 in (45.7 cm)	36 in (91.4 cm)
Crib/toddler bed	28 in (71.1 cm)	52 in (132.1 cm)
Twin	38½ in (97.8 cm)	76 in (193 cm)
Full	53½ in (135.9 cm)	76 in (193 cm)
Queen	60½ in (153.7 cm)	81 in (205.7 cm)
King	76¾ in (194.9 cm)	81 in (205.7 cm)

Sleeping bags
Width: 28 to 30 in (71 to 76.2 cm)
Length: 57 in (144.8 cm)

MATS, SLEEPING BAGS, AND COTS

Rest mats
Width: 24 in (61 cm)
Length: 48 in (121.9 cm)
Thickness: 1 in (2.54 cm)
Folds to 24 × 12 × 4 in (61 × 30.5 × 10.2 cm)

Angels rest cot by The Angeles Group
Width: 22 in (55.9 cm)
Length: 40 in (101.6 cm) and 52 in (132.1 cm)
Height: 4¾ in (12.1 cm)

BASSINETS, CRADLES, CRIBS, AND BEDS

Bassinet with stand
Width: 20 in (50.8 cm)
Length: 38 in (96.5 cm)
Height: 42 in (106.7 cm) to top of hood

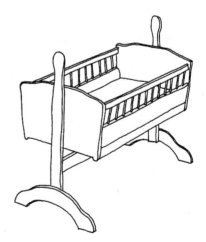

Cradle
Width: 21¾ in (55.2 cm)
Length: 39¾ in (101 cm)
Height: 32¾ in (83.2 cm)

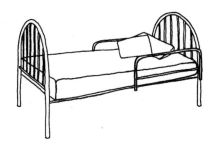

Toddler bed by Cosco
Width: 29 in (73.7 cm)
Length: 53 in (134.6 cm)
Height: 27 in (68.6 cm)

Playpen
Width: 38 in (96.5 cm)
Length: 38 in (96.5 cm)
Height: 30 in (76 cm)
Folded
Width: 9 in (23 cm)
Length: 38 in (96.5 cm)
Height: 33½ in (85 cm)

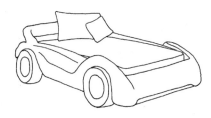

Car bed by Bestar
Width: 54½ in (138.4 cm)
Length: 88 in (223.5 cm)
Height: 25½ in (64.8 cm)

Crib
Width: 30 in (76.2 cm)
Length: 56 in (142 cm)
Height: 46 in (116.8 cm)

Bunk beds
Width: 40 in (101.6 cm)
Length: 80 in (203.2 cm)
Height: 63 to 74 in (160 cm to 195 cm)

Lofts

The configurations and sizes shown are representative of the loft system available from Community Playthings. A list of sources for additional lofts and loft systems may be found in Chapter 6, "Source List."

Loft System Configurations and Sizes Available from Community Playthings

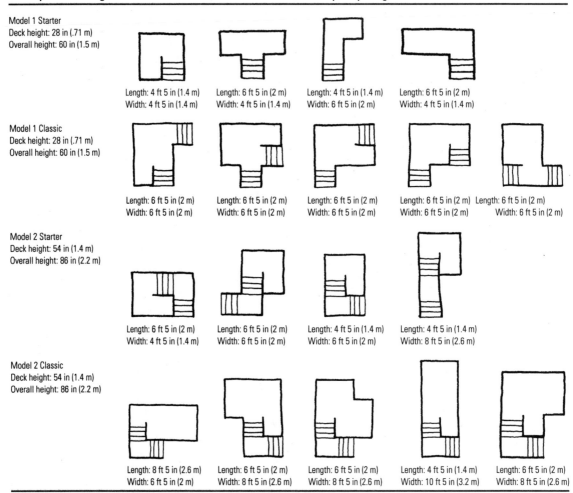

Model 1 Starter
Deck height: 28 in (.71 m)
Overall height: 60 in (1.5 m)

Length: 4 ft 5 in (1.4 m)
Width: 4 ft 5 in (1.4 m)

Length: 6 ft 5 in (2 m)
Width: 4 ft 5 in (1.4 m)

Length: 4 ft 5 in (1.4 m)
Width: 6 ft 5 in (2 m)

Length: 6 ft 5 in (2 m)
Width: 4 ft 5 in (1.4 m)

Model 1 Classic
Deck height: 28 in (.71 m)
Overall height: 60 in (1.5 m)

Length: 6 ft 5 in (2 m)
Width: 6 ft 5 in (2 m)

Length: 6 ft 5 in (2 m)
Width: 6 ft 5 in (2 m)

Length: 6 ft 5 in (2 m)
Width: 6 ft 5 in (2 m)

Length: 6 ft 5 in (2 m)
Width: 6 ft 5 in (2 m)

Length: 6 ft 5 in (2 m)
Width: 6 ft 5 in (2 m)

Model 2 Starter
Deck height: 54 in (1.4 m)
Overall height: 86 in (2.2 m)

Length: 6 ft 5 in (2 m)
Width: 4 ft 5 in (1.4 m)

Length: 6 ft 5 in (2 m)
Width: 6 ft 5 in (2 m)

Length: 4 ft 5 in (1.4 m)
Width: 6 ft 5 in (2 m)

Length: 4 ft 5 in (1.4 m)
Width: 8 ft 5 in (2.6 m)

Model 2 Classic
Deck height: 54 in (1.4 m)
Overall height: 86 in (2.2 m)

Length: 8 ft 5 in (2.6 m)
Width: 6 ft 5 in (2 m)

Length: 6 ft 5 in (2 m)
Width: 8 ft 5 in (2.6 m)

Length: 6 ft 5 in (2 m)
Width: 8 ft 5 in (2.6 m)

Length: 4 ft 5 in (1.4 m)
Width: 10 ft 5 in (3.2 m)

Length: 6 ft 5 in (2 m)
Width: 8 ft 5 in (2.6 m)

Square, rectangular, and diagonal additions are also available.

Bulletin, Chalk, Flannel, and Marker Boards

Standard Sizes
18 in (45.7 cm) × 2 ft (61 cm)
2 ft (61 cm) × 3 ft (91.4 cm)
30 in (76.2 cm) × 40 in (101.6 cm)
3 ft (91.4 cm) × 4 ft (121.9 cm)
3 ft (91.4 cm) × 5 ft (152.4 cm)
3 ft (91.4 cm) × 6 ft (182.9 cm)
3 ft (91.4 cm) × 8 ft (243.8 cm)
3 ft (91.4 cm) × 10 ft (304.8 cm)
3 ft (91.4 cm) × 12 ft (365.8 cm)
3 ft 6 in (106.7 cm) × 5 ft (152.4 cm)
3 ft 6 in (106.7 cm) × 6 ft (182.9 cm)
3 ft 6 in (106.7 cm) × 8 ft (243.8 cm)
3 ft 6 in (106.7 cm) × 10 ft (304.8 cm)
3 ft 6 in (106.7 cm) × 12 ft (365.8 cm)
4 ft (121.9 cm) × 4 ft (121.9 cm)
4 ft (121.9 cm) × 5 ft (152.4 cm)
4 ft (121.9 cm) × 6 ft (182.9 cm)
4 ft (121.9 cm) × 8 ft (243.8 cm)
4 ft (121.9 cm) × 10 ft (304.8 cm)
4 ft (121.9 cm) × 12 ft (365.7 cm)

Storage Furniture

SHELF UNITS

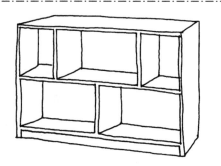

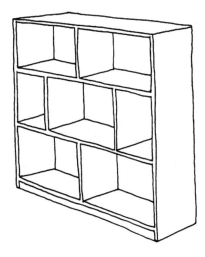

Two-shelf unit
Length: 48 in (121.9 cm)
Depth: 13 to 15 in (33 to 38.1 cm)
Height: 30 in (76.2 cm)

Three-shelf unit
Length: 48 in (121.9 cm)
Depth: 13 to 15 in (33 to 38.1 cm)
Height: 42 in (106.7 cm)

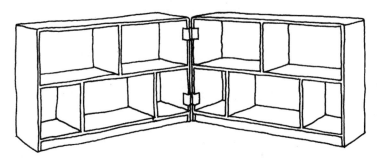

Hinged-shelf unit
Length (each leaf): 48 in (121.9 cm)
Depth: 13 to 15 in (33 to 38.1 cm)
Height: 30 in (76.2 cm)

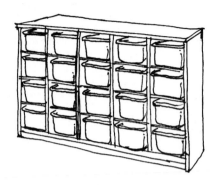

Tote tray storage unit
Length: 48 in (121.9 cm)
Depth: 13 in (33 cm)
Height: 30 in (76.2 cm)
Individual cubby size: 8¾ in (22.2 cm) wide; 12½ in (31.8 cm) deep; 6⅝ in (16.8 cm) high

CUBBIES AND LOCKERS

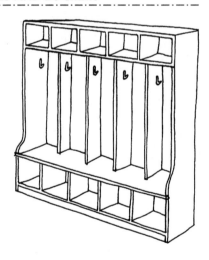

Length: 54 in (137.2 cm)
Depth: 11 in (27.9 cm) at top, 14 in (35.6 cm) at
　　base
Height: 48 in (121.9 cm)

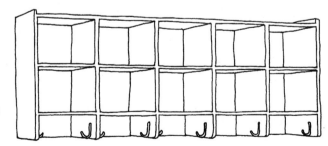

Length: 49¾ in (126.4 cm)
Depth: 13¾ in (34.9 cm)
Height: 19½ in (49.5 cm)

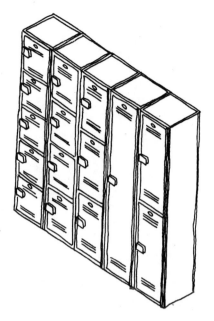

TOY STORAGE

Tub
Diameter: 21½ in (54.6 cm)
Height: 14½ in (36.8 cm)

Toy chest by The Little Tikes Company
Length: 38 in (96.5 cm)
Depth: 24 in (61 cm)
Height: 22 in (55.9 cm)

Lockers
Width of one unit: 12 in (30.5 cm)
Depth: 12, 15, or 18 in (30.5, 38.1, or 45.7 cm)
Height: 60 in (152.4 cm)

BOOK STORAGE

Length: 36 in (91.4 cm)
Depth: 13 in (33 cm)
Height: 29 in (73.7 cm)

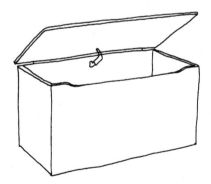

Toy box by Kinderworks
Length: 33 in (83.8 cm)
Depth: 17 in (43.2 cm)
Height: 17 in (43.2 cm)

Car Seats, Strollers, and Other Moving Toys and Equipment

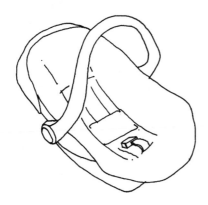

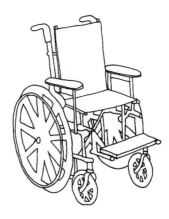

Infant carrier
Width: 18 in (45.7 cm)
Length: 29 in (74 cm)
Height: 24 in (61 cm) with handle in raised position,
   14 in (36 cm) with handle in lowered position

Youth wheelchair
Width: 20 in (51 cm), 12½ in (31 cm) when folded
   for storage
Depth: 40 in (102 cm)
Height: 36 in (91 cm)
Seat height: 19½ in (49.5 cm)

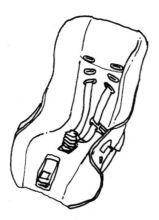

Car seat
Width: 24 in (61 cm)
Depth: 24 in (61 cm)
Height: 16 in (41 cm)

Umbrella stroller
Width: 16 in (41 cm)
Length: 33 in (84 cm)
Height: 36 in (91 cm)

Wagon for six by Community Playthings
Width: 29 in (74 cm)
Length: 62 in (157.5 cm)
Height: 30 in (76 cm) at railing

Stroller
Width: 20 in (51 cm)
Length: 40 in (102 cm)
Height: 40 in (102 cm)

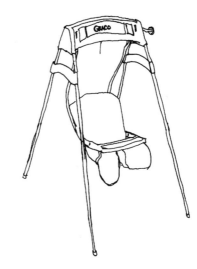

Bye-Bye Buggy by Community Playthings
Four-seat
Width: 28 in (71 cm)
Length: 50 in (127 cm)
High: 38½ in (98 cm)

Swing by Graco
Width: 28 in (71 cm)
Depth: 40 in (102 cm)
Height: 24 in (61 cm)

Six-seat
Width: 28 in (71 cm)
Length: 72 in (183 cm)
Height: 37 in (94 cm)

MOVING TOYS

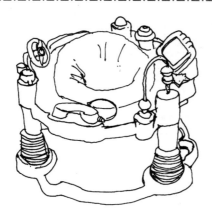

Entertainer/Bouncer by Graco
Diameter: 27 in (69 cm)
Height: 18 in (46 cm)

Radio Flyer Wagon
Width: 18 in (46 cm)
Length: 40 in (102 cm)—not including length of
    handle
Height: 14 in (36 cm) high, 20 in (51 cm) with
    wood sides

Spring horse
Width: 31 in (79 cm)
Length: 42 in (107 cm)
Height: 45 in (114 cm)

Wagon by The Little Tikes Company
Width: 21 in (53.3 cm)
Length: 43 in (109.2 cm)
Height: 21½ in (54.6 cm)

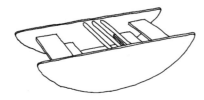

Reversible rocking boat/Step bridge
Width: 24 in (61 cm)
Length: 48 in (121.9 cm)
Height: 11½ in (29.2 cm)

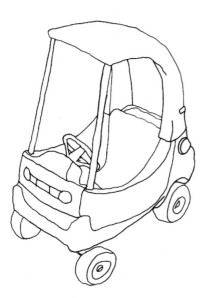

Cozy Coupe by The Little Tikes Company
Width: 17½ in (44.5 cm)
Length: 30 in (76.2 cm)
Height: 34 in (86.4 cm)

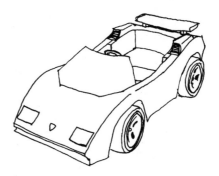

Barbie car by Power Wheels
Width: 22 in (56 cm)
Length: 53 in (135 cm)
Height: 18 in (46 cm)

Tricycles

Front-wheel diameter	10 in (25 cm)	12 in (60.5 cm)
Width	22 in (56 cm)	20 in (51 cm)
Length	26 in (66 cm)	29 in (74 cm)
Height	24 in (61 cm)	26 in (66 cm)

Jeep by Power Wheels
Width: 36 in (91 cm)
Length: 43 in (109 cm)
Height: 36 in (91 cm)

Big Wheels by Empire
Width: 20 in (51 cm)
Length: 40 in (102 cm)
Height: 23 in (58 cm)

Bicycles

Wheel diameter	12 in (30.5 cm)	16 in (41 cm)	18 in (46 cm)
Width	19 in (48 cm)	22 in (56 cm)	27 in (69 cm)
	with training wheels	with training wheels	with training wheels
Length	32 in (81 cm)	44 in (112 cm)	50 in (127 cm)
Height	27 in (68.5 cm)	29 in (74 cm)	34 in (86 cm)
Wheel diameter	20 in (51 cm)	24 in (61 cm)	26 in (66 cm)
Width	57 in (145 cm)	61 in (155 cm)	69 in (175 cm)
Length	27 in (69 cm)	24 in (61 cm)	24 in (61 cm)
Height	35 in (89 cm)	35 in (89 cm)	37 in (94 cm)

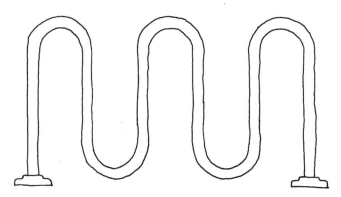

Ribbon Rack bike rack by Brandir
Height: 35¼ in (89.5 cm)
Width: 38⅜ to 110⅜ in (97.5 to 280.4 cm)
Pipe: 2⅜-in (6-cm) diameter, 9⅝ in (24.4 cm) between verticals

Scooter
Width: 28 in (71 cm)
Length: 46 in (117 cm)
Height: 35 in (89 cm)

Skateboard
Width: 8 in (20 cm)
Length: 28 in (71 cm)
Height: 5 in (13 cm)

Games

VIDEO GAME EQUIPMENT

Nintendo 64 System
Width: 7½ in (19 cm)
Length: 10½ in (26.7 cm)
Height: 2¾ in (7 cm)

PlayStation by Sony
Width: 7¼ in (18.4 cm)
Length: 10½ in (27 cm)
Height: 2¼ in (5.7 cm)

ARCADE GAMES

Basketball
Width: 34 in (86.4 cm)
Length: 10 ft 7 in (322.6 cm)
Height: 9 ft (274.3 cm)

Foosball
Width: 39½ in (100.3 cm)
Length: 61 in (154.9 cm)
Height: 36¼ in (92.1 cm)

Width: 34½ in (87.6 cm)
Length: 82 in (208.3 cm)
Height: 86 in (218.4 cm)

Video games
Width: 22 in
Depth: 30 in
Height: 62 in

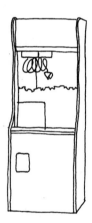

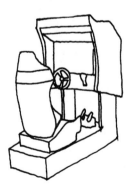

Arcade prize machine
Width: 24 in (61 cm)
Depth: 24 in (61 cm)
Height: 66 in (167.6 cm)

Width: 38 in (95.3 cm)
Depth: 52 in (132 cm)
Height: 52 in (130.2 cm)

Furnishings for Art

Art easel by Childcraft
Width: 24 in (61 cm)
Depth: 27 in (68.6 cm)
Height: 46 in (116.8 cm)

Double art easel by Childcraft
Width: 49½ in (125.7 cm)
Depth: 13 in (33 cm)
Height: 51 in (129.5 cm)

Art easel by The Little Tikes Company
Width: 28 in (71.1 cm)
Depth: 24½ in (62.2 cm)
Height: 43½ in (110.5 cm)

Art drying rack by Childcraft
Width: 38 in (96.5 cm)
Depth: 24 in (61 cm)
Height: 52 in (132.1 cm)

Furnishings for Dramatic Play

The illustrations and dimensions of the following dramatic play elements represent products available through Childcraft Education Corporation. Similar products are available from a variety of sources, many of which are listed in Chapter 6.

Dress-up vanity
Width: 47¼ in (120 cm)
Depth: 11¼ in (28.6 cm)
Height: 40 in (101.6 cm)

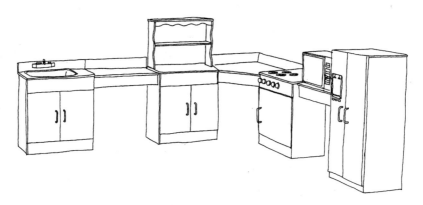

KITCHEN

Dutch cabinet
Width: 24 in (61 cm)
Depth: 13½ in (34.3 cm)
Height: 40 in (101.6 cm)
Counter height: 23¾ in (60.3 cm)

Microwave oven
Width: 17 in (43.2 cm)
Depth: 9½ in (24.1 cm)
Height: 9¾ in (24.8 cm)

Refrigerator
Width: 18 in (45.7 cm)
Depth: 13½ in (34.3 cm)
Height: 36½ in (92.7 cm)

Sink
Width: 24 in (61 cm)
Depth: 13½ in (34.3 cm)
Height: 28 in (71.1 cm)
Counter height: 23¾ in (60.3 cm)

Stove
Width: 24 in (61 cm)
Depth: 13½ in (34.3 cm)
Height: 28 in (71.1 cm)
Counter height: 23¾ in (60.3 cm)

LAUNDRY AND HOUSEKEEPING

Washer/dryer
Width: 30¾ in (78.1 cm)
Depth: 13¾ in (34.9 cm)
Height: 28 in (71.1 cm)
Counter height: 22 in (55.9 cm)

Housekeeping stand
Width: 11¾ in (29.8 cm)
Depth: 11¾ in (29.8 cm)
Height: 23½ in (59.7 cm)
Height of tools: 37 in (94 cm)

LIVING ROOM

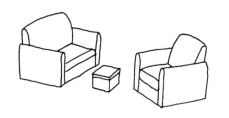

Ironing board
Width: 7½ in (19 cm)
Length: 30 in (76.2 cm)
Height: 22 in (55.9 cm)

Couch
Length: 31 in (78.7 cm)
Depth: 18 in (45.7 cm)
Height: 18 in (45.7 cm)
Ottoman
Length: 10 in (25.4 cm)
Width: 8 in (20.3 cm)
Height: 8 in (20.3 cm)
Chair
Length: 18 in (45.7 cm)
Depth: 18 in (45.7 cm)
Height: 18 in (45.7 cm)

NURSERY

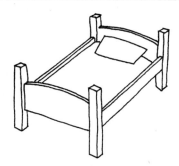

Doll bed
Width: 16 in (40.6 cm)
Length: 30½ in (77.5 cm)
Height: 12 in (30.5 cm)

Doll stroller
Width: 10 in (25.4 cm)
Length: 19 in (48.3 cm)
Height: 23 in (58.4 cm)

Doll cradle
Width: 18 in (45.7 cm)
Length: 31 in (78.7 cm)
Height: 10½ in (26.7 cm)

Puppet theater or market
Width: 45½ in (115.6 cm)
Depth: 31 in (78.7 cm)
Height: 50 in (127 cm)

Doll high chair
Width: 11 in (27.9 cm)
Depth: 10¼ in (26 cm)
Height: 18½ in (47 cm)

Workbench
Length: 44 in (111.8 cm)
Depth: 20 in (50.8 cm)
Height: 25 in (63.5 cm)

References for Part I

American Institute of Architects. *Architectural Graphic Standards,* 6th ed. New York: John Wiley & Sons, 1970.

————. *Architectural Graphic Standards,* 9th ed. New York: John Wiley & Sons, 1994.

American Society for Testing and Materials. *Standard Consumer Safety Performance Specification for Playground Equipment for Public Use.* West Conshohocken, PA: American Society for Testing and Materials, 1995.

————. *Standard Consumer Safety Performance Specification for Home Playground Equipment.* West Conshohocken, PA: American Society for Testing and Materials, 1997.

Department of Health, Education, and Welfare, Public Health Service, Health Resources Administration, National Center for Health Statistics, and Centers for Disease Control. *Weight for Age, Length for Age, Head Circumference for Age, and Weight for Length Charts.* 1995.

Esbensen, Steen B. *The Early Childhood Playground: An Outdoor Classroom.* Ypsilanti, MI: High/Scope Press, 1987.

Nelson, Waldo E. (ed.). *Textbook of Pediatrics.* Philadelphia: Saunders, 1969.

Pheasant, Stephen. *Bodyspace: Anthropometry, Ergonomics and Design.* London: Taylor & Francis, 1986.

————. *Bodyspace: Anthropometry, Ergonomics and the Design of Work,* 2nd ed. London: Taylor & Francis, 1996.

Pollowy, Anne-Marie. *The Urban Nest.* Community Development Series, Vol. 26. Stroudsburg, PA: Dowden, Hutchinson & Ross, Inc., 1977.

Tilley, A. R., and Henry Dreyfuss Associates. *The Measure of Man and Woman: Human Factors in Design.* New York: Whitney Library of Design, 1993.

U.S. Architectural and Transportation Barriers Compliance Board. *Recommendations for Accessibility Standards for Children's Environments; Executive Summary.* Washington, D.C.: U.S. Architectural and Transportation Barriers Compliance Board, 1995.

————. *Americans with Disabilities Act (ADA) Accessibility Guidelines for Buildings and Facilities; Building Elements Designed for Children's Use.* 36 CFR Part 1191 (Docket No. 94-2) RIN 3014 AA17. Washington, D.C.: U.S. Architectural and Transportation Barriers Compliance Board, 1998.

U.S. Consumer Product Safety Commission. *Anthropometry of Infants, Children, and Youths to Age 18 for Product Safety Design.* Washington, D.C.: U.S. Consumer Product Safety Commission, 1977.

————. *Handbook for Public Playground Safety,* Publication No. 325. Washington, D.C.: U.S. Consumer Product Safety Commission, 1997.

————. *Home Playground Safety Tips,* Fact Sheet No. 323. Washington, D.C.: U.S. Consumer Product Safety Commission.

PRODUCTS AND SOURCES

Product Sources

The following source list is the first of its kind. Although there are many categorized lists of resources available to the designer, if products designed for children are even addressed, all these types of products are usually grouped under one general label of children's or juvenile products. The purpose of the present list is threefold. First, it takes the products and companies represented in the usual global children's furnishings categories and breaks them down into more specific types of furnishings. It is hoped that this will prove to relieve the designer of research time to devote more productive time to the design process. Second, the source list represents products for children that are currently being used in a number of different markets. The current list represents companies that typically market their products not only within the design industry, but also the child care, education, pediatric, residential, parks and recreation, and even toy industries. Many of these products may be of interest and value to the designer during the design process. Knowledge of a product's existence and where to find it will allow for a more productive design process. The third purpose of the list is to create an avenue that, through future revisions, will provide manufacturers with a means to market their children's products to a broader range of markets and, thus, encourage development of more products that can enrich the spaces that are created for children.

The list has been divided into three sections: commercially oriented products, residential products, and products for use outdoors. Obviously, many crossovers can occur. For example, picnic tables that are listed in the outdoor portion of the source list can be used quite successfully indoors. Likewise, many commercial products can be used in residential settings and vice versa, if allowed by the codes. Products were placed in the section of the source list where they would most likely be looked for first. Designers are encouraged to not limit their search to one particular section, but to peruse the other sections of the source list to find products that will support their designs.

Some of the categories within each section that have been generated may be confusing for the designer who is making a first foray into the field of children's design. For those categories that may be unknown, such as cubbies and ball pits, photographs have been used to help in describing the type of products represented by that category. The current list may also be viewed as a supplement to source lists that are already being used by designers. For example, many companies listed in traditional resource references have custom capabilities. These companies, unless they specialize in custom work for children, have not been included in this list. Their services may be identified through existing source lists or through resource guides such as McGraw-Hill's *Sweet's Catalog File.* Typically, the products represented in the present source list are stock items which have been designed expressly for use in a child's environment or are of a design that is directly related to a relevant issue. For example, cordless window shades are not a product for use solely in children's environments. However, because of the tremendous safety feature they provide regarding young children, they have been included in the list.

Being the first-of-a-kind source list means that there are some inherent deficiencies that will be reduced in later versions. The first of these deficiencies is that many sources for products have not been identified. The companies listed were identified in one of two ways. Either their names were garnered from a myriad of existing source lists servicing a variety of markets, and they then responded to a single faxed request for information, or they were suggested by designers who have worked in the area of children's design. This process undoubtedly missed many companies who were unaware of the development of the source list. It is hoped that any companies that wish to have their products considered for inclusion in future revisions of this list, or any designers who have discovered a company or product that is not currently in the list, will contact the author so that the next publication of the list can be even more comprehensive and useful.

Another problem that is inherent to all source lists is the fact that between compilation of the list and publication, many things can happen that make the information in the list incorrect. Businesses close, area codes change, web sites are added, and product lines are discontinued. Although efforts have been made to make sure the information is as current as possible, these occurrences are inevitable, and it is hoped that they will not prove to be more of an inconvenience than the source list is helpful.

Some duplication of products may also be represented within each category. Although attempts were made to list original manufacturing sources, in several instances the original source could not be readily identified. Therefore, within any category, some distributors may be listed that carry identical products. It may also be helpful to note that the source list includes a list of suppliers by industry in the hopes of making it somewhat easier for the designer to build a quick reference library for a particular project type.

To meet the designer's requirements for bidding, an effort to list more than one source for each product has been made. However, in some instances, only one company has been identified, meaning one of two things. Either no other company responded to the author's request for product information, or the company listed is truly the only source for that particular product.

Several European companies are also included in the source list. Although some of them have U.S. or Canadian distributors, many do not. This will result in high shipping costs being added to the cost of the product. However, each of the companies has catalogs available, and it is hoped that even if the cost is prohibitive, the exposure to the quality and design of the products offered by these companies will provide stimulation to the design process.

In regard to both the foreign and domestic products included in the following list, it is extremely important to note that it is the responsibility of the reader and user of the list to determine a product's appropriateness for use in an environment being created for children. The reader must also determine a product's adherence to any codes relevant to its design or use. Inclusion in the following list does not denote a level of quality or code compliance, only a product's availability.

COMMERCIAL/CONTRACT PRODUCTS

Accessories

The following child care/early education suppliers carry many accessories and artwork that are educational as well as visually delightful and may double as decorative accessories.

ABC School Supply
Childcraft Education Corporation
Constructive Playthings
Dusyma
Environments
Kaplan
Kinderworks
Lakeshore Learning Materials
Sandy and Sons Educational Supplies
Wehrfritz

CLOCKS

ABC School Supply
Constructive Playthings
Franklin Instrument Company, Inc.
Kaplan

DECORATIVE ACCESSORIES

Safari Ltd.
Taos Drums

Custom-designed Decorative Elements

Barrango, Inc.
F.A.S.T. Corp.
Futura Coatings, Inc.—Composite
    Fabrications Division
Skyline Designs
Straight Line Design

Reading "castle" at Hanover Park Children's Library, Hanover, Pennsylvania. Designed by Chicago Design Group. Constructed by Skyline Design.

Lare-scale Displays

Brio Corporation
F.A.S.T. Corp.

DRAWER/DOOR PULLS

HEWI, Inc.

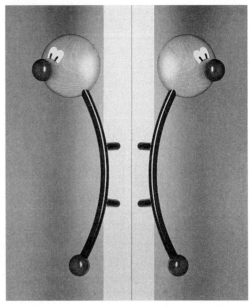

Caterpillar door pulls by HEWI, Inc.

MIRRORS

ABC School Supply
Arredi 3n
Childcraft Education Corporation

Infant wall mirror by Childcraft Education Corp.

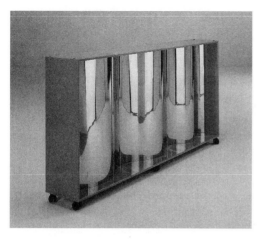

Serpentine mirror by Italiana Societa Arredamenti Fontanili F.lli s.r.l.

Floor cushions by Gressco Ltd.

The Children's Factory
Childs/Play, Inc.
Dusyma
Environments
Haba
Kaplan
Lakeshore Learning Materials
Sandy and Sons Educational Supplies
Texwood Furniture Corporation
Whitney Bros. Co.

Fun Mirrors

Children's Factory
Chime Time
Dusyma
Haba
Interior Systems, Inc.
Italiana Societa Arredamenti Fontanili
    F.lli s.r.l.
People Friendly Places
Playscapes
Wehrfritz

PILLOWS AND CUSHIONS

First Weavers of the Americas
Gressco Ltd.
Haba

Hugg-A-Planet
Lakeshore Learning Materials
Wehrfritz

INDOOR TRASH CONTAINERS

Kaplan
Starplast

Trash containers by Starplast.

WINDOW TREATMENTS
Cordless Window Shades

Comfortex Window Fashions
RollEase, Inc.

Artwork, Graphics, and Wallhangings

WALL-HUNG MANIPULATIVE PANELS

Anatex Enterprises, Inc.
Kinderworks

Kindertracker by Kinderworks.

People Friendly Places
Playscapes

MOBILES

Balitono Incorporated
Clowns 'N' Cases
My Dog Spot
People Friendly Places
Simplex International (PVT) Ltd.
White Eagle

POSTERS, PRINTS, AND SERIGRAPHS

Aaron Ashley, Inc.
Art Beats
Brio Corporation
Dusyma
Eric Holch/Fine Arts
Green Frog Art
Helen Webber Art & Design
Lakeshore Learning Materials
Lexington Furniture Industries
Peaceable Kingdom Press
Portal Publications, Ltd.
Safari Ltd.
Sandy and Sons Educational Supplies
Winn Devon Art Group, Ltd.

Framed Prints

Creative Images
Dragons of Walton Street
Green Frog Art
Portal Publications, Ltd.

FABRIC HANGINGS

ABC School Supply
Environments
Helen Webber Art & Design
People Friendly Places

Custom-designed Fabric Hangings

First Weavers of the Americas
Helen Webber Art & Design

WALL SCULPTURE

Artisan House
Bigame Trophies
Maine Cottage Furniture

Building Products

DISPLAY SYSTEMS

The majority of the following companies carry standard, large, wall-mounted models of chalk/marker boards and bulletin boards. However, some of them also carry smaller versions that can be used as activity walls and room dividers.

Chalk/marker Boards

Aristocrat Industries, Inc.
Bangor Cork Company, Inc.
BBT Group

Mobile marker board and room divider by BBT Group.

The Children's Furniture Co.
Claridge Products & Equipment
Dusyma
Haba
Lakeshore Learning Materials
Marsh Industries, Inc.
Nelson Adams Company
Wehrfritz

Flannel Boards

Aristocrat Industries, Inc.
BBT Group
Lakeshore Learning Materials

Tackboards

Aristocrat Industries, Inc.
Arredi 3n
Bangor Cork Company, Inc.
BBT Group

Claridge Products & Equipment
Dusyma
Haba
Lakeshore Learning Materials
Marsh Industries, Inc.
Nelson Adams Company

Tackless Display Systems

Tackless display systems offer a great way to display children's artwork while eliminating the danger of tacks and staples that may come loose and harm young children. Another advantage of these systems is that they do not require making holes in the "masterpieces."

Advantus Corporation
BBT Group
Claridge Products & Equipment
Haba

DOORS

Accordion Doors

Woodfold-Marco Mfg., Inc.

HANDRAILS

The C/S Group of Companies
HEWI, Inc.

Double handrail by HEWI, Inc.

KITCHEN UNITS

These are actual working kitchens with counters and cabinets lowered to a more accessible height for children. A source list for dramatic play kitchens appears later in this chapter.

Cervitor Kitchens, Inc.
Dusyma
Wehrfritz

LAMINATES

ABET, Inc.

RESTROOM/DRESSING ROOM ENVIRONMENTS

Accessories

HEWI, Inc.

Diaper Deck by American Infant Care Products.

Bathroom accessories by HEWI, Inc.

Changing Tables
American Infant Care Products, Inc.
Koala Corporation/Koala Bear Kare
Diaper Disposal Units
American Infant Care Products, Inc.
Mondial Industries, Ltd.
Safety Seats
American Infant Care Products, Inc.
Koala Corporation/Koala Bear Kare

Faucets and Trim

Hansgrohe
Interbath, Inc.
Watercolors, Inc.

Lavatories

Lavatory/Changing Table Combinations
Stevens Industries
Lavatory/Drinking Fountain Combinations
Elkay Manufacturing Company

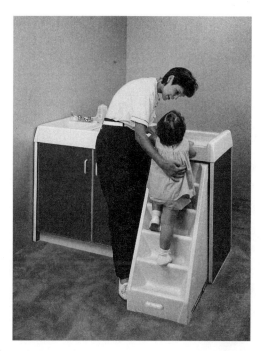

Combination walk-up changing table and sink by Stevens Industries.

Primary toilet and toilet seat by Kohler.

Toilet Partitions

Ampco Products, Inc.
HEWI, Inc.
Wehrfritz

Toilet Seats

Kohler

Toilets

American Standard, Inc.
Eljer Plumbingware
Kohler Company

SIGNAGE

HEWI, Inc.
Interior Systems, Inc.
Scott Sign Systems, Inc.

Restroom signage by HEWI, Inc.

Custom-Designed Environments

CUSTOM-DESIGNED HEALTH CARE ENVIRONMENTS

FunDimensionals

Carolinas Medical Center, Charlotte, North Carolina. Interior Design by Quantrell Mullins & Associates. Production and Installation by FunDimensionals.

CUSTOM-DESIGNED INDOOR ENTERTAINMENT/PLAY ENVIRONMENTS

Calrec Builders & Consultants
Interior Systems, Inc.

CUSTOM-DESIGNED RESIDENTIAL ENVIRONMENTS

Charm & Whimsy
Dragons of Walton Street

CUSTOM-DESIGNED THEMED ENVIRONMENTS

Skyline Design

Fabrics

Anzea
ArcCom*
Carnegie*
DesignTex*
Gretchen Bellinger

Interspec*
Maharam*

Includes fabrics suitable for health care cubicle curtains.

FABRIC ENHANCEMENT SERVICES

Custom Laminations, Inc.

FLAME-RETARDANT FABRICS

Dana Mills, Inc.

Finishes

CEILING FINISHES

Lay-in Ceiling Tiles

Armstrong World Industries, Inc.
USG Interiors, Inc.
Custom-designed Lay-in Ceiling Tiles
Interior Systems
USG Interiors, Inc.

Ceiling Paint

Benjamin Moore & Co.

Cirrus Theme "Train" Ceiling by Armstrong.

FLOOR FINISHES
Hard-Floor Finishes
Vinyl Tile
Wonder Works of America

Cow 'n Moon vinyl floor tile pattern by Wonder Works of America.

Soft-Floor Finishes

Carpet
Collins & Aikman Floorcoverings
Flagship Carpets, Inc.
Mohawk Industries, Inc.

Interactive/Educational Themed Area Rugs and Carpets
ABC School Supply
American Rug Craftsmen
Carpets for Kids
Childcraft Education Corporation
Collins & Aikman Floorcoverings
Couristan
Designs International, Inc.
Dusyma
Environments
Flagship Carpets, Inc.
Joy Carpets, Inc.

The "pond" rug by Carpets for Kids.

Kaplan
Koala Corp./Koala Bear Kare
Lakeshore Learning Materials
Rugs (See Also Interactive/Educational
  Themed Area Rugs and Carpets)
Couristan
Environments
Enzo Artifacts
Lakeshore Learning Materials
Custom-designed rugs
Casa Dos Tapetes de Arraiolos, Inc.
Design Textures
Enzo Artifacts

WALL FINISHES
Wall Bases

Johnsonite

Wall Paint

Benjamin Moore & Co.

Wall Tile

Surving Studios

Wallcoverings

Enzo Artifacts
Wolf Gordon, Inc.

Wallcoverings and borders by Wolf Gordon.

Wallborders
Brewster Wallcovering Company
The Children's Factory
DesignTex
Kaplan
People Friendly Places
Wolf Gordon, Inc.
Wallcovering Enhancement Services
Custom Laminations, Inc.

Furnishings

CUSTOM-DESIGNED FURNISHINGS

Straight Line Designs, Inc.

DRAMATIC PLAY

Role playing is an important part of the development of social skills in very young children. It may look like the furnishings used to encourage dramatic play are toys, but when being included in the layout of a room, they make as much of an impact upon the space, both physically and visually, as their adult-size counterparts. Consideration in their selection and arrangement within the room before the design of the space can enhance the child's dramatic play experience.

Dress-up

ABC School Supply
Biggwood
Childcraft Education Corporation
Childs/Play, Inc.
Dusyma
Kaplan
Kinderworks
Lakeshore Learning Materials
The Little Tikes Company
Sandy and Sons Educational Supplies
The Step2 Company
Wehrfritz

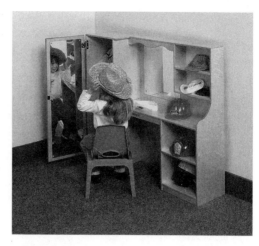

Dress-up vanity by Childcraft.

Fire Engine

Biggwood

Fire engine by Biggwood.

Hospital

Dusyma

House

Angeles Group
Arredi 3n
Dusyma
Italiana Societa Arredamenti Fontanili
    F.lli s.r.l.

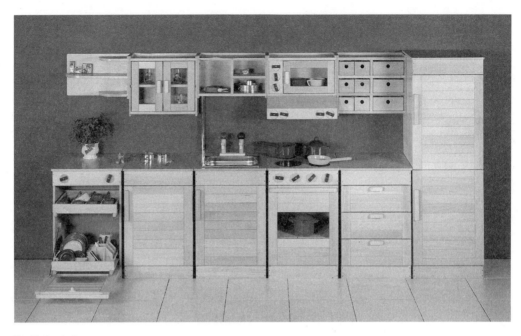

Play kitchen by Dusyma.

Kitchen

ABC School Supply
Arredi 3n
Childcraft Education Corporation
Childs/Play, Inc.
Community Playthings
Dusyma
Environments
Fleetwood
Haba
Italiana Societa Arredamenti Fontanili
    F.lli s.r.l.
Kaplan
Kinderworks
Lakeshore Learning Materials
Learning Products
The Little Tikes Company
Panex Furniture Products, Inc.
Sandy and Sons Educational Supplies
The Step2 Company
Stevens Industries
Texwood Furniture Corporation

Wehrfritz
Whitney Bros. Co.

Laundry

ABC School Supply
Childcraft Education Corporation
Dusyma
Environments
Haba
Kaplan
Lakeshore Learning Materials
Sandy and Sons Educational Supplies
Stevens Industries

Living Room

Depending on its intended use, the soft seating groups listed under the section entitled "Lounge Seating" may be used for dramatic play also. However, lounge seating is typically designed to be more durable with a wider range of upholstery options than the dramatic play living

Living room play set by Kaplan.

room furnishings offered by the following companies.

ABC School Supply
The Children's Factory
Childs/Play, Inc.
Chime Time
Dusyma
Environments
Haba
Italiana Societa Arredamenti Fontanili
 F.lli s.r.l.
Kaplan
Lakeshore Learning Materials
Wehrfritz

Market

Arredi 3n
Childcraft Education Corporation
Dusyma
Lakeshore Learning Materials
The Little Tikes Company   .

Nursery

ABC School Supply
Arredi 3n
Childcraft Education Corporation
Childs/Play, Inc.
Community Playthings
Dusyma
Environments
Kaplan
The Little Tikes Company
The Step2 Company
Wehrfritz

Office

Childcraft Education Corporation

Post Office

Dusyma

School

N.D. Cass Co., Inc.

Telephone Booth

Kaplan
Whitney Bros. Co.

Workbench by Childs/Play.

Telephone booth by Whitney Bros.

ABC School Supply
Childcraft Education Corporation
Childs/Play, Inc.
Community Playthings
Dusyma
Environments
Fleetwood
Kaplan
Lakeshore Learning Materials
The Little Tikes Company
N.D. Cass Co., Inc.
Sandy and Sons Educational Supplies
The Step2 Company
Wehrfritz
Whitney Bros. Co.

Train

Biggwood
Italiana Societa Arredamenti Fontanili
    F.lli s.r.l.
People Friendly Places

Truck

Biggwood

Workbenches

Several of the following companies carry workbenches that are not really dramatic play furnishings, but are actually tough enough for real woodworking projects and at a height that is comfortable for children. Some even come equipped with pegboard and vice grips.

ART EASELS

ABC School Supply
Arredi 3n
BBT Group
Beka Inc.
Childcraft Education Corporation
Childs/Play, Inc.
Community Playthings
Discover Products, Inc.
Dusyma
Environments
Fleetwood
Italiana Societa Arredamenti Fontanili
    F.lli s.r.l.
Kaplan

Kids' Studio
Kinderworks
Lakeshore Learning Materials
The Little Tikes Company
Manta-Ray, Inc.
Marsh Industries, Inc.
N.D. Cass Co., Inc.
Sandy and Sons Educational Supplies
Scandinavian Design
The Step2 Company
Stevens Industries
Texwood Furniture Corporation
Whitney Bros. Co.

INDOOR GROSS MOTOR PLAY EQUIPMENT

Arredi 3n
Community Playthings
Dusyma

Everlast
Haba
Interior Systems, Inc.
Italiana Societa Arredamenti Fontanili F.lli s.r.l.
Lakeshore Learning Materials
Learning Products
SafeSpace Concepts, Inc.
Sandy and Sons Educational Supplies
Wehrfritz

Ball Pits

ABC School Supply
Airspace
Arredi 3n
Belair Recreational Products, Inc.
The Children's Factory
Chime Time
Dusyma
Environments

Ball pit by Environments.

Haba
Italiana Societa Arredamenti Fontanili
    F.lli s.r.l.
Playlofts, Inc.
Playsafe, Inc.
Things From Bell
Wehrfritz

Pedal-go-rounds (Indoor)

Angeles Group

Soft Play Centers

ABC School Supply
Airspace
Arredi 3n
Childcraft Education Corporation
The Children's Factory
Chime Time
Dusyma

Environments
Italiana Societa Arredamenti Fontanili
    F.lli s.r.l.
Kaplan
Lakeshore Learning Materials
PlayDesigns
SafeSpace Concepts, Inc.
Sandy and Sons Educational Supplies
Wehrfritz

LOFTS

ABC School Supply
Childcraft Education Corporation
Community Playthings
Dusyma
Haba
Kaplan
Lakeshore Learning Materials
Lofty Thinkers, L.L.C.

Soft play center by Environments.

Loft by Community Playthings (Photo © Community Playthings. Used by permission).

Playscapes
Playworks, Inc.
Wehrfritz

PUPPET THEATERS

ABC School Supply
Arredi 3n
Beka, Inc.
Childcraft Education Corporation
Childs/Play, Inc.
Community Playthings
Dusyma
Environments
Fleetwood
Kaplan
N.D. Cass Co., Inc.
Whitney Bros. Co.

VIDEO GAME UNITS

Interior Systems, Inc.
Kidzpace Interactive, Inc.
Koala Corp./Koala Bear Kare

CRIBS AND TODDLER BEDS— COMMERCIAL (SEE ALSO BEDS— RESIDENTIAL AND CRIBS—RESIDENTIAL)

ABC School Supply
Arredi 3n
Childcraft Education Corporation
Community Playthings
Dusyma
Environments
Kaplan
L.A. Baby
Lakeshore Learning Materials
Nursery Maid
Old Hickory Furniture Co., Inc.
Sandy and Sons Educational Supplies
Wehrfritz
Whitney Bros. Co.

Pediatric Cribs

Hard Manufacturing Co., Inc.
Midmark

DESKS

American Park and Recreation Company
Childcraft Education Corporation
Instant Products, Inc.
Italiana Societa Arredamenti Fontanili
    F.lli s.r.l.
The Little Tikes Company
The Malnight Company, Inc.
Nemschoff
Wehrfritz

Computer Desks and Tables

ABC School Supply
Anatex Enterprises, Inc.
BBT Group
Childcraft Education Corporation
Childs/Play, Inc.
Environments
Fleetwood
Funblock Tables
Kinderworks
The Little Tikes Company
The Malnight Company, Inc.

Computer desk by Skools, Inc.

Nova Solutions, Inc.
Sandy and Sons Educational Supplies
SIS Human Factors Technologies, Inc.
Skools, Inc.
Stevens Industries
Texwood Furniture Corporation
Whitney Bros. Co.

School Desks

Capitol Seating Company
KI
National School Lines Company
Scholar Craft Products, Inc.

EXERCISE EQUIPMENT

Learning Products

FUTONS

L.A. Baby

LECTERNS

BBT Group

LIBRARY FURNISHINGS

Childcraft Education Corporation
Childs/Play, Inc.
Community Playthings
Decar Educational/Office Furniture
Demco
Fleetwood
Gressco Ltd.
Highsmith, Inc.
McDole Library Furniture
R-Wireworks, Inc.
Texwood Furniture Corporation

School desks by KI.

RESIDENCE LIVING FURNISHINGS (INCLUDES INSTITUTIONAL BEDROOM AND LIVING ROOM FURNISHINGS)

The following companies offer furnishings that are not necessarily scaled to children but are often used in environments in which children live for a temporary, but sometimes extended amount of time. For example, dormitories, halfway homes, foster care facilities, and emergency shelters. Residence living furnishings are constructed to be more durable than standard residential furnishings.

Reading kiosk by Gressco Ltd.

Blockhouse Company, Inc.
Furniture Concepts
University Loft Company

ROOM DIVIDERS

ABC School Supply
Arredi 3n

Room dividers by Arredi 3n dei F.lli Nespoli.

BBT Group
Childcraft Education Corporation
The Children's Factory
The Children's Furniture Company
Childs/Play, Inc.
Chime Time
Community Playthings
Dusyma
Gressco Ltd.
Haba
Italiana Societa Arredamenti Fontanili
    F.lli s.r.l.
Kaplan
Koala Corp./Koala Bear Kare
Lakeshore Learning Materials
Multiplex Display Fixture Company
PlayDesigns

Themed Room Dividers

Angeles Group
Lakeshore Learning Materials
Kidzpace Interactive, Inc.

People Friendly Places
Playscapes
Wehrfritz

SEATING

Beanbags

ABC School Supply
Childcraft Education Corporation
Chime Time
Dusyma
Eazy Bean
Lakeshore Learning Materials

Benches

Anatex Enterprises, Inc.
Arredi 3n
Childs/Play, Inc.
Community Playthings
Dusyma
Fixture Furniture
Gressco Ltd.
Haba
HEWI, Inc.
Highsmith, Inc.
Italiana Societa Arredamenti Fontanili
    F.lli s.r.l.
Learning Products
Playscapes
Scandinavian Design
Texwood Furniture Corporation
Wehrfritz

Chairs (See Also Table and Chair Sets)

Fixed Chairs (Attached to Floor)

The products offered by the following companies are not necessarily scaled to children, but are often used in settings in which children make up a high percentage of the user group, such as fast-food restaurants, food courts, and indoor entertainment facilities.

Falcon Products, Inc.

Folding Chairs

KI

High Chairs

Central Specialties Ltd.
Environments
Community Playthings
Falcon Products, Inc.
Kaplan
Kinderworks
Koala Corp./Koala Bear Kare
Lakeshore Learning Materials
Marston Manufacturing, Inc.
Old Hickory Furniture Co., Inc.

Nonwood Chairs

ABC School Supply
Alar Furniture, Inc.
Anatex Enterprises, Inc.
Angeles Group
Arredi 3n
Capitol Seating Company
Childcraft Education Corporation
Environments
Fixtures Furniture
Haworth
Interior Systems, Inc.
Italiana Societa Arredamenti Fontanili
    F.lli s.r.l.
KI
Kaplan
Koala Corp./Koala Bear Kare
Komponents Laminated Products
Lakeshore Learning Materials
Learning Products
Loewenstein
National School Lines Company
Office Specialty
Panex Furniture Products, Inc.
People Friendly Places
Peter Pepper Products, Inc.
Playscapes
Sandy and Sons Educational Supplies
Scholar Craft Products, Inc.
The Step2 Company
Stevens Industries
Virco Manufacturing Co.

Charlie/Kids by Loewenstein.

Rocking Chairs
ABC School Supply
Childcraft Education Corporation
The Children's Furniture Co.
Community Playthings
Don P. Smith Chair Co.
Environments
Kaplan
Kinderworks
Lakeshore Learning Materials
The Little Tikes Company
Majestic Woodworks
Old Hickory Furniture Co., Inc.
Puzzlecraft Furniture
The Step2 Company

Rocking Toy Seats
For children, rocking toys provide a viable and interesting alternative to traditional seating.

Brio Corporation
Community Playthings
Heirlooms of Tomorrow, Inc.
Horizons International Accents, Inc.

Stackable Chairs
ABC School Supply
Angeles Group

Arredi 3n
Capitol Seating Company
Childcraft Education Corporation
The Children's Furniture Co.
Community Playthings
Danko
Fixtures Furniture
Group Four Furniture
Haworth
KI
Kaplan
Kinderworks
Lakeshore Learning Materials
Loewenstein
McCourt Manufacturing
Sauder Manufacturing Company
Scholar Craft Products, Inc.
Skools, Inc.
Virco Manufacturing Co.

Wood Chairs
ABC School Supply
Arredi 3n
BBT Group
Childcraft Education Corporation
The Children's Furniture Company
Childs/Play, Inc.
Community

Dragon seat by Heirlooms of Tomorrow.

Community Playthings
Danko
Decar Educational/Office Furniture
Demco
Design America
Don P. Smith Chair Co.
Dusyma
Environments
Fleetwood
Group Four Furniture
Haba
Italiana Societa Arredamenti Fontanili
    F.lli s.r.l.
Kaplan
Kinderworks
Lakeshore Learning Materials
Loewenstein
The Malnight Company, Inc.
Nemschoff
Old Hickory Furniture Co., Inc.
People Friendly Places
Puzzlecraft Furniture
Sandy and Sons Educational Supplies
Sauder Manufacturing Company
Scandinavian Design
Simplex International (PVT) Ltd.
Skools, Inc.
Texwood Furniture Corporation
Thonet

Lounge (Soft) Seating

August Incorporated
Design America
Dusyma
Gressco Ltd.
Group Four Furniture
Nemschoff
People Friendly Places

Domino lounge chair by Group Four.

Wood chairs by Thonet.

Loungers

Arconas
Childcraft Education Corporation
The Children's Factory
Environments

Modular

August Incorporated
Dusyma

Linn Jr. modular seating group by August, Inc.   Adult and junior models.

Salon Chairs

Takara Belmont

Stools, Sitting

Anatex Enterprises, Inc.
Capitol Seating Company
The Children's Furniture Company
Community Playthings
Don P. Smith Chair Co.
Funblock Tables
Gressco Ltd.
Haba
Highsmith, Inc.
Peter Pepper Products, Inc.
Skools, Inc.
Texwood Furniture Corporation
Thonet

Wehrfritz
Komponents Laminated Products
The Little Tikes Company
Melodious Music Boxes

STEP STOOLS

Puzzlecraft Furniture
Simplex International (PVT) Ltd.
Wehrfritz

STORAGE

Book Display Units (See Also Library Furnishings)

ABC School Supply
Angeles Group
Arredi 3n
BBT Group

Biggwood
Childcraft Education Corporation
Community Playthings
Demco
Dusyma
Environments
Fleetwood
Gressco Ltd.
Italiana Societa Arredamenti Fontanili
    F.lli s.r.l.
Kaplan
Kinderworks
Lakeshore Learning Materials
Panex Furniture Products, Inc.
People Friendly Places
Sandy and Sons Educational Supplies
Stevens Industries
Texwood Furniture Corporation
Whitney Bros. Co.

Stevens Industries
Wehrfritz

Cubbies

ABC School Supply
Angeles Group
Arredi 3n
Childcraft Education Corporation
Childs/Play, Inc.
Community Playthings
Dusyma
Environments
Fleetwood
Haba
Kaplan
Kinderworks
Komponents Laminated Products
Lakeshore Learning Materials
Nursery Maid
Panex Furniture Products, Inc.
Sandy and Sons Educational Supplies
Scandinavian Design
Stevens Industries
Texwood Furniture Corporation

Two-sided book display unit by Whitney Bros.

Chests

The Children's Furniture Company
Fleetwood
Kinderworks
The Little Tikes Company
The Step2 Company

Cubbies by Childcraft.

Wehrfritz
Whitney Bros. Co.

Drawer Units

Arredi 3n
Haba
Italiana Societa Arredamenti Fontanili
    F.lli s.r.l.
The Malnight Company, Inc.
Nemschoff
Nursery Maid
Old Hickory Furniture Co., Inc.
Wehrfritz

**Hooks, Coatracks,
and Clothes Trees**

Arredi 3n
Beagle Manufacturing Company, Inc.
Childcraft Education Corporation
Childs/Play, Inc.
Dusyma
Haba
HEWI, Inc.
Italiana Societa Arredamenti Fontanili
    F.lli s.r.l.
Kinderworks
Nifty Nob
Wehrfritz
Whitney Bros. Co.

Media Equipment Storage Units

ABC School Supply
Childcraft Education Corporation
Environments
Fleetwood
Kaplan
Kinderworks
Lakeshore Learning Materials
People Friendly Places
Whitney Bros. Co.

Musical Equipment Storage

Haba
Kaplan
Lakeshore Learning Materials
Sandy and Sons Educational Supplies

Wehrfritz
Whitney Bros. Co.

Shelf Units

ABC School Supply
Anatex Enterprises, Inc.
Angeles Group
Arredi 3n
Childcraft Education Corporation
Childs/Play, Inc.
Community Playthings
Dusyma
Environments
Fleetwood
Funblock Tables
Gressco Ltd.
Haba
Italiana Societa Arredamenti Fontanili
    F.lli s.r.l.
Kaplan
Kinderworks
Komponents Laminated Products
Lakeshore Learning Materials
The Malnight Company, Inc.
Old Hickory Furniture Co., Inc.
Panex Furniture Products, Inc.
People Friendly Places
Sandy and Sons Educational Supplies
Scandinavian Design
Simplex International (PVT) Ltd.
The Step2 Company
Stevens Industries
Texwood Furniture Corporation
Virco Manufacturing Co.
Wehrfritz
Whitney Bros. Co.

Tote Tray Storage Units

ABC School Supply
Angeles Group
Childcraft Education Corporation
Childs/Play, Inc.
Chime Time
Community Playthings
Copernicus Educational Products, Inc.
Dusyma

Tote tray storage unit by Childcraft.

Environments
Fleetwood
Funblock Tables
Kaplan
Kinderworks
Lakeshore Learning Materials
Nursery Maid
Panex Furniture Products, Inc.
Sandy and Sons Educational Supplies
Stevens Industries
Texwood Furniture Corporation
Virco Manufacturing Co.
Whitney Bros. Co.

Storage Wall Systems

ABC School Supply
Arredi 3n
Dusyma
Haba
Italiana Societa Arredamenti Fontanili
　　F.lli s.r.l.
Kaplan
Panex Furniture Products, Inc.
Wehrfritz
Whitney Bros. Co.

TABLE AND CHAIR SETS
(SEE ALSO TABLES AND CHAIRS)

Fixed (Attached to Floor) Table and Chair Sets

Falcon Products, Inc.
Interior Systems, Inc.

Nonwood Table and Chair Sets

ABC School Supply
Alar Furniture, Inc.
Angeles Group
Environments
Fixtures Furniture
Haworth
Italiana Societa Arredamenti Fontanili
　　F.lli s.r.l.

Whitco storage wall by Whitney Bros.

Scamps by Haworth.

KI
Kaplan
Lakeshore Learning Materials
Learning Products
The Little Tikes Company
Office Specialty
Panex Furniture Products, Inc.
People Friendly Places
Peter Pepper Products, Inc.
Playscapes
Sandy and Sons Educational Supplies
The Step2 Company
Stevens Industries
Virco Manufacturing Co.

Wood Table and Chair Sets

ABC School Supply
BBT Group
Childcraft Education Corporation
Childs/Play, Inc.
Demco
Design America
Dusyma
Environments
Italiana Societa Arredamenti Fontanili
    F.lli s.r.l.
Kaplan
Kinderworks
Lakeshore Learning Materials
The Malnight Company, Inc.
Nemschoff

Old Hickory Furniture Co., Inc.
People Friendly Places
Sandy and Sons Educational Supplies
Sauder Manufacturing Company
Scandinavian Design
Texwood Furniture Corporation
Thonet
Wehrfritz
Whitney Bros. Co.

Wonderland by Design America.

TABLES (SEE ALSO TABLE AND CHAIR SETS)

Activity Tables

Construction Top Tables (Includes Tables for Use with LEGOs and Similar Building Blocks)

ABC School Supply
Angeles Group
Brio Corporation
Childcraft Education Corporation
Childs/Play, Inc.
Environments
Funblock Tables
Interior Systems, Inc.
Koala Corp./Koala Bear Kare
Lego Dacta, Inc.
Manta-Ray, Inc.
Nursery Maid
Sandy and Sons Educational Supplies

Construction top table by Lego Dacta.

The Step2 Company
Light Tables
ABC School Supply
Angeles Group
Childcraft Education Corporation
Italiana Societa Arredamenti Fontanili
    F.lli s.r.l.
Magnetic-top Manipulative Tables
Childcraft Education Corporation
The Children's Furniture Company

Magnetic top table by The Children's Furniture Co.

Educo International, Inc.
People Friendly Places
Playscapes
Sandy and Sons Educational Supplies
*Manipulative Tables (Includes Bead
    Maze Tables)*
Anatex Enterprises, Inc.
Arredi 3n

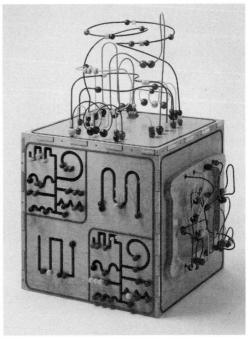

Manipulative cube table by Anatex.

Dusyma
Educo International, Inc.
Kinderworks
Koala Corp./Koala Bear Kare
People Friendly Places
Playscapes
Painting/Drawing Top Tables
The tops of these tables are designed to be painted and drawn on directly with mediums such as finger paints and erasable markers.

ABC School Supply
BBT Group
Manta-Ray, Inc.
Railroad Tables
Brio Corporation
Learning Curve Toys
Roadway Tables
Learning Curve Toys
Sand and/or Water Tables (for Indoor Use)
ABC School Supply
Arredi 3n
Childcraft Education Corporation
Childs/Play, Inc.
Community Playthings
Discover Products, Inc.
Dusyma
Environments
Fleetwood
Haba
Kaplan
Kinderworks
Lakeshore Learning Materials
Learning Products
Manta-Ray, Inc.
Sandy and Sons Educational Supplies
Wehrfritz
Whitney Bros. Co.
Science
Lakeshore Learning Materials

Adjustable-height Tables

ABC School Supply
BBT Group
Berco Tableworks, Ltd.
Childcraft Education Corporation
Decar Educational/Office Furniture
Fleetwood
Lakeshore Learning Materials
Virco Manufacturing Co.

Diaper Changing Tables and Stations

ABC School Supply
Arredi 3n
Childcraft Education Corporation
Childs/Play, Inc.
Community Playthings

Dusyma
Environments
Fleetwood
Kaplan
L.A. Baby
Lakeshore Learning Materials
Nursery Maid
Panex Furniture Products, Inc.
Sandy and Sons Educational Supplies
Stevens Industries
Wehrfritz
Whitney Bros. Co.

Fixed (Secured to Floor) Tables

Falcon Products, Inc.

Folding Tables

McCourt Manufactuirng

Nesting Tables

ABC School Supply
Kaplan

Nonwood Tables

ABC School Supply
Alar Furniture, Inc.
Anatex Enterprises, Inc.
Angeles Group
BBT Group
Childcraft Education Corporation
Decar Educational/Office Furniture
Environments
Falcon Products, Inc.
Fixtures Furniture
Fleetwood
Group Four Furniture
Haworth
Italiana Societa Arredamenti Fontanili
    F.lli s.r.l.
KI
Kaplan
Komponents Laminated Products
Lakeshore Learning Materials
Learning Products
Office Specialty
Panex Furniture Products, Inc.

Flower table by Virco.

People Friendly Places
Peter Pepper Products, Inc.
Peterson Design
Playscapes
Sandy and Sons Educational Supplies
Sico North America, Inc.
The Step2 Company
Stevens Industries
Virco Manufacturing Co.

Pediatric Exam Tables

Goodtime Medical
Hausmann Industries, Inc.
Midmark
Pediatric Designs, Inc.

Wood Tables (Includes Tables with Wooden Legs and Laminate Tops)

ABC School Supply
Arredi 3n
BBT Group

Childcraft Education Corporation
The Children's Furniture Company
Childs/Play, Inc.
Community Playthings

Pediatric exam "bus" table by Goodtime Medical.

Decar Educational/Office Furniture
Design America
Dusyma
Environments
Fleetwood
Gressco Ltd.
Haba
The ICF Group

Aalto multisection table by The ICF Group.

Italiana Societa Arredamenti Fontanili F.lli
    s.r.l.
Kaplan
Kinderworks
The Malnight Company, Inc.
Nemschoff
Old Hickory Furniture Co., Inc.
People Friendly Places
Puzzlecraft Furniture
Sandy and Sons Educational Supplies
Sauder Manufacturing Company
Scandinavian Design
Texwood Furniture Corporation
Thonet
Wehrfritz

Lighting

CEILING LIGHTING

Justice Design Group
Primelite Manufacturing Corp.
Wehrfritz

FLOOR LIGHTING

Merit Wish

TABLE LIGHTING

Dragons of Walton Street
Justice Design Group
Luceplan USA, Inc.
Mark Wilkinson
Melodious Music Boxes
Merit Wish
The Merrymac Collection
MM's Designs
Primelite Manufacturing Corp.
Royal Haeger Lamp Company
Simplex International (PVT) Ltd.
Wehrfritz

WALL LIGHTING

Justice Design Group
Wehrfritz

Wall sconce from the Bogo Collection by Justice Design Group.

Suppliers by Industry

CHILD CARE/EARLY EDUCATION

ABC School Supply
Capitol Seating Company
Childcraft Education Corporation
The Children's Factory
Childs/Play, Inc.
Chime Time
Community Playthings
Constructive Playthings
Demco
Dusyma
Environments
Fleetwood
Funblock Tables
Haba
Kaplan
KI
Kinderworks
Komponents Laminated Products
Lakeshore Learning Materials
The Malnight Company, Inc.
Manta-Ray, Inc.
Nursery Maid
Panex Furniture Products, Inc.
Royal Seating Company
Sandy and Sons Educational Supplies
Scandinavian Design, Inc.
Stevens Industries
Texwood Furniture Company

Things From Bell
Wehrfritz
Whitney Bros. Co.

HEALTH CARE

Goodtime Medical
Hard Manufacturing Co., Inc.
Hausmann Industries, Inc.
Midmark
Nemschoff
Pediatric Designs, Inc.
People Friendly Places
Playscapes

EDUCATIONAL

Aristocrat Industries, Inc.
Bangor Cork Company, Inc.
BBT Group
Capitol Seating Company
Claridge Products & Equipment
Decar Educational/Office Furniture
Demco
Discover Products Inc.
Fleetwood
KI
National School Lines Company
Nelson Adams Company
Royal Seating Company
Scholar Craft Products, Inc.
Sico North America Inc.
Things From Bell

RESIDENTIAL PRODUCTS

ACCESSORIES

Bathroom Accessories

Gusa
Watercolors, Inc.

Bedding

Bed Linens
BananaFish
Belinda Barton Furnishings for Children
California Kids

Dragons of Walton Street
L.A. Baby
My Dog Spot
Sumersault
This End Up Furniture Company
Crib Bedding
BananaFish
Belinda Barton Furnishings for Children.
California Kids
Dragons of Walton Street

Hillcrest Baby
House of Hatten, Inc.
L.A. Baby
Lamby Nursery Collection
My Dog Spot
Noel Joanna, Inc. (NoJo)
Sumersault

Bookends

Merit Wish
MM's Designs
Simplex International (PVT) Ltd.

Clocks

Dragons of Walton Street
Melodious Music Boxes
MM's Designs

Granddaughter clock by Dragons of Walton Street.

Custom-designed Accessories

Charm & Whimsy
Dragons of Walton Street

Decorative Accessories

Dragons of Walton Street
Horizons International Accents, Inc.

Drawer/Door Pulls

D.I.G.S.
Knobs by Susan Goldstick
Nifty Nob
Priss Prints, Inc.

Headboards

d-Scan, Inc.
Design Finland, Inc.
Dragons of Walton Street
Dream Team Design
Merit Wish
Lea Industries
Lexington Furniture Industries
Old Hickory Furniture Co., Inc.

Lamps, table

California Kids
Green Frog Art

Mirrors

Bellini
Cargo Furniture & Accents
d-Scan, Inc.
Dragons of Walton Street
Dream Team Design
Gautier USA, Inc.
Lea Industries
Lexington Furniture Industries
Maine Cottage Furniture
Mark Wilkinson
Melodious Music Boxes
Merit Wish
Moosehead Manufacturing Company
Old Hickory Furniture Co., Inc.
Stevens Industries
Tracers Furniture, Inc.

Pillows and Cushions

Belinda Barton Furnishings for Children
California Kids
Hillcrest Baby

House of Hatten, Inc.
Merit Wish
My Dog Spot

Rugs

California Kids
Couristan
Green Frog Art
MM's Designs

Switchplate Covers

Merit Wish
MM's Designs
Nifty Nob
Priss Prints, Inc.
Rashti & Rashti, The Babi Gift Co.

Wall Art

House of Hatten, Inc.
Priss Prints, Inc.

Wallcoverings

Anna French
Carolyn Ray, Inc.
Dragons of Walton Street
Osborne & Little
Peter Fasano
Spring Street Studio, Inc.
Thibaut Wallcoverings & Fabrics
Wallborders
Anna French
Green Frog Art
Osborne & Little
Priss Prints, Inc.
Thibaut Wallcoverings & Fabrics

Wastebaskets

Dragons of Walton Street
Merit Wish

Window Treatments

Drapery Hardware
Claesson
The Ground Floor
Knobs by Susan Goldstick

Valances
California Kids
Merit Wish

FABRICS

Anna French
Belinda Barton Furnishings for Children
California Kids
Carolyn Ray, Inc.
Dragons of Walton Street
Duralee Fabrics, Inc.
My Dog Spot
Osborne & Little
Peter Fasano
Thibaut Wallcoverings & Fabrics

Faux Furs

Gretchen Bellinger
Spring Street Studio, Inc.

FURNISHINGS

Cradles

Badger Basket Company
Cosco, Inc.
EG Furniture
Generation 2 Worldwide
Mark Wilkinson
Million Dollar Baby
Okla Homer Smith Furniture Manufacturing
    Company
Tracers Furniture, Inc.
Whimsies, Inc.

Bedroom Groups (Typically Includes Bed, Storage Unit(s), Desk, and Chair)

Infant Nursery Groups
Bassett Furniture Industries, Inc.
Bellini
EG Furniture
Generation 2 Worldwide
Lexington Furniture Industries
Moosehead Manufacturing Company

Okla Homer Smith Furniture Manufacturing
Company
Tracers Furniture, Inc.

Festival bedroom grouping by Gautier.

Juvenile/Teen Bedroom Groups
Artisan Studios, Inc.
Bassett Furniture Industries, Inc.
Bellini
Cargo Furniture & Accents
d-Scan, Inc.
Design Finland, Inc.
EG Furniture
Gautier USA, Inc.
Lea Industries
Lexington Furniture Industries
Maine Cottage Furniture
Mark Wilkinson
Moosehead Manufacturing Company
Old Hickory Furniture Co., Inc.
Scandinavian Design
Stevens Industries
Techline
Tracers Furniture, Inc.

Beds
Bassett Furniture Industries, Inc.
Bestar
Cargo Furniture & Accents

Cosco, Inc.
Design Finland, Inc.
Dragons of Walton Street
Dream Team Design
EG Furniture
Gautier USA, Inc.
Kids' Studio
Lexington Furniture Industries
Maine Cottage Furniture
Mark Wilkinson
Million Dollar Baby
Old Hickory Furniture Co., Inc.
Scandinavian Design
The Step2 Company
Stevens Industries
Techline
Tracers Furniture, Inc.
Wild Zoo Design

Goldilocks bed by Mark Wilkinson.

Bunk Beds
Bassett Furniture Industries, Inc.
Cargo Furniture & Accents
Design Finland, Inc.

Dragons of Walton Street
EG Furniture
Gautier USA, Inc.
Lea Industries
Lexington Furniture Industries
Majestic Woodworks
Moosehead Manufacturing Company
Old Hickory Furniture Co., Inc.
Scandinavian Design
The Step2 Company
Stevens Industries
This End Up Furniture Company
Canopy Beds
Bassett Furniture Industries, Inc.
Dragons of Walton Street
Mark Wilkinson
Captain's Beds (Drawer Storage Below)
Bassett Furniture Industries, Inc.
Bellini
Cargo Furniture & Accents
d-Scan, Inc.
Design Finland, Inc.
Dragons of Walton Street
Gautier USA, Inc.
Lea Industries
Lexington Furniture Industries
Moosehead Manufacturing Company
Scandinavian Design
Stevens Industries
Techline
This End Up Furniture Company
Sleigh Beds
Cargo Furniture & Accents
Lea Industries
Lexington Furniture Industries
Tracers Furniture, Inc.
Sofa Beds
Dragons of Walton Street
Trundle Beds
Cargo Furniture & Accents
d-Scan, Inc.
Design Finland, Inc.
EG Furniture
Gautier USA, Inc.
Lea Industries

Lexington Furniture Industries
Maine Cottage Furniture
Moosehead Manufacturing Company
Scandinavian Design
Stevens Industries
This End Up Furniture Company

Cribs

Baby Trilogy, Inc.
Bassett Furniture Industries, Inc.
Bellini
Cosco, Inc.
Dragons of Walton Street
Generation 2 Worldwide
Lexington Furniture Industries
Mark Wilkinson
Million Dollar Baby
Moosehead Manufacturing Company
Scandinavian Design
Simo (USA), Inc.
Tracers Furniture, Inc.

Custom-designed Furnishings

Charm & Whimsy
Dragons of Walton Street
Kathy Foster, Artist
Kids' Studio
Straight Line Design

Desks

Ardley Hall
Bellini
Cargo Furniture & Accents
d-Scan, Inc.
Design Finland, Inc.
Dragons of Walton Street
Gautier USA, Inc.
Lea Industries
Lexington Furniture Industries
Maine Cottage Furniture
Mark Wilkinson
Moosehead Manufacturing Company
N.D. Cass Co., Inc.
Old Hickory Furniture Co., Inc.

Ms. Pearson chest of drawers by Straight Line Design.

Scandinavian Design
Simplex International (PVT) Ltd.
Stevens Industries
This End Up Furniture Company
Tracers Furniture, Inc.

Entertainment Centers

Gautier USA, Inc.
Lea Industries
Lexington Furniture Industries
Moosehead Manufacturing Company
Old Hickory Furniture Co., Inc.
Stevens Industries

Seating

Benches
Ardley Hall
BananaFish

Dream Team Design
Union City Chair Company
Chairs (See Also Table and Chair Sets)
Ardley Hall
Design Finland, Inc.
Dragons of Walton Street
Dream Team Design
Gautier USA, Inc.
Lea Industries
Lexington Furniture Industries
Mark Wilkinson
Moosehead Manufacturing Company
Simplex International (PVT) Ltd.
Union City Chair Company
High chairs
Cosco, Inc.
Dragons of Walton Street
Generation 2 Worldwide
L.A. Baby
Million Dollar Baby
Simo (USA), Inc.
Union City Chair Company
Rocking chairs
Dragons of Walton Street
EG Furniture
Generation 2 Worldwide
Melodious Music Boxes
Million Dollar Baby
N.D. Cass Co., Inc.
Palecek
Union City Chair Company
Wild Zoo Design
UPHOLSTERED
The Joseph Company
National Upholstering Company
Wehrfritz
Ottomans
BananaFish
Belinda Barton Furnishings for Children
Classic Gallery Group
Dragons of Walton Street
Lee Industries
Stools, Sitting
Dragons of Walton Street
Kids' Studio

Rocking chair by National Upholstering Company.

Maine Cottage Furniture
MM's Designs
Simplex International (PVT) Ltd.
Union City Chair Company
Upholstered Seating (Sofas, Love Seats, and Loungers)
Classic Gallery Group
Dragons of Walton Street
Lee Industries, Inc.

Wicker Seating
Palecek
PierceMartin

Storage

Bookcases
Stevens Industries
Wild Zoo Design
Chests of Drawers
Bellini
Cargo Furniture & Accents
d-Scan, Inc.
Design Finland, Inc.
Dragons of Walton Street
EG Furniture
Gautier USA, Inc.
Lea Industries
Lexington Furniture Industries
Mark Wilkinson
Million Dollar Baby
Moosehead Manufacturing Company
Okla Homer Smith Furniture Manufacturing Company
Old Hickory Furniture Co., Inc.
Pilliod Furniture
Scandinavian Design

Upholstered furnishings by Lee Industries, Inc.

Wicker chair by Palecek.

Stevens Industries
Straight Line Design
Techline
This End Up Furniture Company
Tracers Furniture, Inc.
Wild Zoo Design
Clothes Hampers
Badger Basket Company
Hooks, Coatracks, and Clothes Trees
D.I.G.S.
EG Furniture
Merit Wish
MM's Designs
Old Hickory Furniture Co., Inc.
Puzzlecraft Furniture
Simplex International (PVT) Ltd.
Shelf Units
Bellini
Dragons of Walton Street
Dream Team Design
Gautier USA, Inc.
Kids' Studio

Learning Passport Co.
Lexington Furniture Industries
Maine Cottage Furniture
Mark Wilkinson
Moosehead Manufacturing Company
Old Hickory Furniture Co., Inc.
Puzzlecraft Furniture
Scandinavian Design
Straight Line Design
Techline
This End Up Furniture Company
Toy/Hope Chests
Cargo Furniture & Accents
d-Scan, Inc.
Design Finland, Inc.
Dragons of Walton Street
EG Furniture
Generation 2 Worldwide
Majestic Woodworks
Mark Wilkinson
Melodious Music Boxes
Merit Wish
Moosehead Manufacturing Company
N.D. Cass Co., Inc.
Puzzlecraft Furniture
Scandinavian Design
Simplex International (PVT) Ltd.
This End Up Furniture Company
Tracers Furniture, Inc.
Wild Zoo Design

Table and Chair Sets

Badger Basket Company
Cargo Furniture & Accents
Design Finland, Inc.
Dragons of Walton Street
EG Furniture
Eco-sTuff!
Instant Products, Inc.
Kids' Studio
Maine Cottage Furniture
Merit Wish
N.D. Cass Co., Inc.
Scandinavian Design
Simplex International (PVT) Ltd.
This End Up Furniture Company

Table and storage stool by Kids' Studio.

Tracers Furniture, Inc.
Union City Chair Company
Wild Zoo Design

Tables (See Also Table and Chair Sets)

Design Finland, Inc.
Dragons of Walton Street
Kids' Studio
Maine Cottage Furniture
Mark Wilkinson
Simplex International (PVT) Ltd.

Bedside Tables

Cargo Furniture & Accents
d-Scan, Inc.
Dragons of Walton Street
EG Furniture
Gautier USA, Inc.
Lexington Furniture Industries
Maine Cottage Furniture
Mark Wilkinson
Moosehead Manufacturing Company
Old Hickory Furniture Co., Inc.
The Step2 Company

Stevens Industries
Techline
This End Up Furniture Company
Tracers Furniture, Inc.

Infant Changing Tables

Badger Basket Company
Bassett Furniture Industries, Inc.
Bellini
Generation 2 Worldwide
Mark Wilkinson
Million Dollar Baby
Moosehead Manufacturing Company
Okla Homer Smith Furniture Manufacturing
    Company
Scandinavian Design
Tracers Furniture, Inc.
Union City Chair Company

Dressing Tables

Lexington Furniture Industries
Mark Wilkinson
Minic

Goldilocks dressing table by Mark Wilkinson.

OUTDOOR FURNISHINGS AND EQUIPMENT

ACCESSIBLE ELEMENTS

The following companies offer products and services that are specifically designed for outdoor playground use by children with disabilities. Not only can they help make a playground ADA compliant, they can provide added enjoyment of the playground for children with special needs.

Balance Beams

Columbia Cascade Company

Basketball Equipment

The Bankshot Organization
Playkids

Bouncers

Go-Elan, Inc.

Circuit Equipment

Gametime

Horizontal Ladder

PCA Industries, Inc.
Playground Environments

Sand Diggers

Gametime
Henderson Recreation Equipment Limited
Landscape Structures, Inc.
Little Tikes Commercial Play Systems, Inc.
PlayDesigns

Spinners

Things From Bell

Swings

Hammock
Parity, Inc.
PCA Industries, Inc.
Playkids
Things From Bell

Accessible sand digger by Gametime.

Platform Swings
Go-Elan, Inc.
Henderson Recreation Equipment Limited
PCA Industries, Inc.
Playkids
Playland International L.L.C.
Things From Bell
Seat Swings
Chime Time
Gametime
Go-Elan, Inc.
PCA Industries, Inc.
Playkids
Things From Bell
Sphere Swings
Kidstruction

Tables

Sand and/or Water Tables
Playkids

FREESTANDING ACTIVITY EQUIPMENT

Activity Panels and Walls

Belair Recreational Products, Inc.
Howell Equipment Company
Landscape Structures, Inc.
Play & Leisure Systems, Inc.

PlayDesigns
Playkids

Balance Beams

American Park and Recreation Company
BCI Burke Company LLC
Columbia Cascade Company
Dusyma
Environments
Gametime
Go-Elan, Inc.
Kompan, Inc.
Krauss Craft, Inc.
Landscape Structures, Inc.
Little Tikes Commercial Play Systems, Inc.
PCA Industries, Inc.
PlayDesigns
Playlofts, Inc.
Wehrfritz

Ball Walls

L.A. Steelcraft Products, Inc.

Barrel Rolls

Go-Elan, Inc.

Bouncers

ABC School Supply
Kompan, Inc.
Landscape Structures
Playland International L.L.C.

Chin-up and Turning Bars

American Park and Recreation Company
Columbia Cascade Company
Dusyma
Henderson Recreation Equipment Limited
Howell Equipment Company
Kompan, Inc.
Krauss Craft, Inc.
L.A. Steelcraft Products, Inc.
Landscape Structures, Inc.
Little Tikes Commercial Play Systems, Inc.
Play & Leisure Systems, Inc.
Wehrfritz

Climbers

ABC School Supply
American Park and Recreation Company
Belair Recreational Products, Inc.
Big Top Toys, Inc.
BCI Burke Company LLC
Chime Time
Columbia Cascade Company
Dusyma
Gametime
Go-Elan, Inc.
Henderson Recreation Equipment Limited
Howell Equipment Company
Italiana Societa Arredamenti Fontanili
     F.lli s.r.l.
Kompan, Inc.
L.A. Steelcraft Products, Inc.
Landscape Structures, Inc.
Little Tikes Commercial Play Systems, Inc.
PCA Industries, Inc.
PlayDesigns
Playkids
Playland International L.L.C.
Wehrfritz

Crawl Tunnels

Chime Time
Columbia Cascade Company
Gametime
Italiana Societa Arredamenti Fontanili
     F.lli s.r.l.
Kompan, Inc.
Krauss Craft, Inc.
L.A. Steelcraft Products, Inc.
Landscape Structures, Inc.
PlayDesigns

Cyclers

Landscape Structures, Inc.

Horizontal Ladders and Rings

American Park and Recreation Company
Big Top Toys, Inc.
BCI Burke Company LLC

Columbia Cascade Company
Go-Elan, Inc.
Henderson Recreation Equipment Limited
Howell Equipment Company
Kompan, Inc.
Krauss Craft, Inc.
L.A. Steelcraft Products, Inc.
Landscape Structures, Inc.
Little Tikes Commercial Play Systems, Inc.
PCA Industries, Inc.
Playkids
Playland International L.L.C.
Playlofts, Inc.
Wehrfritz

Log Rolls

Columbia Cascade Company
Landscape Structures, Inc.
Little Tikes Commercial Play Systems, Inc.

Mazes

PlayDesigns

Merry-go-rounds

Merry-go-rounds (Push-type)
Big Top Toys, Inc.
BCI Burke Company LLC
Dusyma
Gametime
Go-Elan, Inc.
Henderson Recreation Equipment Limited
Howell Equipment Company
Italiana Societa Arredamenti Fontanili
    F.lli s.r.l.
Landscape Structures, Inc.
Little Tikes Commercial Play Systems, Inc.
Playkids
Merry-go-rounds (Pedal-type)
ABC School Supply
Angeles Group
Big Top Toys, Inc.
Chime Time
Italiana Societa Arredamenti Fontanili
    F.lli s.r.l.
Playkids

Parallel Bars

American Park and Recreation Company
Columbia Cascade Company
Henderson Recreation Equipment Limited
Kompan
L.A. Steelcraft Products, Inc.
Landscape Structures, Inc.
Little Tikes Commercial Play Systems, Inc.
PCA Industries, Inc.
Play & Leisure Systems, Inc.

Punching Bags

Go-Elan, Inc.
Henderson Recreation Equipment Limited

Rope Climbs

L.A. Steelcraft Products, Inc.

Seesaws

BCI Burke Company LLC
Columbia Cascade Company
Dusyma
Go-Elan, Inc.
Henderson Recreation Equipment Limited
Howell Equipment Company
Italiana Societa Arredamenti Fontanili
    F.lli s.r.l.
Kompan, Inc.
Landscape Structures, Inc.
Little Tikes Commercial Play Systems, Inc.
PCA Industries, Inc.
PlayDesigns
Playkids
Playlofts, Inc.
Wehrfritz

Sit-up Benches

Landscape Structures, Inc.
Little Tikes Commercial Play Systems, Inc.
PCA Industries, Inc.

Slides

Belair Recreational Products, Inc.
BCI Burke Company LLC
Chime Time

Columbia Cascade Company
Dusyma
F.A.S.T. Corp.
Gametime
Go-Elan, Inc.
Henderson Recreation Equipment Limited
Howell Equipment Company
Kompan, Inc.
L.A. Steelcraft Products, Inc.
Landscape Structures, Inc.
Little Tikes Commercial Play Systems, Inc.
PCA Industries, Inc.
Peter Pepper Products, Inc.
PlayDesigns
Playkids
Playland International L.L.C.
Wehrfritz

Spring Toys

ABC School Supply
American Park and Recreation Company
American Swing Products
Belair Recreational Products, Inc.
Big Top Toys, Inc.
BCI Burke Company LLC
Chime Time
Columbia Cascade Company
Dusyma
Gametime
Gerber Manufacturing Ltd.

The Scrambler spring rocker by Kompan.

Go-Elan, Inc.
Henderson Recreation Equipment Limited
Howell Equipment Company
Italiana Societa Arredamenti Fontanili
    F.lli s.r.l.
Kompan, Inc.
Krauss Craft, Inc.
L.A. Steelcraft Products, Inc.
Landscape Structures, Inc.
Little Tikes Commercial Play Systems, Inc.
PCA Industries, Inc.
PlayDesigns
Playkids
Wehrfritz

Suspension Bridges

In addition to the following company, most manufacturers of composite playground equipment have the capability of creating a freestanding suspension bridge.

Go-Elan, Inc.

Swings (Includes Tire Swings, Trapeze Bars, and Rings)

Nonwood Frame
American Park and Recreation Company
Belair Recreational Products, Inc.
Big Top Toys, Inc.
BCI Burke Company LLC
Chime Time
Columbia Cascade Company
F.A.S.T. Corp.
Gametime
Go-Elan, Inc.
Henderson Recreation Equipment Limited
Howell Equipment Company
Italiana Societa Arredamenti Fontanili
    F.lli s.r.l.
Kid-Krafters
Kidstruction
L.A. Steelcraft Products, Inc.
Landscape Structures, Inc.
Little Tikes Commercial Play Systems, Inc.
PCA Industries, Inc.
Play & Leisure Systems, Inc.

PlayDesigns
Playkids
Playland International L.L.C.
Tire Swings
Columbia Cascade Company
Gametime
Go-Elan, Inc.
Henderson Recreation Equipment Limited
Howell Equipment Company
Kidstruction
Kompan
Krauss Craft, Inc.
Landscape Structures, Inc.
Little Tikes Commercial Play Systems, Inc.
PCA Industries, Inc.
PlayDesigns
Playkids
Toddler Swings
ABC School Supply
Gametime
Henderson Recreation Equipment Limited
Kompan, Inc.
Landscape Structures, Inc.
Little Tikes Commercial Play Systems, Inc.
Wood Frame
Dusyma
Gametime
Henderson Recreation Equipment Limited
Howell Equipment Company
Italiana Societa Arredamenti Fontanili
    F.lli s.r.l.
Kid-Krafters
Kidstruction
Kompan, Inc.
Krauss Craft, Inc.
PlayDesigns
Playkids
Wehrfritz

Talk Tubes

Gametime
Krauss Craft, Inc.
Landscape Structures, Inc.
Little Tikes Commercial Play Systems,
    Inc.
PlayDesigns

Track Rides

In addition to the following companies, most manufacturers of composite playground equipment have the capability of creating a freestanding track ride.

Columbia Cascade Company
Go-Elan, Inc.
Henderson Recreation Equipment Limited
Kompan
Krauss Craft, Inc.
Landscape Structures, Inc.

Trampolines

Jumpking Outdoor Products
King of Swings
Playlofts, Inc.
Things From Bell

DRAMATIC PLAY (ROLE-PLAYING) PROPS AND EQUIPMENT

Some of the following products may also be suitable for use indoors.

Airplane

Landscape Structures, Inc.

Barn

The Step2 Company

Binoculars

Kompan

Car

Henderson Recreation Equipment Limited
Koala Corp./Koala Bear Kare
Kompan, Inc.
Krauss Craft, Inc.
Little Tikes Commercial Play Systems,
    Inc.

Castle

Kompan, Inc.
PlayDesigns

Fire Engine

Kompan, Inc.
PlayDesigns

Flying Saucer

PlayDesigns

Gas Pump

Environments
Henderson Recreation Equipment Limited
PlayDesigns
The Step2 Company

Helicopter

PlayDesigns

House

Dusyma
Go-Elan, Inc.
Henderson Recreation Equipment Limited
Italiana Societa Arredamenti Fontanili
    F.lli s.r.l.
Kompan, Inc.
Landscape Structures, Inc.
Little Tikes Commercial Play Systems,
    Inc.
Play & Leisure Systems, Inc.
PlayDesigns
Playlofts, Inc.
Wehrfritz

Mailbox

Angeles Group
Environments

Railroad Signs

Go-Elan, Inc.

Sailboat

PlayDesigns

School Bus

Landscape Structures, Inc.
Little Tikes Commercial Play Systems,
    Inc.
PlayDesigns

Ship

Italiana Societa Arredamenti Fontanili
    F.lli s.r.l.
Kompan, Inc.
Wehrfritz

Space Shuttle

Chime Time

Steering Wheels

American Swing Products
American Park and Recreation Company
Cedar Works of Maine
Landscape Structures, Inc.
Polycom Products, Inc.

Telephones

Cedar Works of Maine

Telephone Booth

Kidstruction

Telescopes

American Swing Products
Cedar Works of Maine
Polycom Products, Inc.

Theater

PlayDesigns

Traffic Signs

Angeles Group
Environments
PlayDesigns

Train

Chime Time
Go-Elan, Inc.
Henderson Recreation Equipment
    Limited
Kompan, Inc.
Landscape Structures, Inc.

Train Station

Kompan, Inc.

Trucks

Chime Time
Kompan, Inc.
PlayDesigns

Tugboat

Kompan, Inc.

CIRCUIT EQUIPMENT (FITNESS AND OBSTACLE)

American Park and Recreation Company
Columbia Cascade Company
Gametime
Go-Elan, Inc.
Henderson Recreation Equipment Limited
Howell Equipment Company
Kidstruction
L.A. Steelcraft Products, Inc.
Landscape Structures, Inc.
Little Tikes Commercial Play Systems, Inc.
PCA Industries, Inc.

INFLATABLE PLAY STRUCTURES

Airspace
Things From Bell

MANIPULATIVES—LARGE

ABC School Supply
Discover Products Inc.
Dusyma
Grounds For Play

Large manipulatives by Grounds For Play.

Kaplan
Learning Products
Wehrfritz

COMPONENTS, HARDWARE, AND ACCESSORIES FOR PLAY EQUIPMENT—SOLD SEPARATELY

Components

Activity Panels
American Park and Recreation Company
Bridges
Compass West Corporation
Learning Products
Bubble Panels
American Park and Recreation Company
Compass West Corporation
Kidstruction
L.A. Steelcraft Products, Inc.
Crawl Tunnels
American Park and Recreation Company
Compass West Corporation
Decks
Compass West Corporation
Ramps
Compass West Corporation
Roofs
L.A. Steelcraft Products, Inc.
Slides
American Swing Products
American Park and Recreation Company
Compass West Corporation
L.A. Steelcraft Products, Inc.
Polycom Products, Inc.
Spiral Climbers
Kidstruction
Stairs
West Corporation
Suspension Bridges
Compass West Corporation

Hardware and Accessories

Equipment Supports
Kidstruction
Handgrips
American Swing Products

Kidstruction
Polycom Products, Inc.
Netting
Barbour Threads, Inc.
Pucuda, Inc.
West Coast Netting, Inc.
Pipe Fittings
Hollaender Manufacturing Company
Kee Industrial Products
Custom-molded Plastic
Horizon Plastics Company Ltd.
Posts and Accessories for Net Games
L.A. Steelcraft Products, Inc.
Rope
Crowe Rope Industries LLC
Everlast Sports Manufacturing Corp.
Sleeves for In-ground Wooden Posts
Kidstruction
Swing Accessories
ABC School Supply
American Park and Recreation Company
American Swing Products
Belair Recreational Products, Inc.
BCI Burke Company LLC
Chime Time
Gametime
Go-Elan, Inc.
Hatteras Hammocks, Inc.
Howell Equipment Company
Kidstruction
Krauss Craft, Inc.
L.A. Steelcraft Products, Inc.
Landscape Structures, Inc.
PlayDesigns
Playland International L.L.C.
Polycom Products, Inc.

PLAYGROUND SURFACES
Drainage Systems

Colbond, Inc.
Fibar Systems

Edging

Landscape Structures, Inc.
Little Tikes Commercial Play Systems, Inc.
Playland International L.L.C.

Surfacing
Rubber Surfacing
Rubber chip surfacing
Krauss Craft, Inc.
Landscape Structures, Inc.
Poured-in-place rubber surfacing
BCI Burke Company LLC
Fortco Limited
Futura Coatings, Inc.—Sports Surfaces
    Division
JCH International, Inc.
Kompan, Inc.
Little Tikes Commercial Play Systems, Inc.
No Fault Industries, Inc.
Playland International L.L.C.
Playworks, Inc.
Safeguard Surfacing Corp.
Sof Surfaces, Inc.
Surface America, Inc.
Vitricon, Inc.

Joe DiMaggio Children's Hospital/Visitor's Clubhouse playground, Hollywood, Florida. Vitriturf rubber playground safety surfacing by Vitricon, Inc.

Rubber tile surfacing
Carlisle Surfacing Systems
Dinoflex Manufacturing Ltd.
Dusyma
Island Leisure Products
Italiana Societa Arredamenti Fontanili
    F.lli s.r.l.

JCH International, Inc.
Kompan, Inc.
Krauss Craft, Inc.
Landscape Structures, Inc.
Little Tikes Commercial Play Systems, Inc.
Playland International L.L.C.
Safeguard Surfacing Corp.
Sof Surfaces Inc.
Surface America, Inc.
Tennek Sports Surfaces, Inc.
Wehrfritz

Shock-absorbing turf surfacing
Mat Factory, Inc.
Surface America, Inc.

Wood chip surfacing
Krauss Craft, Inc.

Engineered wood fiber surfacing
Fibar Systems
Sof' Fall

PLAY STRUCTURES

Contained Play Structures

Kidstruction
Koala Corp./Delta Play Division
Little Tikes Commercial Play Systems, Inc.
Pentes Play/Game Time

Playsafe, Inc.
U.S. Playgrounds, Inc.

Custom-designed Play Structures

CalRec Builders & Consultants
Grounds For Play
Henderson Recreation Equipment Limited
Leathers & Associates, Inc. (community-built only)
Wildwood Playgrounds, Ltd. (specialization in accessibility)

Infant Play Structures

Italiana Societa Arredamenti Fontanili F.lli s.r.l.
Landscape Structures, Inc.
PlayDesigns

Nonwood Play Structures

American Park and Recreation Company
Basics, Inc.
Belair Recreational Products, Inc.
Belson Outdoors, Inc.
Big Top Toys, Inc.
BCI Burke Company LLC

Contained play structure by Pentes Play/Game Time.

Infant Fun Center by PlayDesigns.

Columbia Cascade
Gametime
Grounds For Play, Inc.
Henderson Recreation Equipment Limited
Italiana Societa Arredamenti Fontanili
    F.lli s.r.l.
Kidstruction
Koala Corp./Park Structures Division
Kompan

Fun-runner nonwood play structure by Gametime.

Krauss Craft, Inc.
L.A. Steelcraft Products, Inc.
Landscape Structures, Inc.
Little Tikes Commercial Play Systems, Inc.
Mile High Play Systems, Inc.
Play & Leisure Systems, Inc.
PlayDesigns
Playground Environments
Playland International L.L.C.

Teen Play Structures

Kompan
Landscape Structures, Inc.

Toddler/Preschool Play Structures

American Park and Recreation Company
Gametime
Go-Elan, Inc.
Howell Equipment Company
Kidstruction
Kompan, Inc.

Mosaiq toddler playstructure by Kompan.

Landscape Structures, Inc.
Little Tikes Commercial Play Systems, Inc.
PlayDesigns
Playground Environments
Playworks, Inc.
Texwood Furniture Corporation

Wood Play Structures

American Play Systems, Inc.
American Park and Recreation Company
Columbia Cascade Company
Dusyma
Grounds For Play, Inc.
Henderson Recreation Equipment Limited
Howell Equipment Company
Italiana Societa Arredamenti Fontanili
    F.lli s.r.l.
Kid-Krafters
Kidstruction
Kompan, Inc.
Krauss Craft, Inc.
Little Tikes Commercial Play Systems, Inc.
Meyer Design, Inc.
Play & Leisure Systems, Inc.
PlayDesigns
Playkids
Playlofts, Inc.
Playworks, Inc.
Texwood Furniture Corporation
U.S. Playgrounds, Inc.
Wehrfritz

Residential play structure by Cedar Works of Maine.

Wood play structure by Big Toys, a division of Kompan, Inc.

Residential Play Structures

American Play Systems, Inc.
Cedar Works of Maine
ChildLife, Inc.

Hedstrom Corporation
Home & Yard Connection
Kidz Manufacturing
Kid-Krafters
King of Swings
Krauss Craft, Inc.
Leisure Time Products
The Little Tikes Company
Merry Time Play Systems, Inc.
Mile High Play Systems, Inc.
Play & Leisure Systems, Inc.
Playkids
Playlofts, Inc.
Playworks, Inc.
Polycom Products
The Step2 Company
Timbertec, Inc.
The Wood Works
Woodlawn Playcenters
Woodplay

PLAY STRUCTURE INSTALLATION

American Play Systems, Inc. (select areas)
Quality Installations, Incorporated

SAND PLAY

Sand-moving Play Structures

Italiana Societa Arredamenti Fontanili
    F.lli s.r.l.

Sandworks by Kompan.

Kompan, Inc.
Wehrfritz

Sand Tables

Chime Time
Columbia Cascade Company
Environments
Gametime
Italiana Societa Arredamenti Fontanili
    F.lli s.r.l.
Kaplan
Manta-Ray, Inc.
Kompan, Inc.
Landscape Structures, Inc.
Little Tikes Commercial Play Systems, Inc.
Manta-Ray, Inc.
PlayDesigns
Playkids
Texwood Furniture Corporation
Wehrfritz

Sandbox Covers

Italiana Societa Arredamenti Fontanili
    F.lli s.r.l.
Landscape Structures, Inc.
Wehrfritz

Sandboxes

ABC School Supply
Belair Manufacturing Products, Inc.

BCI Burke Company LLC
Cedar Works of Maine
ChildLife, Inc.
Chime Time
Dusyma
Gametime
Howell Equipment Company
Italiana Societa Arredamenti Fontanili
    F.lli s.r.l.
Kompan, Inc.
Landscape Structures, Inc.
Peter Pepper Products, Inc.
PlayDesigns
Playlofts, Inc.
The Step2 Company
Visions Innovated Products, Inc.
Wehrfritz

Sand Diggers

ABC School Supply
Belair Manufacturing Products, Inc.
Dusyma
Gametime
Go-Elan, Inc.

Sand digger by Gametime.

Landscape Structures, Inc.
Little Tikes Commercial Play Systems, Inc.
Play & Leisure Systems, Inc.
PlayDesigns

SHADE AND SHELTER STRUCTURES

Courtesy Shade Tree Co.
Envirodesigns, Inc.

Palm tree by Courtesy Shade Tree Co.

Awnings

Americana Building Products

Fabric Shades

Americana Building Products
BigTop Manufacturing
Dusyma
Henderson Recreation Equipment Limited
Italiana Societa Arredamenti Fontanili
    F.lli s.r.l.
Kompan, Inc.
Lakeshore Learning Materials
PlayDesigns
Wehrfritz

Nonwood Shelters

Americana Building Products
Belair Manufacturing Products, Inc.
Gametime

Litchfield Industries, Inc.
Poligon by W.H. Porter, Inc.

Wood Shelters and Gazebos

Leisure Time Products
Leisure Woods, Inc.
Litchfield Industries, Inc.
Poligon by W.H. Porter, Inc.

SITE FURNISHINGS

Bicycle Racks

American Park and Recreation Company
Belair Manufacturing Products, Inc.
Brandir International, Inc.
BCI Burke Company LLC
Belson Outdoors, Inc.
Canterbury International

Bike rack by Canterbury International.

Columbia Cascade Company
Creative Pipe, Inc.
DuMor, Inc.
Gametime
Gerber Manufacturing Ltd.
Go-Elan, Inc.
Henderson Recreation Equipment Limited
Howell Equipment Company
Krauss Craft, Inc.
L.A. Steelcraft Products, Inc.
Landscape Structures, Inc.

Litchfield Industries, Inc.
Little Tikes Commercial Play Systems, Inc.
PCA Industries, Inc.

Carousels

Barrango, Inc.

Compasses and Sundials

Landscape Structures, Inc.

Drinking Fountains

F.A.S.T. Corp.
Most Dependable Fountains

Gorilla sculpture by Canterbury International.

Drinking fountain by Most Dependable Fountains.

Fencing

Kompan, Inc.
The Step2 Company

Sculpture

Canterbury International
F.A.S.T. Corp.
Futura Coatings, Inc.—Composite
   Fabrications Division

Little Tike Commercial Play Systems, Inc.
Wind & Weather

Seating

Benches
American Park and Recreation Company
Barlow Tyrie
Kompan, Inc.
Visions Innovated Products, Inc.
Chairs
Barlow Tyrie
Cedar Works of Maine
Stools
Educo International, Inc.

Signage

Landscape Structures, Inc.

Storage Units

ABC School Supply
BCI Burke Company LLC
Italiana Societa Arredamenti Fontanili
   F.lli s.r.l.

Tables

Barlow Tyrie
Educo International, Inc.

Activity Top Tables
Go-Elan, Inc.
Landscape Structures, Inc.
Picnic Tables
Combination wood and metal picnic tables
Dusyma
Gametime
Gerber Manufacturing Ltd.
Go-Elan, Inc.
Howell Equipment Company
Italiana Societa Arredamenti Fontanili
    F.lli s.r.l.
Litchfield Industries, Inc.
PlayDesigns
Wehrfritz
Nonwood picnic tables
American Park and Recreation Company
Environments
Fusion Coatings, Inc.
Go-Elan, Inc.
Italiana Societa Arredamenti Fontanili
    F.lli s.r.l.
Litchfield Industries, Inc.
The Little Tikes Company
PlayDesigns

Outdoor garden table-and-chair set by Barlow Tyrie.

Playlofts, Inc.
The Step2 Company
Visions Innovated Products, Inc.
Wood picnic tables—child-size
Cedar Works of Maine
Childs/Play, Inc.
Dusyma
Italiana Societa Arredamenti Fontanili
    F.lli s.r.l.
King of Swings
Kompan, Inc.
Litchfield Industries, Inc.
Wehrfritz

Table and Chair Sets

Barlow Tyrie
Educo International, Inc.

Waste Receptacles

The Fibrex Group, Inc.

SCOREBOARDS

Nevco Scoreboard Company

SPORTS AND GAME EQUIPMENT
Badminton
L.A. Steelcraft Products, Inc.

Picnic table by PlayDesign.

Baseball

AFP Soft Touch
American Park and Recreation Company
Belair Manufacturing Products, Inc.
Everlast Sports Manufacturing Corp.
Henderson Recreation Equipment Limited
Kwik Goal Ltd.
L.A. Steelcraft Products, Inc.
PCA Industries, Inc.

Basketball (Includes Funnel Ball and Rimball)

American Park and Recreation Company
The Bankshot Organization
Belair Manufacturing Products, Inc.
Bison, Inc.
BCI Burke Company LLC
Chime Time
Environments

Bankshot Basketball by The Bankshot Organization.

Future Pro, Inc.
Gametime
Go-Elan, Inc.
Gym-i-nee Associates, Inc.
Henderson Recreation Equipment Limited
Howell Equipment Company
Huffy Sports
Italiana Societa Arredamenti Fontanili
     F.lli s.r.l.
Kaplan
King of Swings
Kompan
Krauss Craft, Inc.
L.A. Steelcraft Products, Inc.
Lakeshore Learning Materials
Landscape Structures, Inc.
Little Tikes Commercial Play Systems, Inc.
PCA Industries, Inc.
Things From Bell

Chess

Italiana Societa Arredamenti Fontanili
     F.lli s.r.l.

Football

American Park and Recreation Company
Belair Manufacturing Products, Inc.
Kwik Goal Ltd.
L.A. Steelcraft Products, Inc.
PCA Industries, Inc.
Things From Bell

Handball

Kwik Goal Ltd.

Hockey

Belair Manufacturing Products, Inc.
Kwik Goal Ltd.

Lacrosse

Kwik Goal Ltd.

Pickle-ball

Pickle-ball, Inc.

Child-size chess board by Italiana Societa Arredamenti Fontanili F.lli s.r.l.

Rugby

Kwik Goal Ltd.

Soccer

American Park and Recreation Company
Belair Manufacturing Products, Inc.
BCI Burke Company LLC
Chime Time
D. Hauptman Co., Inc./Fold-A-Goal
Gametime
Go-Elan, Inc.
Henderson Recreation Equipment Limited
Italiana Societa Arredamenti Fontanili
    F.lli s.r.l.
Kwik Goal Ltd.
L.A. Steelcraft Products, Inc.
PCA Industries, Inc.
Things From Bell

Tennis

Belair Manufacturing Products, Inc.
BCI Burke Company LLC
Gametime
Kwik Goal Ltd.
L.A. Steelcraft Products, Inc.
PCA Industries, Inc.

Tetherball

American Park and Recreation Company
BCI Burke Company LLC
Go-Elan, Inc.
Henderson Recreation Equipment Limited
L.A. Steelcraft Products, Inc.
Landscape Structures, Inc.
PCA Industries, Inc.
Play & Leisure Systems, Inc.
PlayDesigns

Volleyball

American Park and Recreation Company
Bison, Inc.
Kwik Goal Ltd.
L.A. Steelcraft Products, Inc.
Landscape Structures, Inc.
Things From Bell

WATER PLAY

Inflatable In-pool Play Structures

Airspace

Pool Equipment

Adolf Kiefer and Associates

Pool Slides

Kidstruction

Water Play Equipment—Small-scale

Hand Pumps
Dusyma
Henderson Recreation Equipment Limited
Water Tables and Troughs
Chime Time
Columbia Cascade Company
Environments
Henderson Recreation Equipment Limited

Italiana Societa Arredamenti Fontanili
    F.lli s.r.l.
Kaplan
Kompan, Inc.
Little Tikes Commercial Play Systems, Inc.
Manta-Ray, Inc.
PlayDesigns
Wehrfritz

Water Play Structures and Equipment—Large-scale

F.A.S.T. Corp.
Gametime
SCS Interactive, Inc.
Waterplay by LA Systems Ltd.
Whitewater

Whitewater Water Park, Atlanta, Georgia. Large-scale water park equipment by SCS Interactive, Inc.

Water Sports Equipment

Adolf Kiefer and Associates

Waterfall small-scale water play table by Kompan.

CHAPTER 7

Source Information, A to Z

A

Aaron Ashley, Inc.
230 Fifth Ave., Suite 400
New York, NY 10001
212-532-9227
Fax: 212-481-4214

A wide variety of art prints. Folk art prints, including samplers and a variety of contemporary townscapes.

ABC School Supply, Inc.
3312 N. Berkeley Lake Rd., Box 100019
Duluth, GA 30096-9419
800-669-4222
Fax: 770-497-1405
E-mail: sales@abcschoolsupply.com
Website: www.abcschoolsupply.com

A full line of early education furnishings and supplies, including their own line of Korners For Kids furniture, featuring rounded corners as a safety feature.

ABET, Inc.
60 West Sheffield Ave.
Englewood, NJ 07631
800-228-2238 or 201-541-0700
Fax: 201-541-0701

Over 700 high-pressure laminate surfaces, including Lumiphos, a glow-in-the-dark laminate; Magnetico, a laminate that can be drawn on with dry-erase markers; Colours, featuring solid bright colors; Diafos, a translucent laminate; and other exciting, child-oriented patterns in the Seriagrafia line.

Adolph Kiefer and Associates
1700 Kiefer Drive
Zion, IL 60099
800-323-4071
E-mail: catalog@kiefer.com
Web site: www.kiefer.com

Prefabricated swimming pools, pool equipment, and equipment for water sports.

Advantus Corporation
P.O. Box 2017
Orange Park, FL 32067-2017
800-771-0529
Fax: 904-278-2901
E-mail: info@advantus.com
Website: www.advantus.com

Grip-A-Strip (a tackless display system).

AFP Soft Touch
P.O. Box 291
Dousman, WI 53118
800-965-4690 or 414-965-4690
Fax: 414-965-4651

Baseball bases.

Airspace USA, Inc.
89 Patton Avenue
Asheville, NC 28801
800-872-1319
Fax: 828-258-1390
E-mail: airspaceus@aol.com
Website: aimsintl.org/airspace.htm

Aquaplay line of large, inflatable play structures for pools; indoor large-scale soft building blocks, ball pits, themed modular indoor soft play environments; custom-design services.

Alar Furniture, Inc.
158 Oakdale Road
Downsview, Ontario
Canada M3N 2S5
416-743-1925
Fax: 416-743-1827

Kids Stuff line includes welded, steel tube–frame chairs with either upholstered seat or plastic laminate seat to match tabletop, and matching table with steel tube legs and plastic laminate top. Both chairs and tables come in a range of heights.

American Infant Care Products, Inc.
6352 320th St. Way
P.O. Box 128
Cannon Falls, MN 55009
507-263-5354
Fax: 507-263-5350

Restroom/dressing room accessory equipment, including Diaper Deck wall-mounted infant changing tables, the Diaper Dumper diaper disposal units, and wall-mounted infant safety seats.

American Park and Recreation Company
107 North 11th Street
Tampa, FL 33602
800-245-7777 or 813-229-7275
Fax: 813-229-0737
Website: www.APARK.com

A full line of outdoor park and playground equipment and furnishings—including commercial play structures of recycled materials or wood, including models for preschool-age children.

American Play Systems, Inc.
Box 1728
North Sioux City, SD 57049-1728
800-326-4277 or 605-232-9735
Fax: 605-232-9726
E-mail: americanplay
　　@worldnet.att.net
Website: www.americanplay.com

Commercial preschool and residential wood play structures, wood swings, wood preschool and residential play structures.

American Rug Craftsmen
P.O. Box 130
Sugar Valley, GA 30746
800-553-1734
Fax: 706-625-3544

Playmates collection features interactive/educational/themed 30- by 40-in area rugs.

American Standard, Inc.
One Centennial Avenue
P.O. Box 6820
Piscataway, NJ 08855-6820
732-980-3000

Two models of toilets for preschool-age to six-year-old children and two models of ADA-compliant child-size toilets.

American Swing Products
2533 N. Carson Street, #1062
Carson City, NV 89706
800-433-2573
Fax: 775-883-2384
Website: www.americanswing.com

A variety of commercial and residential seats, hardware, and accessories for swings and tire swings; spring toys; play structure components, including a steering wheel, telescope, slides, and handgrips.

Americana Building Products
Hindman Manufacturing Co., Inc.
P.O. Box 1290
Salem, IL 62881
800-851-0865
Fax: 618-548-2890

Fabric shade shelters, retractable awnings, and metal shelters.

Ampco Products, Inc.
11400 NW 36 Avenue
Miami, FL 33167
305-821-5700
Fax: 305-507-1414
E-mail: info@ampco.com
Website: www.ampco.com

Custom commercial restroom partitions scaled to children.

Anatex Enterprises, Inc.
15929 Arminta Street
Van Nuys, CA 91406
800-999-9599 or 818-908-1888
Fax: 818-908-0656

Wire-bead-maze frame manipulative furnishings including wall-mounted panels, the Fleur Rollercoaster Table and the free-standing Play Cube, with manipulative play panels on the sides and top. Laminate- or wood-finished furnishings, including a sitting stool and table, are also available.

Angeles Group
Dailey Industrial Park
9 Capper Drive
Pacific, MO 63069
314-257-0533
Fax: 314-257-5473

BaseLine laminate preschool furnishings, including stackable chairs, tables, book display units, cubbies, shelf units, tote tray units, and construction and light tables; indoor dramatic playhouse/ room divider; indoor and outdoor mini-carousels; outdoor dramatic play props, including traffic signs and a mailbox.

Anna French
108 Shakespeare Rd.
London SE24 0QW
United Kingdom
44-171-7376555
Fax: 44-171-2748913

In the United States:

Classic Revivals, Inc.
1 Design Center Place
Suite 534
Boston, MA 02210
617-574-9030
Fax: 617-574-9027

Residential fabrics, wallcoverings, and wall borders.

Anzea
520 Greenleaf Street
Fort Worth, TX 76107
817-336-2310
Fax: 817-336-9548
E-mail: info@anzea.com

... Under the Big Top (a collection of patterned fabrics for upholstery and wall applications).

ArcCom Fabrics, Inc.
33 Ramland South
Orangeburg, NY 10962
914-365-1100
Fax: 914-365-3627

Fabrics for drapery, upholstery, wallcoverings, and cubicle curtains.

Arconas Corporation
580 Orwell St.
Mississauga, Ontario
Canada L5A 3V7
800-387-9496 or
905-272-0727
Fax: 905-897-7470
E-mail: info@arconas.com

Bouloum (upholstered or fiberglass-molded loungers for indoor or outdoor use). These loungers are not child-sized, but their playful, sculptural quality has been used successfully in children's environments.

Ardley Hall
P.O. Box 2143
High Point, NC 27261
336-475-7600
Fax: 336-475-7601

Residential carved mahogany desk with leather top, wood chairs, and wood bench.

Aristrocrat Industries, Inc.
7555 Sharp Road
P.O. Box 1117
Mt. Vernon, OH 43050
800-221-7875 or 740-393-2121
Fax: 740-393-2200
E-mail: aristocrat@ecr.net
Website: aristocrat.com

Chalk/marker boards, flannel boards, bulletin boards.

Armstrong World Industries, Inc.
P.O. Box 3001
Lancaster, PA 17604
888-234-5464
In Canada: 514-733-9981
Fax: 800-572-8324

Cirrus Themes Ceilings feature acoustical lay-in ceiling tiles with a variety of cut-in patterns, including trains, stars, leaves, and others.

Arredi 3n dei F.lli Nespoli
20034 Giussano, Milan
Via Rossini 11, Italy
39-0362-850128
Fax: 39-0362-354820

A variety of child care furnishings from Milan's Studio G3 including room dividers, a unique playhouse with arched windows, a dramatic play fruit-and-vegetable stand, and manipulative tables for infants.

Art Beats
33 River Road
Cos Cob, CT 06807

or

P.O. Box 1469
Greenwich, CT 06836-1469
800-338-3315 or 203-661-5477
Fax: 800-574-2787 or 203-661-2480

Posters and prints.

Artisan House, Inc.
P.O. Box 26566
1755 Glendale Blvd.
Los Angeles, CA 90026
800-354-6873 or 323-664-1111
Fax: 323-664-5679

Hand-painted metal wall sculptures featuring cartoon and storybook characters.

Artisan Studios, Inc.
3664 Cherry Road
Memphis, TN 38118
901-547-1448
Fax: 901-547-1920

The Safari line of the Amy Howard Collection features an alligator-skinned poster bed, a nightstand painted like the skin of a giraffe, and a faux bamboo animal chest with sculpted safari animal pulls.

August, Inc.
354 Congress Park Dr.
Centerville, OH 45459
800-318-5242 or 937-434-2520
Fax: 937-434-9087
E-mail: solutions@augustinc.com
Website: www.augustinc.com

R & R® and Petite Stuff® lines feature upholstered chairs, sofas, and ottomans. Linn, Jr.® and Laurel, Jr. lines feature upholstered modular lounge seating designed to match their adult lines.

B

Baby Trilogy, Inc.
Rt. 1, Box 649 A
Lubbock, TX 79401
888-874-9596 or 806-829-2122
Fax: 806-829-2107

The residential Tri-Bed fits into a corner with a rounded front (available with or without a canopy).

Badger Basket Company
111 Lions Drive, Suite 220
Barrington, IL 60010
847-381-6200
Fax: 847-381-6218

Residential juvenile and nursery furnishings include a wood table-and-chair set, hampers, changing/dressing tables, cradles, and a glider cradle that converts to a child's glider bench.

Balitono, Inc.
26 Pleasant Valley Way
Princeton Junction, NJ 08550-3308
609-936-8807
Fax: 609-936-8869
E-mail: info@Balitono.com

Mobiles.

BananaFish
8821 Shirley Avenue
Northridge, CA 91324
818-727-1645
Fax: 818-727-1307

Residential bed and crib bedding, benches, and ottomans.

Bangor Cork Company, Inc.
William and D Streets
Pen Argyl, PA 18072-0125
610-863-9041
Fax: 610-863-6275

Bulletin boards, chalk/marker boards.

The Bankshot Organization
785F Rockville Pike, PMB 504
Rockville, MD 20852
800-933-0140 or 301-309-0260
Fax: 301-309-0263
E-mail: Bankshotbb@aol.com
Website: www.Bankshot.com

Nonaggressive basketball with angled, curved, and unconventionally configured, brightly colored bankboards (ADA accessible).

Barbour Threads, Inc.
20 Blue Mountain Avenue
Anniston, AL 36201
256-237-9461
Fax: 256-237-8816

Custom-designed nets and netting for use on play structures.

Barlow Tyrie, Inc.
1263 Glen Ave., Suite 230
Moorestown, NJ 08057
609-273-7878
Fax: 609-273-9199
Website: www.teak.com

Outdoor teakwood benches, chairs, and tables.

Barrango, Inc.
360 Swift Avenue, Suite #1
So. San Francisco, CA 94080
650-871-1931
Fax: 650-872-3107

Custom design and construction of decorative elements, including carousels and displays for retail environments, amusement parks, and exterior/interior playgrounds.

Basics, Inc.
P.O. Box M, 9071 Hwy. 12 East
Delano, MN 55328
612-972-2153
Fax: 612-972-2803

Nonwood commercial play structures.

Bassett Furniture Industries, Inc.
P.O. Box 626
3525 Fairystone Park Highway
Bassett, VA 24055
540-629-6450
Fax: 540-629-6332

Residential infant and juvenile/teen bedroom groups, including beds, bunk beds, canopy beds, chest beds, cribs, and changing/dressing tables.

BBT Group (Best-Rite, Balt, and Trinity)
201 North Crockett
Cameron, TX 76520
800-749-2258 or 254-697-4953
Fax: 800-697-6258
E-mail: boards@bestrite.com,
    furniture@baltinc.com,
    church@pews.com
Website: www.bestrite.com,
    www.baltinc.com, www.pews.com

A variety of chalkboards, flannel boards, tackboards, and tackless display systems, including large boards at child's level that double as movable room dividers, art easels, nonwood painting/drawing top tables, adjustable-height computer furnishings, lecterns, wood chairs with optional vinyl seat and/or back, wood tables, and book display units.

BCI Burke Company LLC
P.O. Box 549
660 Van Dyne Road
Fond du Lac, WI 54936-0549
920-921-9220
Fax: 920-921-9566

Nonwood commercial play structures, nonwood swings, and a variety of freestanding activity and sports equipment. Cushiondeck, poured-in-place rubber resilient surfacing.

Beagle Manufacturing Company, Inc.
4377 North Baldwin Avenue
El Monte, CA 91731
800-233-1878 or 213-686-0607
Fax: 626-442-2064

Wire-frame valets, coatracks, and clothes trees.

Beka, Inc.
542 Selby Avenue
St. Paul, MN 55102
888-999-2352 or 651-222-7005
Fax: 651-222-3965

Easels and puppet theaters.

Belair Recreational Products, Inc.
18 Spalding Dr.
P.O. Box 4679
Brantford, Ontario
Canada N3T 6H2
800-387-6318 or 519-752-7529
Fax: 519-752-6875
E-mail: belair.rec@sympatico.ca
Website: www.belairplayground.com

A wide variety of outdoor products, including nonwood commercial play structures and sports equipment; indoor ball pits also available.

Belinda Barton Furnishings for Children
P.O. Box 552
Cutchogue, NY 11935
516-734-2872
Fax: 516-734-2873
Website: www.belindabarton.com

Residential bed and crib bedding, blankets, throw pillows, fabrics, and upholstered ottoman.

Bellini
165 Oval Drive
Islandia, NY 11722
800-332-2229
Website: www.bellini.com

Residential infant and juvenile bedroom groups, including beds, captain's beds, cribs, desks, mirrors, armoires, chests of drawers, shelf units, and changing/dressing tables.

Belson Outdoors, Inc.
111 North River Road
P.O. Box 207
North Aurora, IL 60542-0207
800-323-5664 or 630-897-8489
Fax: 630-897-0573

Nonwood commercial play structures and bike racks.

Benjamin Moore & Co.
51 Chestnut Ridge Road
Montvale, NJ 07645-1862
800-972-4685 or 201-573-9600
Fax: 201-573-9046

Crayola Paints line offers ceiling and wall paints in the colors of Crayola crayons and an F/X line of special effects finishes, such as chalkboard paint, glitter finish, and glow-in-the-dark paint.

Berco Tableworks, Ltd.
1120 Montrose Ave.
St. Louis, MO 63104
888-772-4788 or 314-772-4700

Fax: 888-772-4789 or 314-772-6241
E-mail: info@berco.org

Adjustable-height tables.

Bestar
4220 Villeneuve
Lac-Megantic, Québec
Canada G6B 1C3
819-583-1017
Fax: 819-583-5370

Residential toddler and twin "car" beds.

Big Top Manufacturing
3255 North U.S. 19 North
Route 5, Box 425
Perry, FL 32347
850-584-7786
Fax: 850-584-7713
E-mail: sales@bigtopshelters.com
Website: www.bigtopshelters.com

Outdoor vinyl shade/shelters units with galvanized-steel frames.

Big Top Toys, Inc.
217 Sparkman St. SW
P.O. Box 1464
Hartselle, AL 35640
800-368-8861 or 256-751-0933
Fax: 256-751-0927

Nonwood commercial play structures, swings, and climbers.

BigGame Trophies
Box 4, 1040 Fifth Avenue
Lyons, CO 80540
800-424-7695 or 303-823-0105

Large, wall-hung wild animal head puppets made of synthetic furs and velours.

Biggwood
2901 Bowen Rd.
P.O. Box 306
Elma, NY 14059-0306
716-652-3764
Fax: 716-652-3764

E-mail: Biggwood1@aol.com
Website: www.biggwood.com

Book display unit and large play-on dramatic play furniture, including a dress-up castle, fire engine, train, and truck.

Bison, Inc.
603 "L" Street
Lincoln, NE 68508
800-247-7668 or 402-474-3353
Fax: 800-638-0698 or 402-474-6720
Website: www.bisoninc.com

Basketball and volleyball equipment.

Blockhouse Company, Inc.
3285 Farmtrail Road
York, PA 17402
717-764-5555
Fax: 717-767-8939

Bedroom groups for residence living.

Brandir International, Inc.
521 Fifth Avenue, 17th Floor
New York, NY 10175
212-505-6500
Fax: 212-505-6813

The Ribbon Rack bike racks.

Brewster Wallcovering Company
67 Pacella Park Drive
Randolph, MA 02368
800-717-5651 or 781-963-4800
Fax: 781-963-4975
E-mail: brewstersamples
   @brewsterwallcovering.com
Website:
   www.brewsterwallcovering.com

Stock wall borders. Digitally-printed borders are also available.

Brio Corporation
N120 W18485 Freistadt Road
Germantown, WI 53022
888-274-6869 or 414-250-3240

Railroad-top play tables that are designed to be used with Brio's wooden train systems, and construction-top tables that are to be used with Brio's building block system. Decorative accessories include a 36-in- and a 61-in-tall Brio clown. A series of four posters and rocking seats are also available.

C

California Kids
621 Old County Road
San Carlos, CA 94070
800-548-5214 or 650-637-9054
Fax: 800-637-5648 or 650-637-0810

Residential bed and crib bedding, throw pillows, window valances, fabric, and matching table lamps. Ten brightly colored 3- by 5-ft rugs are also available.

CalRec Builders & Consultants
P.O. Box 636
Orange, CA 92856-0636
714-639-4091
Fax: 714-639-1336

Custom indoor and outdoor play environments and play structures.

Canterbury International
5632 West Washington Blvd.
Los Angeles, CA 90016
800-935-7111 or 323-936-7111
Fax: 323-936-7115

Bike racks and wooden site sculptures.

Capitol Seating Company
P.O. Box 938
2802 South Loop Drive
Belton, TX 76513
800-460-1272 or 254-939-1853
Fax: 254-939-0917
Website: www.CapitolSeating.com

Plastic melamine and tubular metal school desks, chairs, and stools in a variety of heights and colors. Some chair models are stackable.

Cargo Furniture & Accents
1400 Everman Parkway
Suite A
P.O. Box 40607
Fort Worth, TX 76140
817-551-9663
Fax: 817-551-9673

Residential juvenile/teen bedroom groups, including bunk beds, trundle beds, captain's beds, sleigh beds, desks, chests of drawers, toy chests, bedside tables, mirrors, and table and chair sets.

Carlisle Surfacing Systems
P.O. Box 10
Carlisle, PA 17013
800-851-4746
Website: www.carlsurf.com

Rubber tile playground surfacing.

Carnegie
110 North Centre Avenue
Rockville Centre, NY 11570
516-678-6770
Fax: 516-678-6848
E-mail: mail@carnegiefabric.com
Website: www.carnegiefabrics.com

Xorel's patterned fabrics, Twinkle Star and Circus, for walls, panels, and upholstery. Also available: Pattern 4120 and Alphabet Soup for cubicle curtains and draperies.

Carolyn Ray, Inc.
578 Nepperhan Avenue
Yonkers, NY 10701
914-476-0619
Fax: 914-476-0677

Residential fabrics and matching wall-coverings.

Carpet For Kids etc.
115 SE Ninth Ave.
Portland, OR 97214
503-232-1203
Fax: 503-232-1394
Website: www.carpetsforkids.com

5-ft 10-in by 8-ft 4-in and 8-ft 4-in by 11-ft 8-in interactive/educational/themed area rugs.

Casa Dos Tapetes de Arraiolos, Inc.
D&D, 979 Third Avenue, Room 1519
New York, NY 10022
212-688-9330
Fax: 212-688-9802

Custom-designed Portuguese needle-point rugs.

Cedar Works of Maine
Route 1, P.O. Box 990
Rockport, ME 04856
800-462-3327 or 207-596-1010
Fax: 207-596-7900
E-mail: info@cedarworks.com
Website: www.cedarworks.com

Residential wood play structures, wood chairs, picnic tables, and sandboxes, and a variety of play structure components.

Central Specialties Ltd.
220-D Exchange Dr.
Crystal Lake, IL 60014
815-459-6000
Fax: 815-459-6562
E-mail: gaychrome@csltd.com

Commercial wood stackable high chairs.

Cervitor Kitchens, Inc.
10775 Lower Azusa Road
El Monte, CA 91731-1351
800-523-2666 or 626-443-0184
Fax: 626-443-0400

Unit kitchens custom-built to a child's scale.

Channel Craft & Distribution, Inc.
P.O. Box 101
Charleroi, PA 15022
800-232-4386 or 724-489-4900
Fax: 724-489-0773
Website: www.channelcraft.com

Decorative three-dimensional puzzles and brain-teasers in wood and metal.

Charm & Whimsy
114 E. 32nd St., Suite 603
New York, NY 10016
212-683-7609
Fax: 212-725-7512

Custom-designed residential themed environments, accessories, and hand-painted furnishings.

Childcraft Education Corp.
P.O. Box 3239
Lancaster, PA 17604
800-631-5652
Fax: 888-532-4453
E-mail: cec@epix.net

A full line of child care/early education furnishings, supplies, and equipment, including their own lines of birch and maple furniture.

ChildLife, Inc.
55 Whitney Street
Holliston, MA 01746
800-467-9464
Fax: 508-429-3874
E-mail: goswing@childlife.com
Website: www.childlife.com

Residential play structures and wood sandboxes.

The Children's Factory
245 West Essex Ave.
St. Louis, MO 63122
314-821-1441
Fax: 314-821-3916
E-mail: childfact@stlnet.com
Website: www.ece2.com

Soft play centers, ball pits, room dividers, and a variety of mirrors including fun mirrors.

The Children's Furniture Company
3800 Buena Vista Avenue
Baltimore, MD 21211
800-697-3408 or 410-243-7488
Fax: 410-243-7489
Website: www.childrens-furniture.com

Commercial furnishings, including chairs in a variety of leaf-shaped or geometric backs, available in six analine-dye finishes; table-top and wall-mounted manipulatives, room dividers, sitting stools, benches, rockers, and toy chests. Tables come in any shape or height.

Childs/Play, Inc.
P.O. Box 448
Eureka Springs, AR 72632
800-447-8375 or 501-253-8686
Fax: 501-253-7196

A variety of products and wood furnishings for early education environments.

Chime Time
One Sportime Way
Atlanta, GA 30340
800-677-5075 or 770-449-5700
Fax: 800-845-1535 or 770-263-0897
E-mail: catalog.request@sportime
    .com

A variety of indoor soft play centers and ball pits and outdoor nonwood play and sports equipment.

Claesson
P.O. Box 130
Cape Neddick, ME 03902
800-344-9128
Fax: 864-429-8243

Drapery hardware in the Safari, Noah's Ark, Playroom, and Jungle Group collections.

Claridge Products & Equipment
P.O. Box 910
601 Hwy. 62-65 South
Harrison, AR 72602-0910
870-743-2200
Fax: 870-743-1908

Chalkboards, tackboards, and tackless display systems for the school industry.

Classic Gallery Group
211 Fraley Road
High Point, NC 27263
336-886-4191
Fax: 800-211-2311

Residential upholstered residential chairs, sofas, and ottomans.

Clowns 'N' Cases
P.O. Box 23032
Belleville, IL 62223
800-256-9672
Fax: 618-397-1003

Mobiles featuring hand-painted papier-mâché clowns hanging from balloons and parachutes.

Colbond, Inc.
Sand Hill Road
P.O. Box 1057
Enka, NC 28728
800-365-7391
Fax: 828-665-5009

Playground drainage systems.

Collins & Aikman Floorcoverings
311 Smith Industrial Boulevard
Dalton, GA 30720

or

P.O. Box 1447
Dalton, GA 30722-1447
800-248-2878 or 706-259-9711

Interactive/educational area rugs include a 10- by 10-ft rug of the alphabet and numbers and an 8- by 6-ft map of the United States. Powerbond carpet, manufactured specifically for the school environment, offers custom inlay capabilities.

Columbia Cascade Company
1975 S.W. Fifth Avenue
Portland, OR 97201-5293
800-547-1940 or 503-223-1157
Fax: 503-223-4530
E-mail: hq@timberform.com
Website: www.timberform.com

Features a full line of playground equipment and site furnishings including Pipeline (commercial nonwood play structures) and Timber-Form (commercial wood play structures), outdoor fitness systems, and bike racks.

Comfortex Window Fashions
21 Elm St.
Maplewood, NY 12189
800-843-4151
Fax: 518-273-4079
Website: www.comfortex.com

Cordless window shades.

Community
P.O. Box 231
Jasper, IN 47547-0231
800-622-5661 or 812-482-3204
Fax: 812-482-1548
E-mail: mktg@jasperseating.com

Commercial wood chairs available in eight wood finishes and six color stains. Matching adult versions available.

Community Playthings
P.O. Box 901, Route 213
Rifton, NY 12471
800-777-4244
Fax: 800-336-5948

A full line of maple furnishings for the child care/early education environment.

Compass West Corporation
1838 N.E. Laurelwood Loop
Canby, OR 97013
503-266-7277
Fax: 503-266-6270

Play structure components.

Constructive Playthings
13201 Arrington Road
Grandview, MO 64030
800-448-1412 or 816-761-5900
Fax: 816-761-9295
E-mail: ustoy@ustoyco.com

A full line of furnishings, equipment, and supplies for child care/early education environments.

Copernicus Educational Products
RR3, Box 577
Arthur, Ontario
Canada N0G 1A0
800-267-8494 or 519-848-3664
Fax: 519-848-5516

A variety of tote tray storage units and cubbies.

Cosco, Inc.
2525 State Street
Columbus, IN 47201-7494
800-544-1108
Fax: 800-207-8182
E-mail: consumer@cosco.inc
Website: www.coscoinc.com

Wood and nonwood toddler beds, cradles, cribs, and high chairs.

Couristan
Two Executive Drive
Fort Lee, NJ 07024
800-223-6186 or 201-585-8500
Fax: 201-585-8552

A variety of residential rugs, including the lines of Wild Beauty, Awakenings, Kids Care, Wild Asia, and Couristan Kids. Rugs featuring Winnie the Pooh, Mickey Mouse, and interactive themes are also available.

Courtesy Shade Tree Co.
P.O. Box 118
Lexington, NE 68850
800-962-8254
Fax: 308-324-6688

9- to 15-ft artificial fiberglass palm shade trees.

Creative Images
6100 U.S. 1 North
St. Augustine, FL 32095
904-825-6700
Fax: 904-825-4998
E-mail: joy@crimages.com
Website: www.crimages.com

Framed prints with a safe nonglass, cleanable surface.

Creative Pipe, Inc.
2629 Manhattan Avenue, Suite 289
Hermosa Beach, CA 90254-2447
310-376-9536 or 800-644-8467
Fax: 310-798-1785
E-mail: sales@creativepipe.com
Website: www.creativepipe.com

Bike racks.

Crowe Rope Industries, LLC
P.O. Box 600
Waterville, ME 04901
207-877-2224

Natural fiber and synthetic ropes for use in play environments.

The C/S Group of Companies
P.O. Box 380
Muncy, PA 17756
717-546-5941 or 800-233-8493 (Eastern and Central United States)
800-234-0010 (West Coast, Texas, and Hawaii)
Fax: 570-546-5169

In Canada:

895 Lakefront Promenade
Mississauga, Ontario
Canada L5E 2C2
905-274-3611
Fax: 905-274-6241
Website: www.c-sgroup.com

Acrovyn handrail features a dual line of rails with the lower rung being more accessible to children. Additional Acrovyn wall protection products include corner/bumper guards and high-impact wallcovering and panels.

Custom Laminations, Inc.
932 Market Street
P.O. Box 2066
Paterson, NJ 07509
973-279-9332
Fax: 973-279-6916

Fabric and wallcovering treatments, including flame proofing, laminating, vinylizing, and application of moisture barriers and stain repellants.

D

D. Hauptman Co., Inc./Fold-A-Goal
4856 W. Jefferson Blvd.
Los Angeles, CA 90016
800-542-4625 or 323-734-2507
Fax: 323-734-0731
E-mail: info@fold-a-goal.com
Website: www.fold-a-goal.com

Soccer equipment.

d-Scan, Inc.
Highway 58 West
P.O. Box 1067
South Boston, VA 24592
804-575-0900
Fax: 804-575-0946

Residential juvenile/teen bedroom groups.

Dan Moffett's Rustic Furniture
P.O. Box 21186
Louisville, KY 40221-0186
502-448-5166
Fax: 603-251-5964
E-mail: dan@moffetts.net
Website: www.moffetts.net

Wood twig chairs, love seats, tables, and ottomans.

Dana Mills, Inc.
650 Heathrow Dr.
Lincolnshire, IL 60069-4221
847-913-9700
Fax: 847-913-9232

Flame-retardant fabrics.

Danko
102 Cypress Lane
Red Lion, PA 17356
800-882-5300 or 717-244-5252
Fax: 717-246-8120

Wood tables and chairs, including the stackable Childform chair, a smaller version of the Bodyform chair.

Decar Educational/Office Furniture
7615 University Avenue
P.O. Box 620188
Middleton, WI 53562-0188
800-653-3227 or 608-836-1911
Fax: 608-836-8255

Library furnishings, including wood chairs with upholstery options and adjustable-height high-pressure laminate activity tables.

Demco
P.O. Box 7488
Madison, WI 53707-7488
800-462-9809
Fax: 800-245-1329 (orders)
E-mail: quote@demco.com
Website: www.demco.com

Features several lines of library and classroom furnishings for early education and school environments.

Design America
4200 Aurora Street, Suite G
Coral Gables, FL 33146
800-367-3003 or 305-448-0600
Fax: 305-567-0946
Website: www.dsgnonline.com

Three-color wood table-and-chair set with matching rocker. Production of company's lounge seating in children's sizes is also available.

Design Finland, Inc.
Pacific Design Center
8687 Melrose Avenue #8273
Los Angeles, CA 90069
310-659-2075
Fax: 310-659-1290
E-mail: info@designfinland.com
Website: www.designfinland.com

Features the laminate Muurame line of residential juvenile/teen bedroom groups that includes headboards, beds, bunk beds, captain's beds, trundle beds, desks, chairs, chests of drawers, toy chests, and table-and-chair sets.

Design Textures
175 Colorado Blvd.
Denver, CO 80206
303-322-5807
Fax: 303-377-0229

Custom rugs.

Designs International, Inc.
P.O. Box 1503
Chatsworth, GA 30705
800-517-5101 or 706-517-5100
Fax: 706-517-2500
E-mail: designsintl@alltel.net

Interactive/educational themed area rugs up to 12 ft by 18 ft, including bilingual rugs.

DesignTex, Inc.
200 Varick Street
8th Floor
New York, NY 10014
212-886-8100
Fax: 212-886-8111

Fabrics include cubicle curtain fabric.

D.I.G.S.
P.O. Box 2064
New York, NY 10013-2064
888-868-3447 or 212-966-9651
Fax: 212-966-9651
E-mail: digs@pipeline.com

Bronze fossils, bones, and shell-inspired drawer and door pulls, and hooks.

Dinoflex Manufacturing Ltd.
5590 46th Ave. SE
Salmon Arm, British Columbia
Canada V1E 4S1
250-832-7780
Fax: 800-305-2109 or 250-832-7788
E-mail: sales@dinoflex.com
Website: dinoflex.com

Rubber tile playground surfacing.

Discover Products, Inc.
800 Brandi Lane
Round Rock, TX 78681
800-728-2330 or 512-388-2327
Fax: 512-388-4757
E-mail: sales@discoverproducts.com
Website: www.discoverproducts.com

Easels, chart stands, a sand/water table, and a large manipulative set.

Don P. Smith Chair Co.
P.O. Box 157
Loudon, TN 37774
423-458-2602
Fax: 423-458-4680

Wood ladder-back chairs, rocking chairs, and sitting stools.

Dragons of Walton Street Ltd.
23 Walton Street
London SW3 2HX
United Kingdom
44-171-5893795
Fax: 44-171-5844570
E-mail: dragons@solutions-inc.co.uk

In the United States:

In The Children's Shop
289 Greenwich Ave.
Greenwich, CT 06830
203-862-9255
Fax: 203-862-9015
E-mail: DragonsUSA@aol.com

Hand-painted furnishings, upholstered seating, granddaughter clocks, and custom-designed accessories and residential environments.

Dream Team Design
Hunts Green House
Hunts Green, Berkshire RG20 8BY
United Kingdom
44-1488-608807
Fax: 44-1488-608827

Colorful and uniquely designed residential furnishings.

DuMor, Inc.
P.O. Box 142
Mifflintown, PA 17059
800-598-4018 or 717-436-2106
Fax: 717-436-9839
E-mail: dumorsales@acsworld.net
Website: www.dumor.com

Bike racks.

Duralee Fabrics, Ltd.
1775 Fifth Ave.
Bay Shore, NY 11706
800-275-3872 or 516-273-8800
Fax: 516-273-8996
E-mail: duralee1@aol.com

Fabrics.

Dusyma
c/o Guidecraft USA
P.O. Box 324
Industrial Park, Building 30
Garnerville, NY 10923
914-947-3500
Fax: 914-947-3770
E-mail: GDCRAFT324@AOL.COM

A full line of German furnishings, indoor and outdoor play equipment, and supplies for the child care/early education environment.

E

eazy bean
42 Rausch Street
San Francisco, CA 94103
415-255-8516
Fax: 415-255-8014
E-mail: eazybean@aol.com

Beanbag seating.

Eco-sTuff
131 Spring Street
New York, NY 10012
212-431-3723
Fax: 212-431-7465
E-mail: mcd7@ix.netcom.com

Residential ready-to-assemble-and-paint table and chairs made from compressed, recycled newspapers.

Educo International, Inc.
123 Cree Road
Sherwood Park, Alberta
Canada T8A 3X9
800-661-4142 or 780-467-9772
Fax: 780-467-4014
E-mail: mazes@educo.com
Website: www.educo.com

A variety of manipulative and magnetic-top tables and outdoor wood tables with steel coil legs; matching stools available.

EG Furniture
381 Principale
P.O. Box 294
LaPerade, Québec
Canada G0X 2J0
418-325-2050
Fax: 888-329-8634 or 418-325-2545
E-mail: eg@egfurniture.com
Website: www.egfurniture.com

Residential infant and juvenile/teen bedroom groups.

Eljer Plumbingware
14801 Quorum Drive
Dallas, TX 75240
972-560-2000

Child-size toilets.

Elkay Manufacturing Company
2222 Camden Court
Oak Brook, IL 60523
630-574-8484

Classroom sinks with built-in drinking fountains.

Envirodesigns, Inc.
10546 105th Street
Edmonton, Alberta
Canada T5H 2W7
780-448-1044
Fax: 780-448-1042
E-mail: envirodesigns@compusmart
    .ab.ca
Website: www.envirodesigns.com

Large-scale shade umbrellas.

Environments, Inc.
P.O. Box 1348
Beaufort Industrial Park
Beaufort, SC 29901-1348
800-342-4453 or 803-846-8155
Fax: 800-343-2987

A complete source for furnishings, equipment, and supplies for the child care/early education environment, in-cluding a variety of banners and soft play centers.

Enzo Artifacts, Inc.
P.O. Box 457
East Amherst, NY 14051-0457
800-621-4544 or 716-636-5114
Fax: 716-636-4696

Commercial wallcoverings and five pat-terns of commercial stock 6- by 9-foot contemporary rugs. Custom services available.

Eric Holch Gallery
5 Pine Street
Nantucket, MA 02554
508-228-7654
Fax: 508-228-1537
E-mail: eric@nantucket.net
Website: www.ericholch.com

Serigraph prints and posters of New England townscapes and harbor themes, all in mostly primary colors.

Everlast Sports Manufacturing Corp.
750 East 132nd St.
Bronx, NY 10454
718-993-0100
Fax: 718-665-4116

Indoor boxing/martial arts equipment, including punching bags and mats. Manila climbing ropes and baseball bases are also available.

F

Falcon Products, Inc.
9387 Dielman Industrial Drive
St. Louis, MO 63132
800-873-3252 or 314-991-9200
Fax: 314-991-9227

Commercial high chairs, fixed and nonfixed fiberglass tables, chairs, and stools. These products are not scaled to children, but are often used in com-mercial fast-food environments areas.

F.A.S.T. Corp. (Fiberglass Animals Shapes and Trademarks)
P.O. Box 258, Hwy. 21
Sparta, WI 54656
608-269-7110
Fax: 608-269-7514

Large-scale stock and custom decorative fiberglass accessories, displays, and water play equipment.

Fibar Systems
Suite 300, 80 Business Park Drive
Armonk, NY 10504-1705
800-342-2721 or 914-273-8770
Fax: 914-273-8659
E-mail: fibar@fibar.com
Website: www.fibar.com

Engineered wood fiber playground surfacing and drainage systems.

The Fibrex Group, Inc.
3734 Cook Boulevard
Chesapeake, VA 23323
800-346-4458
Fax: 757-487-5876

Two models of outdoor polyethylene waste receptacles shaped like a frog (Froggo) and a porpoise (Splash).

First Weavers of the Americas
825 Locust St.
Lawrence, KS 66044-5449
800-571-0156
Fax: 785-838-4486

South American Indian designs on wool throw pillows and tapestries. Custom design services are available.

Fixtures Furniture
1642 Crystal
P.O. Box 266346
Kansas City, MO 64126-0346
800-821-3500 or 816-241-4500
Fax: 816-241-4027

Features the Bola Junior and Baby Bola lines of epoxy-painted metal-frame chairs and tables with optional upholstered, thermoplastic, or wood seats and backs. Matching adult chairs are available.

Flagship Carpets, Inc.
P.O. Box 1189
3295 Hwy. 411 N.
Chatsworth, GA 30705
800-848-4055 or 706-695-4055
Fax: 706-695-6632
E-mail: flagship@alltel.net
Website: flagshipcarpetsinc.com

Interactive/educational themed area rugs and carpets, including black light, fluorescent, and bilingual patterns.

Fleetwood Furniture Company
P.O. Box 1259
Holland, MI 49422-1259
800-257-6390 or 616-396-1142
Fax: 616-396-8022

Furnishings for the early education and school environments.

Fortco Limited
1190 Old Oak Dr.
Oakville, Ontario
Canada L6M 3K7
416-736-3455
Fax: 905-825-5887
E-mail: sandro.forte@sympatico.ca
Website: www3.sympatico.ca
   /sandro.forte/

Seamless rubber playground surfacing.

Franklin Instrument Company, Inc.
P.O. Box 2949
Warminster, PA 18974
215-355-7942
Fax: 215-322-1022

The battery-powered Kid Klok was designed to help children learn to read analog time.

Funblock Tables
6515 Railroad
Raytown, MO 64133
800-283-8625 or 816-353-2090
Fax: 816-353-5175
E-mail: funblock@micro.com or
    sales@funblock.com
Website: www.funblock.com

A variety of construction-top tables and computer furnishings, including preschool and accessible models.

FunDimensionals
3710 Patterstone Drive
Alpharetta, GA 30022
800-270-5005
Fax: 770-410-5754

Custom-designed health care environments.

Furniture Concepts
The Courtland East Building
29225 Chagrin Boulevard, Suite 110
Pepper Pike, OH 44122
800-969-4100 or 216-292-9100
Fax: 216-292-7460

Residence living furnishings.

Fusion Coatings, Inc.
P.O. Box 143
1101 East 8th Street
Winona, MN 55987
507-452-1112
Fax: 507-452-9099
Website: www.fusioncoatings.com

PVC-coated 4-ft square picnic table with seating on all four sides.

Futura Coatings, Inc.—Composite Fabrications and Sports Surfaces Divisions
9200 Latty Avenue
Hazelwood (St. Louis), MO 63042-2805
314-521-4100
Fax: 314-521-7255

E-mail: futura@inlink.com
Website: www.inlink.com/~futura/

Large-scale indoor and outdoor decorative elements and displays and seamless playground rubber surfacing.

Future Pro, Inc.
P.O. Box 486
200 N. Main
Inman, KS 67546
800-328-4625 or 316-585-6405
Fax: 316-585-6799

Basketball equipment.

G

Gametime
P.O. Box 680121
Fort Payne, AL 35967
800-235-2440 or 256-845-5610
For Pentes contained play structures:
    800-617-2158
Fax: 256-845-9361
E-mail: infor@gametime.com
Website: www.gametime.com

A full line of playground equipment and site furnishings, including non-wood play structures, a TotTime line for preschool-age children, and the Pentes contained play equipment.

Gautier USA, Inc.
Copans Business Park
1521 W. Copans Rd., Suite 109
Pompano Beach, FL 33064-1513
800-793-6075 or 954-975-3303
Fax: 954-975-3359
E-mail: gautier@iamerica.net
Website: www.gautierusa.com

Residential juvenile/teen bedroom groups, including bunk beds, captain's beds, and trundle beds.

Generation 2 Worldwide
113 Anderson Court, Suite #1
Dothan, AL 36301

334-792-1144
Fax: 334-794-2251

Residential infant bedroom groups that include cradles, cribs, high chairs, rockers, toy chests, and changing tables.

Gerber Manufacturing Ltd.

2917 Latham Drive
Madison, WI 53713
800-393-9923 or 608-271-2777
Fax: 608-271-1920
Website: www.gerbertables.com

Outdoor spring toys, bike racks, and wood top and metal-frame picnic tables.

GINGER/GUSA, Inc.

460-N Greenway Industrial Drive
Fort Mill, SC 29715-8102
888-469-6511 or 803-547-5786
Fax: 803-647-6356

Colorella line of bathroom accessories available in a variety of finishes and colors, including primary yellow and red.

Go-Elan, Inc.

630, boulevard Becancour
C.P. 447
Gentilly, Québec
Canada G0X 1G0
819-298-3431
Fax: 819-298-2299
E-mail: info@goelan.com
Website: goelan.com

A full line of commercial nonwood playground equipment and site furnishings.

Goodtime Medical

5410 W. Roosevelt Road
Chicago, IL 60644
888-386-8225
Fax: 773-626-5015
Website: www.goodtimemedical.com

A variety of pediatric exam tables, including models designed as a train, fire engine, school bus, 4 × 4, and caboose.

Green Frog Art

Four Sawgrass Village #230
Ponte Vedra, FL 32082
800-833-5024 or 904-280-3903
Fax: 904-280-9920
Website: www.greenfrogart.com

Framed and unframed prints of a variety of artistic styles and subject matters. Handpainted products including mats and frames, wallpaper borders, lamps, and floor rugs.

Gressco Ltd.

328 Moravian Valley Road
P.O. Box 339
Waunakee, WI 53597-0339
800-345-3480 or 608-849-6300
Fax: 608-849-6304
E-mail: info@gresscoltd.com

A unique line of library furnishings, including large reading cushions.

Gretchen Bellinger

P.O. Box 64
31 Ontario Street
Cohoes, NY 12047-0064
518-235-2828
Fax: 518-235-4242
E-mail: gretchenbellinger@juno.com

Contract and residential fabrics, including faux animal prints.

The Ground Floor

Division of John Ragsdale Interiors, Inc.
95½ Broad Street
Charleston, SC 29401
843-722-3576
Fax: 843-577-5880
Website: www.ragsdalefinials.com

Drapery hardware, including The Animal Series line of finials.

Grounds For Play, Inc.

3501 Ave. E East
Arlington, TX 76011

800-552-7529 or 817-640-4374
Fax: 817-649-8552
E-mail: gfp@onramp.net
Website: www.groundsforplay.com

Large outdoor manipulatives, and wood and nonwood commercial play structures. Custom design services also available.

Group Four Furniture Inc.
25-5 Connell Court
Toronto, Ontario
Canada M8Z 1E8
877-585-1478 or 416-251-1128
Fax: 416-251-6285
E-mail: g4furn@aol.com
Website: members.aol.com/g4furn

Tubular steel–framed seating; Domino, an upholstered lounge chair; and the 7000 table, which features a crayon cup in the center.

Gym-i-nee Associates, Inc.
3305 Rutherford Rd., Suite C
Taylors, SC 29687
800-496-1114 or 864-292-2626
Fax: 864-322-5466

Funnel ball equipment.

H

Haba
c/o t.c. timber
Habermaass Corporation
P.O. Box 42
4407 Jordan Road
Skaneateles, NY 13152
800-468-6873
Fax: 315-685-3792

A line of German furnishings featuring unique room dividers and modular storage systems for the child care/early education environment.

Hansgrohe, Inc.
1465 Ventura Drive
Cumming, GA 30130

800-719-1000 or 770-844-7414
Fax: 770-889-1783

Features Alfie, the Aquasaur, a children's handshower designed as a dinosaur in primary colors.

Hard Manufacturing Co., Inc.
230 Grider St.
Buffalo, NY 14215-3797
800-873-4273 or 716-893-1800
Fax: 716-896-2579
E-mail: hardmfg@aol.com

Pediatric cribs and beds.

Hatteras Hammocks, Inc.
P.O. Box 1602
Greenville, NC 27834
800-334-1078 or 252-758-0641
Fax: 252-758-0375

Belt swings for residential use.

Hausmann Industries, Inc.
130 Union Street
Northvale, NJ 07647
888-428-7626 or 201-767-0255
Fax: 201-767-1369
Website: www.hausmann.com

Pediatric exam tables.

Haworth, Inc.
One Haworth Center
Holland, MI 49423-9576
800-344-2600 or 616-393-3000
Fax: 616-393-3420
Website: www.haworth-furn.com

Scamps Children's Furniture line includes nonwood tables, stools, and stackable chairs with an upholstery option.

Hedstrom Corporation
585 Slawin Court
Mt. Prospect, IL 60056-2183
800-323-5999 or 847-803-9200
Fax: 847-803-9223

In Canada:

400 Main Street East
Milton, Ontario
Canada L9T 4X5
905-693-0071
Fax: 905-693-0091

Residential play structures and trampolines.

Heirlooms of Tomorrow Ltd.
2591 B¾ Road
Grand Junction, CO 81503
970-241-6778
Fax: 970-241-0771

Upholstered rocking seats designed as ponies, swans, dragons, dinosaurs and geese.

Helen Webber Art & Design
14 Commercial Blvd. #101
Novato, CA 94949
415-883-6604
Fax: 415-883-0886
E-mail: hwdes@ix.netcom.com

Custom and limited edition art pieces in a variety of mediums, including tapestry, metal, clay, wood, glass, and prints.

Henderson Recreation Equipment Limited
c/o Goric Marketing Group, Inc.
P.O. Box 117
Ashland, MA 01721
508-429-3870
Fax: 508-429-3048
E-mail: goric@goric.com

In Canada:

11 Gilbertson Drive, Box 68
Simcoe, Ontario
Canada N3Y 4K8
800-265-5462 or 519-426-9380
Fax: 519-426-1132
Website: www.henderson-recreation.com

A full line of commercial playground equipment and site furnishings, includ-ing the lines of Children's Playgrounds (custom-designed wood) and Playsteel Playstructures.

HEWI, Inc.
2851 Old Tree Drive
Lancaster, PA 17603
877-439-4462 or 717-293-1313
Fax: 800-827-3270 or 717-293-3270
E-mail: hewi@hewi.com

Imaginative "caterpillar" door pulls and coatracks, and an "elephant" coatrack/bench unit. Restroom accessories, boy and girl symbols for restroom signage, and double handrails also available.

Highsmith, Inc.
W5527 Highway 106
P.O. Box 800
Fort Atkinson, WI 53538-0800
800-558-2110
Fax: 800-835-2329
E-mail: service@highsmith.com
Website: www.highsmith.com

A variety of lines of library furnishings and accessories.

Hillcrest Baby
295 Fifth Avenue, Suite 1616
New York, NY 10016
212-447-9090
Fax: 212-447-9801

Residential crib bedding and pillows.

Hollaender Manufacturing Company
10285 Wayne Avenue
P.O. Box 156399
Cincinnati, OH 45215-6399
800-772-8800 or 513-772-8800
Fax: 800-772-8806 or 513-772-8806

Pipe fittings for play structures.

Home & Yard Connection
112 Shadowlawn Dr.
Fishers, IN 46038

800-566-7722 or 317-577-2227
Fax: 317-577-3765
Residential play structures.

Horizon Plastics Company Ltd.
Bldg. 3W, Northam Industrial Park
P.O. Box 474
Cobourg, Ontario
Canada K9A 4L1
905-372-2291
Fax: 905-372-9397

Custom plastic molder for play struc-ture components.

Horizons International Accents, Inc.
400 Talbert Street
Daly City, CA 94014
415-330-9881
Fax: 415-330-9900
E-mail: HorizonIA@aol.com

Wall art and decorative accessories, in-cluding the Monkeypod line of wood accessories and rocking seats.

House of Hatten, Inc.
301 Inner Loop Rd.
Georgetown, TX 78626
512-819-9600
Fax: 512-819-9033

Residential crib bedding, pillows, and fabric wallhangings.

Howell Equipment Company
c/o Potomac Engineering Corporation
919 North Michigan Avenue
Chicago, IL 60611-1601
800-562-7901 or 312-787-7262
Fax: 312-787-3407
Park and playground equipment, in-cluding commercial wood play struc-tures.

Huffy Sports
N53 W24700 S. Corporate Circle
Sussex, WI 53089
414-820-3440

Fax: 414-820-1395
Website: www.huffysports.com
Basketball equipment.

Hugg-A-Planet
159 Catamount Drive
Milton, VT 05468
800-839-3334 or 802-893-3334
Fax: 802-893-3345
E-mail: hugearth@together.net
Website: Huggaplanet.com

Pillows with prints of maps of the United States and the world.

I

The ICF Group
Clarkstown Executive Park
704 Executive Blvd.
Valley Cottage, NY 10989
800-237-1625
Fax: 888-784-8209
Website: www.icfgroup.com

A multisectioned table with birch legs and a variety of surfacing options (nat-ural, wood veneer, laminate, linoleum). Designed by Alvar Aalto for the Viipuri Library in Viipuri, Finland.

Interbath, Inc.
665 N. Baldwin Park Blvd.
City of Industry, CA 91746
800-423-9485
Fax: 626-369-3316
Website: www.interbath.com

In Canada:

5556 Tomken Road
Mississauga, Ontario
Canada L4W 1P4
800-661-5361
Fax: 905-624-0796

Colorful showerheads, handshowers, and bath organization accessories.

Interior Systems
1541 Miller St.
La Crosse, WI 54601
800-782-0070
Fax: 608-782-8575
Website: www.interiorsystems.com

Arkidtecture Funscapes provide for custom-cut, lay-in ceiling tiles.

Interior Systems, Inc.
Atrium School Environments
525 West Rolling Meadows Drive
Fond du Lac, WI 54936
800-837-8373 or 414-923-4313
Fax: 414-923-1677
Website: www.isiamerica.com

Fixed tables and seating, and signage designed for different age groups.

Interspec
P.O. Box 705
Allenwood, NJ 08720
800-526-2800 or 732-938-4114

Commercial fabric for cubicle curtains, draperies, and bedspreads.

Island Leisure Products
3431 Benton Drive NW
Calgary, Alberta
Canada T2L 1W7
403-282-3845
Fax: 403-282-3845

In the United Kingdom:

Church Road Business Centre
Sittingbourn, Kent ME10 3RS
United Kingdom
44-1795-436500
Fax: 44-1795-436700

Rubber tile playground surfacing.

Italiana Società Arredamenti Fontanili F.lli s.r.l.
42020 Quattro Castella
Reggio Emilia, Italy
39-0522-887421
Fax: 39-0522-887129

A line of Italian early education furnishings, products, and outdoor play equipment from the manufacturers of furniture and equipment for the schools of Reggio Emilia, including a large outdoor chess set and a variety of mirror furnishings.

J

JCH International, Inc.
978 Hermitage Road NE
Rome, GA 30161-9641
800-328-9203 or 706-295-4111
Fax: 706-295-4114

Seamless poured-in-place and tile rubber playground surfacing.

Johnsonite
16910 Munn Rd.
Chagrin Falls, OH 44023
800-899-8916
Fax: 440-543-8920

In Canada:

560 Weber Street N.
Waterloo, Ontario
Canada N2L 5C6
800-661-2162

Rubber and vinyl wall bases in nontraditional colors.

The Joseph Company
P.O. Box 417
Dothan, AL 36302
334-702-6761 or 334-671-4917
E-mail: toddlerock@ala.net
Website: www.toddlerock.com

The Toddle Rock, an upholstered child's rocker.

Joy Carpets, Inc.
P.O. Box 5379
104 W. Forrest Rd.
Ft. Oglethorpe, GA 30742-0579
800-645-2787 or 706-866-3335
Fax: 706-866-7928

E-mail: joycarpets@joycarpets.com
Website: www.joycarpets.com

Commercial interactive/educational themed area rugs and carpets.

Jumpking Outdoor Products
901 W. Miller Rd.
Garland, TX 75041
800-322-2211 or 972-271-5867
Fax: 972-494-2726
E-mail: jumpking@airmail.net

Trampolines.

Justice Design Group, Inc.
P.O. Box 2429
Culver City, CA 90231
310-397-8300
Fax: 310-397-7170
E-mail: sales@jdg.com
Website: www.jdg.com

Bogo collection features wooden juvenile theme wall, table, and ceiling-hung light fixtures. The Ambiance Collection of wall lighting features sun, moon, stars, and ABC block themes.

K

Kaplan School Supply Corp.
1310 Lewisville-Clemmons Rd.
P.O. Box 609
Lewisville, NC 27023-0609
800-334-2014 or 336-766-7374
Fax: 800-452-7526 or 336-766-5652

A full line of furnishings and supplies for the child care/early education environment.

Kathy Foster, Artist
6721 Deane Hill Drive
Knoxville, TN 37919
423-558-3008

Hand-painted, custom-designed, themed wood table-and-chair sets.

Kee Industrial Products
P.O. Box 207
Buffalo, NY 14225-0207
800-851-5181 or 716-896-4949
Fax: 716-896-5696

In Canada:

219 Connie Crescent, Unit 9
Concord, Ontario
Canada L4K 1L4
Fax: 716-896-5696

Pipe fittings for play structures.

KI
1330 Bellevue St.
Green Bay, WI 54302
800-454-9796
Website: www.ki-inc.com

Furnishings for the educational environment, including the Versa line of commercial chairs and tables with matching adult furnishings. Folding metal chairs and school desks are also available.

Kid-Krafters, Inc.
310 Liberty Pike
Franklin, TN 37064
800-323-0282 or 615-790-2485
Fax: 615-790-3779

Commercial and residential play structures.

Kids' Studio
8342 West Fourth Street
Los Angeles, CA 90048
323-655-4028
Fax: 323-655-4178
E-mail: kids_studio@juno.com

Contemporary residential furnishings, including beds, stools, shelf units, and table-and-chair sets. Custom design services available.

Kidstruction
P.O. Box 162048
Austin, TX 78716-2048

800-245-8449 or 512-442-3502
Fax: 512-442-4410

Commercial play structures and accessories, including an accessible sphere swing for disabled children.

Kidz Manufacturing
405 Riverview Drive
Manitowoc, WI 54220
920-682-8386
Fax: 920-682-8386

Residential play structures.

Kidzpace Interactive, Inc.
P.O. Box 550
Collingwood, Ontario
Canada L9Y 4B2
705-444-2300
705-444-0007

Video entertainment centers and themed room dividers (barn, jungle, sea) with interactive activities.

Kinderworks Corporation
P.O. Box 1441
Somersworth, NH 03878
888-692-8697 or 603-692-2777
Fax: 603-692-4545

A variety of furnishings and accessories for child care/early education environments, including storage units, wall-hung manipulative activities, and tables with attached manipulative activities.

King of Swings
5182 Brookhollow Pkwy., Suite D
Norcross, GA 30071
770-448-5464

Residential play structures.

Knobs by Susan Goldstick
2 Parker #305
San Francisco, CA 94118
415-332-6719
Fax: 415-332-6830

Highly decorative drawer/door pulls and finials designed with jewel-tone colors and crystals.

Koala Corp./Delta Play Division
200-14666 64th Ave.
Surrey, British Columbia
Canada V35 1X7
604-591-6612
Fax: 604-591-6636
Website: www.deltaplay.com

Indoor/outdoor contained play structures.

Koala Corp./Koala Bear Kare
11600 E. 53rd Avenue, Unit D
Denver, CO 80239-2312
800-666-0363
Fax: 303-574-9000

Restroom/dressing room equipment (wall-mounted changing tables and safety seats) and commercial high chairs. Interactive/educational themed area rugs and carpets, manipulative-top tables, room dividers, nonwood chairs, and video game units.

Koala Corp./Park Structures Division
12325 West Sample Road
Coral Springs, FL 33065
954-340-9100
Fax: 954-340-0131
Website: www.parkstructures.com

Commercial nonwood play structures.

Kohler Co.
444 Highland Drive
Kohler, WI 53044
920-457-4441
Fax: 920-459-1656
Website: www.kohler.com

Child-sized toilet, Primary, with colorful seat options.

Kompan, Inc.

7717 New Market Street
Olympia, WA 98501
800-426-9788 or 360-943-6374
Fax: 360-943-6254
Website: www.kompan.com

A complete line of park and playground products, including three lines of commercial play structures: Kompan, specializing in early childhood structures; Big Toys; and 10 Plus, featuring play structures for teenagers.

Komponents Laminated Products

39741 Industrial Rd.
P.O. Box 162
Oconomowoc, WI 53066
888-567-6061 or 414-567-6061
Fax: 414-567-6906
Website: www.funfurniture.com

Cubbies shaped like dinosaurs, cows, and space shuttles. Nonwood tables and chairs and shelf units are also available.

Krauss Craft, Inc.

30400 Redwood Hwy.
P.O. Box 2111
Cave Junction, OR 97523
800-333-8519
Fax: 541-592-6356
E-mail: kcraft@cdsnet.net
Website: www.krausscraft.com

Commercial and residential play structures.

Kwik Goal Ltd.

140 Pacific Drive
Quakertown, PA 18951
215-536-2200
Fax: 215-536-4309

Youth and small-sided goals for soccer, floor hockey, and other goal specific activities.

L

L.A. Baby

2050 E. 49th St.
Los Angeles, CA 90058
800-584-3094
Fax: 323-584-4819
E-mail: LABABYCO@aol.com

A metal toddler's sofa, The Little Futon, which converts to a bed, and The Cradle, which converts to a love seat for toddlers. Metal toddler beds, institutional-quality folding cribs, changing/ dressing tables, and cradle and crib bedding are also available.

L.A. Steelcraft Products, Inc.

1974 Lincoln Ave.
P.O. Box 90365
Pasadena, CA 91109-0365
800-371-2438 or 626-798-7401
Fax: 626-798-1482
E-mail: stlcraft@aol.com
Website: lasteelcraftproducts.com

A full line of park and playground equipment, including commercial nonwood play structures.

Lakeshore Learning Materials

2695 E. Dominguez St.
P.O. Box 6261
Carson, CA 90749
800-421-5354 or 310-537-8600
Fax: 310-537-5403
Website: www.lakeshorelearning.com

Furnishings, equipment, and supplies for the child care/early education environment, including a science activity–top table.

Lamby Nursery Collection

305 Grover St.
Lynden, WA 98264
800-669-0527 or 360-354-6719
Fax: 360-354-6513

E-mail: info@lamby.com
Website: www.lamby.com
Lambskin crib bedding.

Landscape Structures, Inc.
601 7th St. South
P.O. Box 198
Delano, MN 55328
800-328-0035 or 612-972-3391
Fax: 612-972-5291
Website: www.playlsi.com

A full line of park and playground equipment and accessories. Commercial nonwood play structures, including models for toddlers and teens.

Lea Industries
One Plaza Center
Box HP3
High Point, NC 27261-1500
336-294-5233
Fax: 800-933-0243

Residential juvenile/teen bedroom groups, including bunk beds, captain's beds, sleigh beds, and trundle beds.

Learning Curve Toys
311 W. Superior St. #416
Chicago, IL 60610
800-704-8697
Fax: 312-654-1729

In Canada:

Brigitta's Import Inc.
282 N. Rivermede Rd.
Concord, Ontario
Canada L4K 3N6
800-263-8117 or 905-669-1570
Fax: 905-669-3529
Website: www.learningtoys.com

Railroad and roadway activity–top tables.

Learning Passport Co.
7104 Loch Lomond Drive
Bethesda, MD 20817

800-853-2762 or 301-229-5940
Fax: 301-229-5940
Website: www.LearningPassport.com

Residential shelf units and seating that double as dollhouses, puppet theater, and fortress.

Learning Products
700 Fee Fee Road
Maryland Heights, MO 63043
888-338-5437 or 314-997-6400
Fax: 314-997-4489

A variety of large manipulative systems, including the Snap Wall System and Edublocs. Indoor gross motor play manipulatives and Kindersize exercise equipment are also available.

Leathers & Associates, Inc.
Design for Community Built
99 Eastlake Road
Ithaca, NY 14850
607-277-1650
Fax: 607-277-1433
E-mail: leathers@dreamscape.com
Website: leatherassociates.com

Community-built, custom-designed wood play structures.

Lee Industries, Inc.
P.O. Box 26
Newton, NC 28658
800-892-7150
Fax: 828-465-0614
Website: www.leeindustries.com

The Lee 4 Kids group features upholstered love seats, lounge chairs, and ottomans for residential use.

LEGO Dacta, Inc.
113 North Maple Street
Enfield, CT 06082
800-510-5773
Fax: 860-763-7477

E-mail: kenneth.hunt@america
.lego.com
Website: www.lego.com/dacta

A construction-top table, the Lego Dacta Flip-Top Playtable features a reversible top for use with either Duplo or Lego building blocks.

Leisure Time Products
P.O. Box 459
Siloam Springs, AR 72761
501-524-4138 or 501-524-6481

Residential wood play structures.

Leisure Woods, Inc.
P.O. Box 177
Genoa, IL 60135
815-784-2497
Fax: 815-784-2499

Gazebos.

Lexington Furniture Industries
P.O. Box 1008
Lexington, NC 27293-1008
800-539-4636 or 336-249-5300
Fax: 336-249-5365
Website: www.lexington.com

Residential infant and juvenile/teen bedroom groups, including the Locker Room line and Betsy Cameron's Children line of furnishings and prints.

Litchfield Industries, Inc.
4 Industrial Drive
Litchfield, MI 49252
800-542-5282 or 517-542-2988
Fax: 517-542-3939
E-mail: info@litchfieldindustries.com
Website: www.litchfieldindustries.com

A variety of site furnishings, including gazebos and metal shelters.

Little Tikes Commercial Play Systems
One Iron Mountain Drive
P.O. Box 897
Farmington, MO 63640

800-325-8828 or 573-756-4591
Fax: 573-756-0319

In Canada:

21 Scott Avenue
P.O. Box 125
Paris, Ontario
Canada N3L 3E7
800-265-9953 or 519-442-6331
Fax: 519-442-8200

A full line of commercial park and playground equipment, including contained and nonwood play structures.

The Little Tikes Company
2180 Barlow Road
P.O. Box 2277
Hudson, OH 44236
800-321-4424
Fax: 330-650-3956

A variety of indoor dramatic play equipment, computer furnishings, nonwood table-and-chair sets, and residential outdoor play structures and equipment.

Loewenstein
P.O. Box 10369
Pompano Beach, FL 33061-6369
954-960-1100
Fax: 954-960-0409

Several lines of chairs, including Padova II, Dine, Charlie, and Fast, and a table base from the Activity line. Each line of chairs includes matching adult chairs.

Lofty Thinkers, L.L.C.
P.O. Box 1388
Carrollton, GA 30117
800-692-6343 or 770-832-6660
Fax: 770-832-6687
Website: www.superiorinternational
.com

Lofts.

Luceplan USA, Inc.
315 Hudson Street
New York, NY 10013
212-989-6265
Fax: 212-462-4349
E-mail: info@luceplanusa.com
Website: www.luceplanusa.com

The On Off table light, made of molded polyurethane, operates by being tilted side to side.

M

Maharam
45 Rasons Court
Hauppauge, NY 11788
800-645-3943 or 516-582-3434
Fax: 516-582-1026
E-mail: www.maharam.com

Cubicle curtain fabric, including a design called Gameboard.

Maine Cottage Furniture
P.O. Box 935
Yarmouth, ME 04096-1935
207-846-1430
Fax: 207-846-0602
E-mail: info@mainecottage.com
Website: www.mainecottage.com

Residential wood juvenile/teen bedroom groups.

Majestic Woodworks, Inc.
1147 61st St.
Brooklyn, NY 11219
718-851-2700
Fax: 718-851-0655

Residential furnishings, including a child's glider rocker.

The Malnight Company, Inc.
146 Monroe Center
1400 McKay Tower
Grand Rapids, MI 49503

616-454-0979
Fax: 616-454-6781
E-mail: JimM@malcofurn.com
Website: www.malcofurn.com

The Bright Kids Collection includes a variety of wood furnishings for the early education environment.

Manta-Ray, Inc.
502 E. North Parkway
West Unity, OH 43570
800-252-0276 or 419-924-2328
Fax: 419-924-5543
E-mail: mantaray@brightnet.net
Website: www.childbrite.com

The ChildBrite line features a variety of activity furnishings for child care/early education environments.

Mark Wilkinson
Dalia Kitchen Design, Inc.
One Design Center Place
Suites 635 and 643
Boston, MA 02210
617-482-2566
Fax: 617-482-2744

In the United Kingdom:

Overton House
High Street, Bromham, Chippenham
Wiltshire SN15 2HA
United Kingdom
44-1380-850184
E-mail: gadi@mwf.com

Residential furnishings for infant and juvenile/teen bedroom groups.

Marsh Industries, Inc.
Visual Products Group
P.O. Box 509
Dover, OH 44622
800-426-4244 or 330-343-8825
Fax: 330-343-9515
E-mail: wdsinghaus@marsh-ind.com
Website: www.marsh-ind.com

Chalk/marker boards, tackboards, and art easels. Chalk/marker boards are also available at children's height.

Marston Manufacturing, Inc.
3028 N. Hopkins Rd.
P.O. Box 24407
Richmond, VA 23224
804-233-0020
Fax: 804-232-4950

Commercial wood high chairs.

Mat Factory, Inc.
760 W. 16th Street, Bldg. E
Costa Mesa, CA 92627
949-645-3122
Fax: 949-645-0966
E-mail: MATFACT@pop3.concentric
    .net
Website: www.matfactoryinc.com

Safety Deck II (recycled rubber/PVC mats with holes that allow for natural grass to grow through).

McCourt Manufacturing
1001 North Third Street
Fort Smith, AR 72901
800-333-2687 ext. 217
Fax: 501-783-7306
E-mail: info@mccourtmfg.com
Website: www.mccourtmfg.com

Lightweight folding tables (4 or 6 ft by 30 in); high-pressure laminate tops in three heights and ABS plastic tops in adjustable heights. Stacking chairs in four heights and four colors.

McDole Library Furniture
323 Brooke Rd.
Winchester, VA 22603
540-667-7983
Fax: 540-722-4786
E-mail: mcdole@visuallink.com
Website: www.mcdole.net

Library furnishings.

Melodious Music Boxes
65 West Commercial Street
Portland, ME 04101
207-774-5519
Fax: 207-774-2810
E-mail: musicbox@ime.net

A variety of residential accessories and furnishings incorporating music boxes into their designs.

Merit Wish
P.O. Box 5085
New Castle, PA 16105
724-458-4811
Fax: 724-458-9286

Hand-painted residential accessories and furnishings.

The Merrymac Collection
P.O. Box 81572
Las Vegas, NV 89180
888-221-2044
Fax: 702-221-7119

Residential table lamps.

Merrytime Play Systems, Inc.
1520 15th Street
Two Rivers, WI 54241
800-678-4967
Website: www.merrytime.com

Residential play structures.

Meyer Design, Inc.
100 High St.
Akron, OH 44308-1918
800-543-9176 or 330-434-9176
Fax: 330-434-9110

Commercial wood play structures.

Midmark Corporation
60 Vista Dr.
Versailles, OH 45380
800-643-6275
Fax: 800-365-8631
Website: www.midmark.com

Pediatric exam table.

Mile High Play Systems, Inc.
3629 S. Fox Street, Suite C
Englewood, CO 80110
888-803-3385 or 303-762-9441
Fax: 303-762-9431
Website: milehiplay.com

Commercial and residential play structures and site amenities.

Million Dollar Baby
1520 Beach Street
Montebello, CA 90640
800-282-3886 or 323-728-9988
Fax: 323-722-2805

Residential cradles, beds, cribs, high chairs, child's rockers, chests of drawers, and changing/dressing tables.

Minic
524 East 117th Street
New York, NY 10035
212-410-5500
Fax: 212-410-5533
E-mail: Minic1@aol.com
Website: www.minic.net

Dressing tables.

MM's Designs
1555 W. Sam Houston Parkway N.
Houston, TX 77043-3112
713-461-2600
Fax: 713-827-7071

Residential accessories.

Mohawk Industries, Inc.
P.O. Box 12069
160 South Industrial Boulevard
Calhoun, GA 30703-7002
800-241-4494 or 706-629-7721

Kid Proof carpet line.

Mondial Industries, Ltd.
600 Mondial Parkway
Streetsboro, OH 44241
330-626-4490
Fax: 330-626-4491

Jumbo Diaper Genie, diaper disposal units for commercial use.

Moosehead Manufacturing Company
P.O. Box 287
Monson, ME 04464-0287
207-997-3621
Fax: 207-997-9611

Residential infant and juvenile/teen bedroom groups.

Most Dependable Fountains
4697 Winchester Road
Memphis, TN 38118
800-552-6331 or 901-794-4072
Fax: 901-794-4272
Website: www.mostdependable.com

Outdoor drinking fountains.

Multiplex Display Fixture Company
1555 Larkin Williams Rd.
Fenton, MO 63026-3008
800-325-3350
Fax: 314-326-1716
E-mail: mplex@inlink.com

Display panels that double as room dividers.

My Dog Spot
11588 Sorrento Valley Road, Suite 22
San Diego, CA 92121
619-259-7200
Fax: 619-259-7365
Website: www.mydogspot4kids.com

Residential crib bedding, pillows, mobiles, and fabric.

N

N. D. Cass Co., Inc.
P.O. Box 907
Athol, MA 01331
508-249-3205
Fax: 508-249-3454

Residential furniture, including dramatic play furniture.

National School Lines Company
606 East Murdock Avenue
P.O. Box 707
Oshkosh, WI 54901-0707
920-236-3535
Fax: 920-236-3520
E-mail: sales@nsl-inc.com
Website: www.nsl-inc.com

School desks and chairs.

National Upholstering Company
4000 Adeline St.
Emeryville, CA 94608
510-653-8915
Fax: 510-652-4754

Upholstered child's rocker for residential use.

Nelson Adams Company
180 N. Sherman Avenue
Corona, CA 91720
909-340-2800
Fax: 909-340-2885
E-mail: www.sales@nelsonadams
     .com
Website: www.nelsonadams.com

Chalk/marker boards and tackboards.

Nemschoff
2218 Julson Court
Sheboygan, WI 53081
920-457-7726
Fax: 920-459-1234

Commercial and healthcare furnishings, including lounge (soft) seating, wood tables and chairs, and desks.

Nevco Scoreboard Company
301 E. Harris Avenue, P.O. Box 609
Greenville, IL 62246-0609
800-851-4040 or 618-664-0360
Fax: 618-664-0398
E-mail: nevco@nevcoscoreboards
     .com
Website: www.nevcoscoreboards.com

Scoreboards.

Nifty Nob
3051 NW 104th St., Suite A
Urbandale, IA 50322
515-252-7447
Fax: 515-252-7449
E-mail: ideas@niftynob.com
Website: www.niftynob.com

Drawer/door pulls, switchplate covers, and hooks in a variety of shapes, including animals, fish, sun, moon, stars, sports balls, and wild animals.

No Fault Industries, Inc.
11325 Pennywood Ave.
Baton Rouge, LA 70809
800-232-7766 or 225-293-7760
Fax: 225-291-3821
E-mail: nofaultl@lx.netcom.com
Website: www.nofault.com

Saf Dek seamless rubber playground surfacing.

Noel Joanna, Inc. (NoJo)
22942 Arroyo Vista
Rancho Santa Margarita, CA 92688
949-858-9717
Fax: 949-858-9686

Residential crib bedding.

Nova Solutions, Inc.
421 W. Industrial Avenue
Effingham, IL 62401
800-730-6682
Fax: 800-940-6682
E-mail: Novadesk@effingham.net
Website: www.novadesk.com

Computer furnishings.

Nursery Maid
P.O. Box 922
151 South "N" Street
Dinuba, CA 93618
800-443-8773 or 559-591-0839
Fax: 559-591-0848

A variety of furnishings for the child care environment.

O

Office Specialty
67 Toll Road
Holland Landing, Ontario
Canada L9N 1H2
905-836-7676
Fax: 905-836-6000

Geni Kids line features chairs and tables of tubular steel construction, available in a range of standard finish and upholstery options, plus custom colors and COM.

Old Hickory Furniture Co., Inc.
403 South Noble Street
Shelbyville, IN 46176
800-232-2275 or 317-392-6740
Fax: 317-398-2275
Website: www.old-hickory.com

Hospitality and residential furnishings constructed of natural bark hickory. The company's entire line of furnishings can be built to sizes suitable for children.

Olka Homer Smith Furniture Manufacturing Company
P.O. Box 1148
Fort Smith, AR 72902
501-783-6191
Fax: 501-783-5767

Commercial cribs and residential infant bedroom groups.

Osborne & Little
90 Commerce Road
Stamford, CT 06902
203-359-1500
Fax: 203-353-0854

Residential fabrics, wallcoverings, and wall borders.

P

Palecek
P.O. Box 225
Richmond, CA 94808-0225

800-274-7730
Fax: 510-234-7234

Wicker chairs and rockers for residential and contract use.

Panex Furniture Products, Inc.
109 North West Second Street
Smithville, TX 78957
800-688-6556 or 512-237-3300
Fax: 512-237-3327

A variety of furnishings for child care/early education environments.

Parity, Inc.
P.O. Box 231
N. Aurora, IL 60542-0231
800-848-3585
Fax: 630-906-0556

The AeroSling Swing provides swing accessibility.

pca industries, inc.
1121 Grandview Drive
South San Francisco, CA 94080
650-871-5938
Fax: 650-871-5996

Outdoor activity and sports equipment and site furnishings.

Peaceable Kingdom Press
707-B Heinz Avenue
Berkeley, CA 94710
510-644-9801
Fax: 510-644-9805
E-mail: pkp@pkpress.com
Website: www.pkpress.com

Posters of the artwork from classic children's books.

Pediatric Designs, Inc.
2151 Oak Glen Trail
Stillwater, MN 55082
800-766-7257 or 651-429-0018
Fax: 651-439-0213
Website: www.zoopals.com

Zoopals features pediatric exam tables designed as a dinosaur, hippo, elephant, lion, and polar bear.

People Friendly Places, Inc.
853 Sanders Road #306
Northbrook, IL 60062
800-369-6331 or 847-267-9028
Fax: 847-267-9029
E-mail: sales@peoplefriendlyplaces
    .com
Website: www.peoplefriendlyplaces
    .com

A variety of furnishings and accessories selected for use in waiting rooms.

Peter Fasano Ltd.
964 South Main Street
Great Barrington, MA 01230
413-528-6872
Fax: 413-528-6851

Residential fabrics and wallcoverings.

Peter Pepper Products, Inc.
17929 S. Susana Road
Compton, CA 90224
310-639-0390
Fax: 310-639-6013
E-mail: customerservice
    @peterpepperproducts.com
Website: www.peterpepperproducts
    .com

Fiberglass tables, chairs, stools, slides, and sandboxes.

Peterson Design
740 105th Ave.
P.O. Box 6789
Oakland, CA 94603
800-932-5166 or 510-632-1750
Fax: 510-489-8029
Website: www.petersondesign.com

Cherokee Club and Mesa Series feature commercial tables with decorative inlaid laminate tops. Lamination of black-and-white or color photographs into tops is also available.

Pickle-Ball, Inc.
4700 Ninth Ave. N.W.
Seattle, WA 98107
206-784-4723
Fax: 206-781-0782

Pickle ball (paddle tennis–type game) equipment.

PierceMartin
129 Armour Drive
Atlanta, GA 30324
800-334-8701 or 404-872-0800
Fax: 404-872-0859

Upholstered wicker chair for residential use.

Pilliod Furniture
P.O. Box 26777
4620 Grandover Parkway
Greensboro, NC 27417-6777
336-294-5233
Fax: 336-315-4377
Website: www.pilliodfurniture.com

Features a Tots & Up line of residential chests of drawers.

Play & Leisure Systems, Inc.
3255 E. Washington Street
Phoenix, AZ 85034
602-275-5555
Fax: 602-275-5556
Website: www.playandleisure.com

Commercial and residential play structures and a variety of freestanding outdoor activity equipment.

Playground Environments
P.O. Box 578
22 Old Country Road
Quogue, NY 11959
800-662-0922 or 516-653-5465 ext. 133

Fax: 516-653-2933
E-mail: PEPlay@mindspring.com
Website: PlaygroundEnvironments
.com

Commercial nonwood play structures, including models for toddlers.

Playkids
4281 SW 75th Ave.
Miami, FL 33155
800-958-5437 or 305-267-5437
Fax: 305-267-0530
Website: www.playkids.com

Commercial wood and residential play structures.

Playland International L.L.C.
150 Adamson Industrial Blvd.
Carrollton, GA 30117
800-356-4727 or 770-834-6120
Fax: 770-834-6495
E-mail: playlandin@aol.com
Website: www.playland-inc.com

Nonwood commercial play structures and playground equipment.

Playlofts, Inc.
2296 Maple Ave.
Cortlandt Manor, NY 10567
914-739-2774

Commercial and residential wood play structures and a variety of other playground products.

Playsafe, Inc.
401 E. Walnut Street
Garland, TX 75040-6605
972-487-8877
Fax: 972-487-0588
E-mail: info@playsafe-inc.com
Website: www.playsafe-inc.com

Ball pits and soft contained commercial play structures.

Playscapes
2600 Daniels Street
Madison, WI 53704
800-248-7529 or 608-222-9600
Fax: 608-222-8100

A variety of furnishings and accessories designed for use in waiting rooms.

Playworks, Inc.
6411 River Parkway
Wauwatosa, WI 53213
414-453-5253

Commercial and residential play structures, including models for toddlers; indoor play lofts.

Playworld Systems, Inc.
1000 Buffalo Road
Lewisburg, PA 17837-9795
800-233-8404 or 570-522-9800
Fax: 570-522-3030
Website: www.playworldsystems.com
Website: www.playdesigns.com

A complete line of outdoor dramatic play equipment, site furnishings, and accessories (including commercial play structures and the Playdesign line for infants and toddlers).

Poligon by W. H. Porter, Inc.
4240 N. 136th Avenue
Holland, MI 49424
616-399-1963
Fax: 616-399-9123
E-mail: sales@poligon.com
Website: www.poligon.com

Poligon line of metal gazebos and shelters.

Polycom Products
67 Beaver Ave., Suite A
Annandale, NJ 08801
908-735-7373
Fax: 908-730-7467

Swing hardware and accessories and play structure components.

Portal Publications, Ltd.
201 Almeda Del Prado
Novato, CA 94949
800-227-1720 or 415-884-6200
Fax: 415-382-3377
Website: www.portalpub.com
Posters and framed prints.

Primelite Manufacturing Corp.
407 South Main Street
Freeport, NY 11520
800-327-7583 or 516-868-4411
Fax: 516-868-4609

Juvenile Gems line features ceiling and table lighting.

Priss Prints, Inc.
585 Slawin Court
Mount Prospect, IL 60056-2183
800-323-5999 or 847-803-9200
Fax: 847-803-9223

Decorative accessories for residential use, including drawer pulls, switchplate covers, and precut self-stick wall appliqués in a variety of themes, such as Winnie the Pooh, Looney Tunes and Disney movies, Barbie, and Barney.

Pucuda, Inc.
500 Main Street
P.O. Box 1019
Deep River, CT 06417
800-241-7330 or 860-526-8004
Fax: 860-526-4858
Website: www.netting.com

A wide range of nets and netting products for use in play environments.

Puzzlecraft Furniture
4804 Strawberry Lane
Louisville, KY 40209
800-862-6688 or 502-367-2266
Fax: 502-368-6958

Ready-to-assemble furniture for residential and light commercial use, using interlocking pieces that require no hammers, nails, or glue in its assembly.

Q

Quality Installations Incorporated
P.O. Box 271064
Salt Lake City, UT 84127
801-359-9516
Fax: 801-359-9519
E-mail: qiinc@vii.com
Installation of all major manufacturers' play structures and freestanding play equipment.

R

R-WIREworks, Inc.
P.O. Box 1118
Elmira, NY 14902
607-733-7169, ext. 26
Fax: 607-734-8859

Art easels, book displays, shelf storage units, and tote tray storage units.

Rally Racks
Division of Guard-Nut, Inc.
P.O. Box 1675
Santa Rosa, CA 95402
800-533-6423
Fax: 707-528-8085
E-mail: guardnut@GUARDNUT.COM
Bike racks.

Rashti & Rashti, The Babi Gift Co.
Division of HJ Rashti & Co., Inc.
112 West 34th Street, Suite 921
New York, NY 10120
212-594-2939
Fax: 212-594-9102
E-mail: rashtiny@emi.com

Nursery room accessories, including switchplate covers.

Recreation Technology, Inc.
P.O. Box 1048
Brick House Road
Dunkirk, MD 20754-1048
800-368-2573 or 301-855-5348
Fax: 410-257-7579

Freestanding commercial outdoor activity equipment.

Reed Brothers
Turner Station
Sebastopol, CA 95472
707-795-6261
Fax: 707-823-5311

Hand-carved residential furnishings.

Remploy Limited Furniture Group
Bruce Road, Swansea Industrial Estate
Fforestfach, Swansea SA5 4HY
United Kingdom
44-1792-560100
Fax: 44-1792-560167

Library furnishings available in England.

Rocky Duron & Associates, Inc.
2965 Congressman Lane
Dallas, TX 75220
800-875-5457 or 214-358-3455
Fax: 214-358-5713

Wood table-and-chair units in which chairs telescope from table on sliding rails. Detachment is optional.

RollEase, Inc.
200 Harvard Avenue
Stamford, CT 06902
800-552-5100 or 203-964-1573
Fax: 203-964-0513
E-mail: sales@rollease.com
Website: www.rollease.com

Window-covering cord tension devices (cordless).

Room Plus, Inc.
91 Michigan Avenue
Paterson, NJ 07503
800-766-6758 or 973-523-4600
Fax: 973-669-0781
Website: www.roomplus.com

Residential infant and juvenile/teen bedroom groups.

Royal Haeger Lamp Company
Contract Sales Office
P.O. Box 769
Westport, CT 06881
203-226-9920
Fax: 203-227-5631

Ceramic table lamp with sports theme.

Royal Seating Corporation
P.O. Box 753
Cameron, TX 76520
254-697-6421 or 254-697-4916
Fax: 254-697-4900

Nonwood tables, chairs, desks, and a variety of furnishings for the child care/early education and school environments.

Rugs by Vicki Simon
442 Post Street, Suite 302
San Francisco, CA 94102
415-576-0500
Fax: 415-576-0501

Custom-designed rugs.

Russ Berrie and Company, Inc.
111 Bauer Drive
Oakland, NJ 07436
800-631-8465 or 201-337-9000

In Canada:

Amram's
315 Attwell Drive
Etobicoke (Toronto), Ontario
Canada M9W 5C1

416-675-1040
Website: www.RussBerrie.com

Decorative accessories, including a wide variety of teddy bears.

S

Safari Ltd.
1400 NW 159th St.
P.O. Box 630685
Miami, FL 33163
800-554-5414 or 305-621-1000
Fax: 305-621-6894
Website: www.safariltd.com

Decorative accessories and posters.

Safe Guard Surfacing Corp.
P.O. Box 801
St. James, NY 11780
800-899-8703 or 516-862-1276
Fax: 516-862-2217
E-mail: safeguard@playsurface.com
Website: www.playsurface.com

Rubber seamless poured-in-place and tile playground surfacing.

SafeSpace Concepts, Inc.
1424 North Post Oak
Houston, TX 77055
800-622-4289
Fax: 713-956-6416
E-mail: safespace@aol.com
Website: www.safespaceconcepts.com

Indoor gross motor play equipment and soft play centers for infants and toddlers to 3 years old.

Sandy and Son Educational Supplies
1360 Cambridge Street
Cambridge, MA 02139
800-841-7529 or 617-491-6290
Fax: 617-491-6821

A full line of child care/early education furnishings, accessories, and supplies.

Sauder Manufacturing Company
930 W. Barre Road
Archbold, OH 43502-0230
800-537-1530 or 419-446-9384
Fax: 419-446-3697

The Kidz line features bentwood chairs and matching table.

Scandinavian Design, Inc.
347 Fifth Avenue, Suite 1009
New York, NY 10016
212-213-0009
Fax: 212-684-7931

Distributors of the Finnish lines of Jysky, child care/early education furnishings and Muurame, juvenile/teen bedroom groups.

Scholar Craft Products, Inc.
P.O. Box 170748
Birmingham, AL 35217
205-841-1922
Fax: 205-841-1992

Melamine and tubular steel school desks and chairs, nonwood and stackable chairs.

Scott Sign Systems, Inc.
7524 Commerce Place
Sarasota, FL 34243-5020

or

P.O. Box 1047
Tallevast, FL 34270-1047
800-237-9447 or 941-355-5171
Fax: 941-351-1787
E-mail: scottsigns@mindspring.com
Website: www.scottsign.com

ADA-compliant boys and girls restroom plaques.

SCS Interactive, Inc.
6260 Blimp Boulevard
Tillamook, OR 97141
408-378-7611

Fax: 408-378-5812
Website: www.scsinteractive.com

Large-scale interactive waterplay attractions.

Sico North America, Inc.
7525 Cahill Road
P.O. Box 1169
Minneapolis, MN 55440
800-328-6138 or 612-941-1700
Fax: 612-941-6688

Folding, nonwood tables (10 ft by 24 in), with attached seating.

Simo (USA), Inc.
142 Hamilton Avenue
Stamford, CT 06902
203-348-7466
Fax: 203-324-0380
E-mail: simo_perskaas@compuserve
　.com
Website: www.simostrollers.com

Residential high chairs and cribs.

Simplex International (PVT) Ltd.
328, Madapatha Road
Batakettara, Sri Lanka
94-1-614046
Fax: 94-1-614050
E-mail: simplex@slt.lk

A variety of accessories and furnishings.

SIS human factor technologies, inc.
55C Harvey Road
Londonderry, NH 03053
603-432-4495
Fax: 603-434-8456
E-mail: SIShft@aol.com

Computer furnishings.

Skools, Inc.
40 Fifth Avenue, Suite 15A
New York, NY 10011-8843
800-545-4474 or 212-674-1150

Fax: 212-674-2426
E-mail: skoolsinc@aol.com
Website: www.kinderlink.com

Features Kinderlink's chairs and interconnecting stools and a solid birch computer desk.

Skyline Design
2653 West Chicago Avenue
Chicago, IL 60622
773-278-4660
Fax: 773-278-3548
E-mail: kent.y@skydesign.com
Website: www.skydesign.com

Decorative elements sculptures, murals, and signage to create custom-designed environments.

Sof' Fall Incorporated
P.O. Box 667
Draper, UT 84020
800-523-8690
Fax: 888-763-3255
E-mail: soffall@nstep.net
Website: www.Sof-Fall.com

Engineered wood fiber playground surfacing.

Sof Surfaces, Inc.
1702 London Road
Sarnia, Ontario
Canada N7T 7H2
800-263-2363
Fax: 519-542-5977
E-mail: altinfo@sofsurfaces.com
Website: www.sofsurfaces.com

Rubber poured-in-place and tile playground surfacing.

Spring Street Studio, Inc.
P.O. Box 19317
Sarasota, FL 34276
941-922-3452
Fax: 941-922-5608

Faux fur fabrics and several lines of wallcoverings.

Starplast
230 Fifth Ave., Suite #1805
New York, NY 10001
212-679-2010
Fax: 212-679-2008
E-mail: strplst@mail.idt.net
Website: www.starplast-crown.com

*Trash containers designed as a croco-
dile and an ice cream cone.*

The Step2 Company
10010 Aurora-Hudson Road
P.O. Box 2412
Streetsboro, OH 44241-0412
330-656-0440
Fax: 330-655-9685

*A variety of accessories, furnishings,
and residential play structures.*

Stevens Industries
704 W. Main St.
Teutopolis, IL 62467
800-500-5437 or 217-857-6411
Fax: 217-857-9144

*Commercial Tot Mate line includes
sinks with attached changing tables, including ADA-compliant models. Other
furnishings for the child care/early education environment are also available. Residential juvenile/teen bedroom
groups available in the I.D. Kids line.*

Straight Line Designs, Inc.
1000 Parker St.
Vancouver, British Columbia
Canada V6A 2H2
604-251-9669
Fax: 604-251-1676
E-mail: sld@axion.net
Website: www.straightlinedesigns
   .com

*Large-scale decorative elements. Lim-
ited edition and custom-designed commercial and residential furnishings.*

Sumersault Ltd.
P.O. Box 269
Scarsdale, NY 10583
800-232-3006 or 201-768-7890
Fax: 201-768-4909
Website: Sumersault.com

Residential bed and crib bedding.

Surface America, Inc.
P.O. Box 157
Williamsville, NY 14231
800-999-0555 or 716-632-8413
Fax: 716-632-8324
E-mail: surface@surfaceamerica
Website: www.surfam.com

*Rubber seamless poured-in-place and
tile playground surfacing, and shock-
absorbing turf.*

Surving Studios
17 Millsburg Rd.
Middletown, NY 10940
800-768-4954 or 914-355-1430
Fax: 914-355-1517
E-mail: surving@warwick.net

Wall tiles.

T

Takara Belmont
One Belmont Drive
Somerset, NJ 08873
800-526-3847 ext. 58
Fax: 732-469-9430

*Kid's World salon chairs with cast alu-
minum animal bodies for seats.*

Taos Drums
P.O. Box 1916
Taos, NM 87571
800-424-3786
Fax: 505-758-9844

*Authentic Native American log drums
as decorative accessories.*

Techline, a product of Marshall Erdman & Associates
500 South Division Street
Waunakee, WI 53597
800-356-8400
Fax: 608-849-8371
E-mail: techline@mailbag.com
Website: www.techline-furn.com

Residential juvenile/teen bedroom groups.

Tennek Sports Surfaces, Inc.
460 Park County Rd. 43, Suite 2
Bailey, CO 80421
800-845-6724 or 303-838-0922
Fax: 303-838-0924

Rubber tile playground safety surfacing.

Texwood Furniture Company
P.O. Box 431
Taylor, TX 76574-0431
888-878-0000
Fax: 512-352-3084
E-mail: info@texwood.com

Library furnishings and child care/early education furnishings.

Thibaut Wallcoverings & Fabrics
480 Frelinghuysen Avenue
Newark, NJ 07114
800-823-0704 or 973-643-1118
Fax: 973-643-3133

Residential fabrics, wallcoverings, and wall borders.

Things From Bell
75 Mill St.
P.O. Box 513
Colchester, CT 06415-0513
800-543-1458
Fax: 800-566-6678

A variety of outdoor play equipment and indoor ball pits.

This End Up Furniture Company
1309 Exchange Alley
Richmond, VA 23219
800-627-5161
Fax: 804-321-7338

Residential juvenile/teen bedroom groups and bedding.

Thonet
403 Meacham Road
P.O. Box 5909
Statesville, NC 28677
800-551-6702 or 704-878-2222
Fax: 704-873-6124
E-mail: service@thonet.com

Primaries line features molded-plywood chairs, stools, and tables. Chairs have optional foam-padded upholstered seat.

Timbertec, Inc.
P.O. Box 812
Kentville, Nova Scotia
Canada B4N 4H8
902-679-1020
Fax: 902-679-1959

Residential play structures.

Tracers Furniture, Inc.
30 Warren Place
Mt. Vernon, NY 10550
914-668-9372
Fax: 914-668-9368
E-mail: tracersjuv@worldnet.att.net

Residential infant and juvenile/teen bedroom groups.

U

Union City Chair Company
18 Market Street
Union City, PA 16438
800-822-4247 or 814-438-3878
Fax: 814-438-7536
Website: www.ncinter.net/~ucchair

A variety of residential furnishings.

University Loft Company
433 E. Washington St.
Indianapolis, IN 46204
317-631-5433
Fax: 317-631-1516

Residence living furnishings.

U.S. Playgrounds, Inc.
39307 Auburn/Enumclaw Road
Auburn, WA 98092
800-326-7529 or 253-735-2003
Fax: 253-735-6016 or 509-882-5010

Commercial contained nonwood and wood play structures. Residential play structures.

USG Interiors, Inc.
P.O. Box 4470
Chicago, IL 60680-4124
800-874-4968
Fax: 312-606-4093
Website: www.usg.com

Lay-in ceiling tiles. Stock designs include pawprints, aquarium fish, a train, animals, and others. Custom designs are also available.

V

Virco Manufacturing Company
2027 Harpers Way
Torrance, CA 90501
800-448-4726
Fax: 800-258-7367

or

Highway 65, South
Conway, AR 72032
800-448-4726
Fax: 800-396-8232
Website: www.virco-mfg.com

A commercial line of nonwood chairs and tables and storage units for child care/early education environments.

Visions Innovated Products, Inc. (Nebcoat products)
P.O. Box 3160
McAlester, OK 74502
800-505-5101 or 918-426-5100
Fax: 918-426-5924
E-mail: webcoat@webcoat.com
Website: www.webcoat.com

Plastisol-coated site furnishings.

Vitricon, Inc.
65 Davids Drive
Hauppauge, NY 11788
800-777-6596 or 516-231-1300
Fax: 516-231-1329

Seamless rubber playground surfacing.

W

Watercolors, Inc.
Garrison on Hudson
New York, NY 10524
914-424-3327

Bathroom accessories, sinks, and faucets in bright primary colors.

Waterplay by LA Systems
Box 909
Penticton, British Columbia
Canada V2A 7G1
250-493-1693
Fax: 250-493-1675
E-mail: admin@waterplay.com
Website: waterplay.com

Large-scale water playground equipment.

Wehrfritz
c/o t.c. timber
Habermaass Corporation
P.O. Box 42
4407 Jordan Road
Skaneateles, NY 13152

800-468-6873
Fax: 315-685-3792

A full line of German furnishings, equipment, supplies, and outdoor play equipment for child care/early education environments.

West Coast Netting, Inc.
5075 Flightline Dr.
Kingman, AZ 86401
800-854-5741 or 520-692-1144
Fax: 520-692-1501

Netting for use on play structures.

Whimsies, Inc.
33 El Paso Drive
P.O. Box 4249
Alamogordo, NM 88311-4249
800-437-3688
Fax: 505-437-4191

Residential nursing cradle that converts to a toddler's love seat.

White Eagle
P.O. Box 40
Willits, CA 95490
800-959-5811 or 707-459-0311
Fax: 707-459-6602
E-mail: whiteeagle@zapcom.net
Website: WhiteEagleRainbows.com

Celestialights—holographic 3-D mobiles and crystalites-holographic spiral mobiles.

Whitewater West Industries Ltd.
6700 McMillan Way
Richmond, British Columbia
Canada V6W IJ7
604-273-1068
Fax: 604-273-4518
E-mail: whitewater@whitewaterwest
.com

Designers and planners of water park and large-scale water play equipment.

Whitney Bros. Co.
P.O. Box 644
Keene, NH 03431
800-225-5381
Website: www.whitneybros.com

A complete line of furnishings for the child care/early education environments, including the Whitco Storage Wall System.

Wild Zoo Design
63025 O.B. Riley Road, #9
Bend, OR 97701
888-543-8588 or 541-388-2443
Fax: 541-388-7317
E-mail: wildzoo@teleport.com

A variety of residential furnishings, including "animal" beds.

Wildwood Playgrounds, Ltd.
3707 NE Columbia Blvd.
Portland, OR 97211
800-875-7529 or 503-288-5797
Fax: 503-288-7908

Custom-designed, highly accessible play structures. Standard commercial wood and nonwood play structures are also available.

Wind & Weather
P.O. Box 2320
Mendocino, CA 95460
800-922-9463
E-mail: customerservice
@windandweather.com
Website: www.windandweather.com

Outdoor sculptures.

Winn Devon Art Group, Ltd.
6015 Sixth Avenue South
Seattle, WA 98108
206-763-9544
Fax: 206-762-1389

Posters and prints.

Wolf Gordon, Inc.
33-00 47th Avenue
Long Island City, NY 11101-2430
718-361-6611
Fax: 718-361-1090
E-mail: info@wolf-gordon.com
Website: www.wolf-gordon.com

Commercial wallcoverings and wall borders.

Wonder Works of America
Brooklyn Navy Yard
Building 292, Suite 402
Brooklyn, NY 11205
800-338-1029 or 718-858-4000
Fax: 718-855-3522

Kids' Play line features brightly colored vinyl floor tile in four collections: Sprinkles, Cow 'N Moon, Tik Tak Toe, and Animal Krackers.

The Wood Works
264 Brookfield Road
Charlton, MA 01507
508-248-3770

Residential play structures.

Woodfold-Marco Mfg., Inc.
P.O. Box 346
Forest Grove, OR 97116-0346
503-357-7181
Fax: 800-257-9282
E-mail: info@woodfold.com
Website: www.woodfold.com

Accordion doors with option of application of decorative murals or wallcoverings to panels.

Woodlawn Playcenters
13961 Woodlawn Hills
Cedar Springs, MI 49319
616-696-9600
Fax: 616-696-9935
Website: www.playcenters.com

Residential play structures.

Woodplay
2101 Harrod St.
Raleigh, NC 27604
800-982-1822 or 919-875-4499
Fax: 919-875-4264
Website: www.woodplay.com

Residential play structures.

ADDITIONAL CHILD DEVELOPMENT AND RESOURCE INFORMATION

CHAPTER 8

Development of Abilities and Perceptions in Young Children: A Brief Overview

Whereas the anthropometric charts in the beginning of this book document the physical growth of a child's body, the following information is meant to serve as a brief overview of the development of abilities and perceptions of children at various ages up to adolescence. Obviously, each child is a unique individual, and developmental progress will occur at different times. Some children will progress more quickly in one area and not as quickly in another area. There will also be variations among cultures. Different environments tend to strongly impact development in all areas. It is hoped that the following information, although very generalized, will serve as an initial resource that directs the designer toward a better understanding of the stages of capabilities, social skills, and perceptions of children at various ages.

Birth to 3 months	Visually follows moving objects.
	Reaches toward but misses objects.
	Grasps rattles.
	Cannot discern fine details of objects.
	Shows a visual preference for the human face at close range.
	Begins to smile.
	Listens to voices and coos.
	Sustains social contact.
	Listens to music.
3–6 months	Reaches and grasps objects and brings them to mouth.
	Sits with support.
	Laughs out loud.
	Shows displeasure if social contact is broken.
	Has difficulty tolerating separation from mother or primary caregiver.
	Can distinguish color in a manner similar to an adult's.
	Perceives distances as being close or far.
6–9 months	Rolls over.
	Transfers objects from hand to hand.

Sits alone.
Babbles.
Enjoys looking in mirror.

9–12 months   Crawls.
Pulls to standing position.
Stands alone.
Walks alone.
Responds to name.
Plays peek-a-boo and pat-a-cake.
Waves bye-bye.
Repeats consonant sounds (mama, dada).

12–15 months   Crawls up stairs.
Descends stairs by crawling backward or sliding while in seated position.
Plays "catch the ball" and "hide and seek."
Indicates desires and needs by pointing.
Gives hugs.
Can identify location of sounds.
Can say a few words.
Can follow simple commands.
Can name simple objects (e.g., ball, dog, and so forth).

15–18 months   Feeds self.
Runs stiffly.
Sits on small chair.
Walks up stairs with one hand held.
Explores everything (e.g., drawers, wastebaskets, and so forth).
Seeks help when in trouble.
May complain when wet or soiled.
Imitates scribbling.
Knows up to 50 words.
Names pictures.
Identifies one or more parts of the body.

18–21 months   Can jump in place.
Begins running.
Walks up a few stairs alone.
Walks down stairs with help.

2 years   Runs well.
Walks a greater distance, but at a slow pace.
Walks up and down stairs, unaided, one step at a time.
Opens doors.
Climbs on furniture.
Likes to fill, dump, and throw.
Sand, rock, and water play are enjoyed.

Dramatic play (imitating adult roles) begins.

Can use a variety of simple outdoor play equipment.

Actively works to maintain a close proximity [20 ft (6 m)] to mother or primary caregiver.

Enjoys being with other children and will play alongside them, but not with them (parallel play).

Listens to stories with pictures.

Vision is comparable to an adult's.

Develops spatial awareness (e.g., inside/outside, top/bottom, front/back, and so forth).

Puts three words together (noun, verb, subject).

3 years
Rides tricycles.

Washes hands.

Can jump a distance of 15 to 24 in (38.1 to 60.1 cm).

Climbs stairs alternating feet.

Can stand momentarily on one foot.

Combines playthings (sand and water, miniature cars and blocks).

Accepting of temporary absence of mother or primary caregiver when familiar people are present.

Plays in small groups of two to three children for brief periods of time.

Increasingly able to wait for a play turn.

Will put toys away with some supervision.

Helps in dressing.

Can count up to three objects.

Grammar is close to adult speech.

4 years
Can hop on one foot.

Can jump a distance of 24 to 33 in (61 to 83.8 cm).

Goes down stairs alternating feet, if supported.

Throws ball overhand.

Can use scissors to cut out pictures.

Climbs well.

Performs stunts.

Plays in small groups for longer periods of time.

Can go to toilet alone.

Can tell a story.

5 years
Skips.

Can make a running jump of 28 to 38 in (71.1 to 96.5 cm).

Can walk down stairs alternating feet, unsupported.

Requires less intense supervision.

Can run and climb with sureness.

Shows interest in roller skates.

Builds complicated three-dimensional structures that combine several materials.

Extensive role playing.
Recognizes specific landmarks, but does not understand geographic relationships between them.
Play groups increase to five and six and will last longer.
Friendships are stronger.
Dresses and undresses without help.
Thinks that own point of view is the only one.

6–8 years

Roller skates.
Rides bicycles.
Swims.
Can play games requiring considerable motor coordination, such as hopscotch and football.
Can play games with rules, such as board games and card games.
Can hop into small squares with accuracy.
Plays organized games.
Understands geographic relationships of landmarks.
Begins collections of various types.
Plays cooperatively with others.
Understands that others may have differing points of view.

8–10 years

Can jump vertically 8½ to 10 in (21.6 to 25.4 cm).
Can throw a ball between 40 and 70 ft (12.2 and 21.3 m).
Can run approximately 17 ft (5.2 m) per second.

10–12 years

Can complete a standing broad jump between 4½ and 5 ft (1.4 and 1.5 m).
Standing high jump of 3 ft (91.4 cm) is possible.
Girls become temporarily taller than boys.
Can take into account several different points of view.

CHAPTER 9

Organizations and Bibliographical Information Related to Designing Environments for Children

The following lists contain numerous organizations and references that may be of help to the designer as he or she begins to design environments for children. Along with a category that lists general resources that address several issues of designing for children, the information is divided into the various project types that might be encountered: accessibility and special needs, child care and preschool, health care, museum, outdoor play, and schools. Creating a complete bibliography on books and articles that have been written on the design of children's environments would easily be a book within itself. Sifting through numerous pages of references may defeat the well-intentioned designer to the point of giving up on research, especially when faced with a quickly approaching deadline. Therefore, in an effort to aid and not overwhelm the information-gathering process, only the most comprehensive and helpful resources have been listed.

General Design Resources

Children's Environments Review (series). New York: Children's Environments Research Group at The Graduate School and University Center of the City University of New York.

Weinstein, C. S., and T. G. David (eds.). *Spaces for Children: The Built Environment and Child Development.* New York: Plenum Press, 1987.

For a comprehensive bibliography of resources, refer to:

Moore, Gary T., Carol G. Lane, and Lisa Lindberg. *Bibliography on Children and the Physical Environment.* Milwaukee, WI: The School of Architecture and Urban Planning, University of Wisconsin, 1979.

Accessibility and Special Needs Design

RESOURCE ORGANIZATIONS

U.S. Architectural and Transportation Barriers Compliance Board
1331 F Street, NW, Suite 1000
Washington, D.C. 20004-1111
800-872-2253 Ext. 27 or 202-272-5434 Ext. 27
800-993-2822 or 202-272-5449 (TTY)

The Center for Accessible Housing
School of Design
North Carolina State University
P.O. Box 8613
Raleigh, NC 27695-8613
800-647-6777 or 919-515-3082
Fax: 919-515-3023
E-mail: cud@ncsu.edu
Website: www.design.ncsu.edu/cud

RESOURCES FOR ACCESSIBLE DESIGN FOR CHILDREN

Architectural and Transportation Barriers Compliance Board. *Americans with Disabilities Act (ADA) Accessibility Guidelines for Buildings and Facilities; Building Elements Designed for Children's Use.* Washington, D.C.: Architectural and Transportation Barriers Compliance Board, 1998.

Center for Accessible Housing. *Accessibility Standards for Children's Environments: Summary of the Final Technical Report Prepared for The Architectural and Transportation Barriers Compliance Board.* Raleigh, NC: Center for Accessible Housing, North Carolina State University, 1992.

Cohen, U., Jeffrey Beer, Elizabeth Kidera, and Wendy Golden. *Mainstreaming the Handicapped: A Design Guide.* Milwaukee, WI: Center for Architecture and Urban Planning Research, University of Wisconsin—Milwaukee, 1979.

Moore, G. T., and U. Cohen. *Designing Environments for Handicapped Children.* New York: Educational Facilities Laboratories, 1979.

Olds, A. R. "Designing Classrooms for Children with Special Needs." In *Special Education and Development: Perspectives on Young Children with Special Needs,* S. Meisels (ed.). Baltimore, MD: University Park Press, 1979.

Child Care and Preschool Design

RESOURCE ORGANIZATIONS

National Association for the Education of Young Children (NAEYC)
1509 16th Street, NW
Washington, D.C. 20036
800-424-2460 or 202-232-8777
Fax: 202-328-1846
E-mail: naeyc@naeyc.org
Website: www.naeyc.org

In the appendix are listed the state offices of each state that are responsible for the licensing of child care facilities within that state. Because the majority of state regulations address in some way the physical requirements of the facility, it is helpful for the designer to become aware of these requirements at the start of the design process.

RESOURCES FOR THE DESIGN OF CHILD CARE AND PRESCHOOL FACILITIES

Dudek, Mark. *Kindergarten Architecture: Space for the Imagination.* London: E & FW Spon, 1996.

Moore, G. T., C. G. Lane, A. B. Hill, U. Cohen, and T. McGinty. *Recommendations for Child Care Centers.* Milwaukee, WI: Center for Architecture and Urban Planning Research, University of Wisconsin—Milwaukee, 1994.

For a comprehensive bibliography, refer to:

Moore, Gary T. (ed.). *Comprehensive Bibliography on Child Care and Preschool Design.* Washington, D.C.: American Institute of Architects; Milwaukee, WI: Center for Architecture and Urban Planning Research, University of Wisconsin—Milwaukee, 1994.

Health Care Design

RESOURCE ORGANIZATION

Association for the Care of Children's Health (ACCH)
19 Mantua Road
Mt. Royal, NJ 08061
609-224-1742
609-423-3420
E-mail: acchhq@talley.com
Website: look.net/acch

RESOURCES FOR THE DESIGN OF HEALTH CARE FACILITIES FOR CHILDREN

Malkin, Jain. *Hospital Interior Architecture.* New York: Van Nostrand Reinhold, 1992.

Olds, Anita R. "Psychological Considerations in Humanizing the Physical Environment of Pediatric Outpatient and Hospital Settings." In *Psychosocial Aspects of Pediatric Care,* E. Gellert (ed.), pp. 111–131. New York: Grune & Stratton, 1980.

Shepley, M., M. Fournier, and K. Ward. *Healthcare Environments for Children and Families.* Dubuque, IA: Kendall/Hunt Publishing, 1998.

For a complete bibliography on the design of health care facilities for children, see:

Olds, A., and P. Daniel. *Child Health Care Facilities: Design Guidelines—Literature Outline.* Bethesda, MD: The Association for the Care of Children's Health, 1987.

Museum Design

RESOURCE ORGANIZATION

Association of Youth Museums
1300 L St., NW, Suite 975
Washington, D.C. 20005
202-898-1080
Fax: 202-898-1086
E-mail: aymdc@aol.com
Website: www.aym.org/

RESOURCES FOR THE DESIGN OF CHILDREN'S MUSEUMS

Cohen, U., and R. McMurtry. *Museums and Children: A Design Guide.* Milwaukee, WI: University of Wisconsin—Milwaukee, Center for Architecture and Urban Planning Research, 1985.

Maher, Mary (ed.). *Collective Vision: Starting and Sustaining a Children's Museum.* Washington, D.C.: American Youth Museums, 1997.

Outdoor Play Design

RESOURCES FOR THE DESIGN OF CHILDREN'S OUTDOOR PLAY ENVIRONMENTS

Cohen, U., A. B. Hill, C. G. Lane, T. McGinty, and G. T. Moore. *Recommendations for Child Play Areas.* Milwaukee, WI: University of Wisconsin—Milwaukee, Center for Architecture and Urban Planning Research, 1991.

Esbensen, S. B. *The Early Childhood Playground: An Outdoor Classroom.* Ypsilanti, MI: High Scope Press, 1987.

Frost, J. L., and B. Klein. *Children's Play and Playgrounds.* Melrose, MA: Allyn & Bacon, 1991.

Moore, R. C. *Plants for Play: A Planting Guide for Children's Play Environments.* Berkeley, CA: MIG Communications, 1993.

Moore, R. C., S. M. Goltsman, and D. S. Iacofano. *Play for All Guidelines: Planning, Design and Management of Outdoor Play Settings for All Children,* 2nd ed. Berkeley, CA: MIG Communications, 1992.

Senda, Mitsuru. *Design of Children's Play Environments.* New York: McGraw-Hill, 1992.

School Design

RESOURCES FOR THE DESIGN OF SCHOOL FACILITIES

Lackney, Jeffrey A. *Educational Facilities: The Impact and Role of the Physical Environment of the School in Teaching, Learning, and Educational Outcomes.* Milwaukee, WI: University of Wisconsin—Milwaukee, Center for Architecture and Urban Planning Research, 1994.

Moore, Gary T., and Jeffrey A. Lackney. *Educational Facilities: Analysis & Design Patterns.* Milwaukee, WI: University of Wisconsin—Milwaukee, Center for Architecture and Urban Planning Research, 1994.

STATE AGENCIES RESPONSIBLE FOR THE LICENSING OF CHILD CARE CENTERS

Alabama

Adult, Child, and Family Services Division
Department of Human Resources
50 Ripley St.
Montgomery, AL 36130-4000
334-242-9500
Fax: 334-242-0939

Alaska

Division of Family and Youth Services
Department of Health and Social Services
P.O. Box 110630
Juneau, AK 99811-0630
907-465-2817
Fax: 907-465-3190

Arizona

Administration for Children, Youth, and Families
Division of Children and Family Services
Site Code 940A
P.O. Box 6123
Phoenix, AZ 85005
602-542-2277
Fax: 602-542-3330

Arkansas

Child Care Licensing Unit
Division of Children and Family Services
P.O. Box 1437, Slot #720
Little Rock, AR 72203-1437
501-682-8590
Fax: 501-682-8666

California

Community Care Licensing Division
Department of Social Services
744 P St., Mail Stop 17-17
Sacramento, CA 95814
946-657-2346
Fax: 916-657-3783

Colorado

Division of Child Care
Office of Children, Youth, and Families Services
1575 Sherman St., First Floor
Denver, CO 80203-1714
303-866-6468
Fax: 303-866-4453

Connecticut

Community Nursing/Day Care
Department of Public Health
410 Capitol Ave.
Hartford, CT 06134-0308
860-509-8000
Fax: 860-509-7111

Delaware

Office of Child Care Licensing
Division of Family Services
Department of Services for Children, Youth, and Their Families
Delaware Youth and Family Center
1825 Faulkland Rd.
Wilmington, DE 19805
302-892-5800
Fax: 302-633-2652

District of Columbia

Service Facility Regulation Administration
Consumer and Regulatory Affairs
Department of Health
614 H St., NW, Rm. 1003
Washington, DC 20001
202-727-7190
Fax: 202-645-0526

Florida

Family Safety and Preservation Program Office
Department of Children and Families
2811 Industrial Plaza
Tallahassee, FL 32301
850-488-4900
Fax: 850-488-9584

Georgia

Day Care Licensing Section
Office of Regulatory Services
Department of Human Resources
2 Peachtree St., 20th Floor
Atlanta, GA 30303
404-657-5701
Fax: 404-657-5708

Guam

Bureau of Social Services Administrator
Government of Guam
P.O. Box 2816
Agana, GU 96932
011 (671) 475-2607
Fax: 011 (671) 472-6649

Hawaii

Social Services Division
Department of Human Services
P.O. Box 339
Honolulu, HI 96809
808-586-5701
Fax: 808-586-5700

Idaho

Bureau of Family and Children's Services
Division of Family and Community Services
Department of Health and Welfare
P.O. Box 83720
Boise, ID 83720-0036
208-334-5691
Fax: 208-334-6699

Illinois

Division of Child Protection
Department of Children and Family Services
406 East Monroe St., Station #60
Springfield, IL 62701-1498
217-785-2688
Fax: 217-524-3347

Indiana

Family Protection and Preservation Bureau
Division of Family and Children
Family and Social Services Administration
W364 Government Center South
402 West Washington St.
Indianapolis, IN 46207-7083
317-232-4420
Fax: 317-232-4436

Iowa

Division of Adult, Children, and Family Services
Department of Human Services
Hoover Building, Fifth Floor
Des Moines, IA 50319-0114
515-281-5521
Fax: 515-281-4597

Kansas

Child Day Care Services
Commission on Income Maintenance/Employment Preparation Services
Docking State Office Building, Room 651-W
915 SW Harrison
Topeka, KS 66612-1570
785-296-3374
Fax: 785-296-0146

Kentucky

Division of Licensing and Regulations
Office of the Inspector General Cabinet for Health Services
275 East Main St., Fourth Floor
Frankfort, KY 40621
502-564-2800
Fax: 502-564-6546

Louisiana

Bureau of Licensing
Department of Social Services
P.O. Box 3078
Baton Rouge, LA 70821
225-922-0015
Fax: 225-922-0014

Maine

Division of Child Care and Licensing
Bureau of Child and Family Services
Department of Human Services
11 State House Station
Augusta, ME 04333
207-287-5060
Fax: 207-287-5282

Maryland

Licensing
Child Care Administration
Department of Human Resources
Saratoga State Center
311 West Saratoga St.
Baltimore, MD 21201
410-767-7810
Fax: 410-333-8699

Massachusetts

Office of Child Care Services
1 Ashburton Place, Room 1111
Boston, MA 02108
617-727-8900
Fax: 617-626-2028

Michigan

Child Care Licensing
Bureau of Regulatory Services
Department of Consumer and Industry Services
P.O. Box 30650
Lansing, MI 48909-8150
517-373-6614
Fax: 517-335-6121

Minnesota

Licensing Division
Department of Human Services
444 Lafayette Rd.
St. Paul, MN 55155-3842
651-296-6117
Fax: 651-296-6244

Mississippi

Division of Family and Children's Services
Department of Human Services
750 North State St.
Jackson, MS 39202
601-359-4999
Fax: 601-359-4363

Missouri

Child Care Licensing
Child Care Unit
Department of Health
P.O. Box 570
Jefferson City, MO 65102-0570
573-751-6001
Fax: 573-526-5345

Montana

Protection/Intervention/Treatment Services
Program Management Bureau
Department of Public Health and Human Services
P.O. Box 8005
Helena, MT 59604-8005
406-444-5906
Fax: 406-444-5956

Nebraska

Child Care
Department of Health and Human Services
301 Centennial Mall, South
P.O. Box 95044
Lincoln, NE 68502-5044
402-471-9431
Fax: 402-471-7763

Nevada

Division of Child and Family Services
711 East Fifth St.
Carson City, NV 89710
702-687-5982
Fax: 702-687-4722

New Hampshire

Licensing and Regulation
Office of Program Support
Department of Health and Human Services
6 Hazen Dr.
Concord, NH 03301-6527
603-271-5069
Fax: 603-271-5590

New Jersey

Bureau of Licensing
Division of Youth and Family Services
CN 717
Trenton, NJ 08625-0717
609-292-1018
Fax: 609-984-0507

New Mexico

Child Care Licensing Bureau
Prevention and Intervention Division
Children, Youth, and Families Department
P.O. Drawer 5160
Santa Fe, NM 87502-5160
505-827-7687
Fax: 505-827-9978

New York

Division of Services and Community Development
Department of Social Services
40 North Pearl St.
Albany, NY 12243
518-474-9428
Fax: 518-474-1842

North Carolina

Interstate Services Team
Division of Social Services
325 North Salisbury St.
Raleigh, NC 27603
919-733-4319
Fax: 919-733-0023

North Dakota

Children and Family Services Division
Department of Human Services
State Capitol—Judicial Wing
600 East Boulevard Ave.
Bismarck, ND 58505
701-328-2316
Fax: 701-328-3538

Ohio

Bureau of Child Care
Department of Human Services
30 East Broad St., 32nd Floor
Columbus, OH 43266-0423
614-466-3822
Fax: 614-728-6803

Oklahoma

Office of Child Care
Children and Family Services Division
Department of Human Services
4545 North Lincoln Blvd., Suite 100
Oklahoma City, OK 73105
800-347-2276 or 405-521-3561
Fax: 405-521-0391

Oregon

Licensing/Registration
Child Care Division
Employment Department
875 Union St., NE
Salem, OR 97311
503-378-3178
Fax: 503-378-5417

Pennsylvania

Bureau of Child Day Care Services
Office of Children, Youth, and Families
Bertolino Building, Fourth Floor
1401 North Seventh St.
Harrisburg, PA 17102
717-787-8691
Fax: 717-787-1529

Puerto Rico

Licensing Office
Department of the Family
P.O. Box 11398
San Juan, PR 00910
787-724-0767
Fax: 787-723-1223

Rhode Island

Program Development, Contracts, and Standards
Division of Community Resources
Department of Children, Youth, and Families
610 Mount Pleasant Ave.
Providence, RI 02908-1935
401-457-4550
Fax: 401-457-5388

South Carolina

Child Day Care Licensing and Regulatory Services
Office of Program Policy and Oversight
P.O. Box 1520
Columbia, SC 29202-1520
803-734-5740
Fax: 803-734-6093

South Dakota

Child Protection Services
Department of Social Services
700 Governors Dr.
Pierre, SD 57501
605-773-3227
Fax: 605-777-6834

Tennessee

Social Services
Department of Children's Services
Cordell Hull Building, Eighth Floor
436 Sixth Ave., North
Nashville, TN 37243
615-741-9699
Fax: 615-532-8079

Texas

Child Care Licensing
Department of Protective and Regulatory Services, Mail Code E-550
P.O. Box 149030
Austin, TX 78714-9030
512-438-3269
Fax: 512-438-3848

Utah

Bureau of Health Facilities Licensure
Department of Health
P.O. Box 142851
Salt Lake City, UT 84114-2851
801-538-6101
Fax: 801-538-6306

Vermont

Interstate Compact Correspondent
Division of Social Services
Department of Social and Rehabilitation Services
Agency of Human Services
103 South Main St.
Waterbury, VT 05671-1601
802-241-3110
Fax: 802-241-1220

Virginia

Children's Programs
Division of Licensing
Department of Social Services
730 East Broad St.
Richmond, VA 23219-1849
804-692-1760
Fax: 804-692-2370

Virgin Islands (U.S.)

Division of Children, Youth, and Families
Department of Human Services
Government of the Virgin Islands
3011 Golden Rock
Christiansted, Saint Croix, VI 00820-4355
340-773-2323
Fax: 340-773-6121

Washington

Division of Licensed Resources
Children's Services Administration
Department of Social and Health Services
P.O. Box 45700
Olympia, WA 98504-5700
360-902-8038
Fax: 360-902-7903

West Virginia

Licensing/Day Care
Office of Social Services
Bureau for Children and Families
Building 6, Room 850, State Capital Complex
Charleston, WV 25305
304-558-7980
Fax: 304-558-8800

Wisconsin

Bureau of Programs and Policies
Division of Children and Family Services
Department of Health and Family Services
1 West Wilson St., Rm. 465
P.O. Box 8916
Madison, WI 53708-8916
608-266-6799
Fax: 608-264-6750

Wyoming

Community Services
Department of Family Services
Hathaway Building, Third Floor
2300 Capital Ave.
Cheyenne, WY 82002-0490
307-777-5366
Fax: 307-777-3659

GAME, FIELD, AND COURT DIMENSIONS

APPENDIX B

Following are diagrams of the areas required by popular games and sports that are often incorporated into the designs of children's areas. These diagrams are to be used during the initial planning stages of a project. In the cases of fields and courts to be used for regulation play, the athletic organization governing the use of the facility should be contacted for current regulations and final layouts. When available, possible variations in court or field sizes according to age have been given.

Badminton

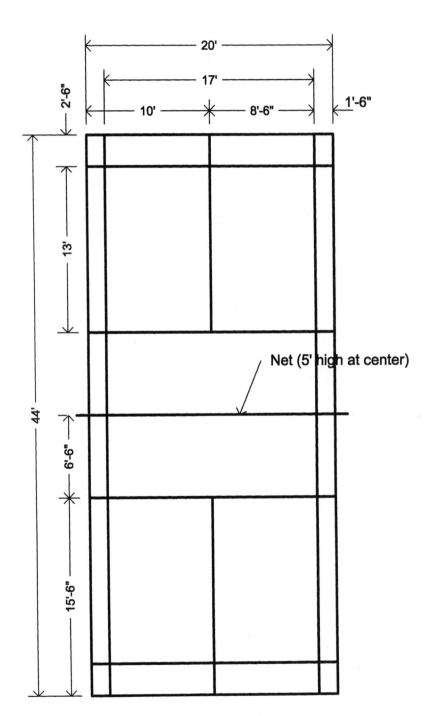

Baseball—60-ft Base Lines

This field is appropriate for ages 5 to 12 and for T-ball.

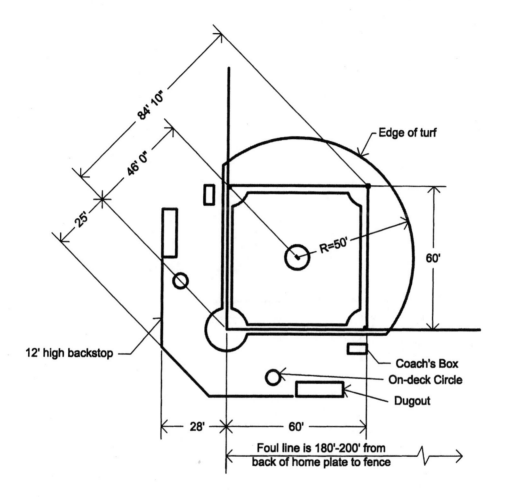

84' 10"

46' 0"

25'

Edge of turf

R=50'

60'

12' high backstop

Coach's Box

On-deck Circle

Dugout

28'

60'

Foul line is 180'-200' from
back of home plate to fence

Baseball—80-ft Base Lines

This field is appropriate for ages 13 and 14.

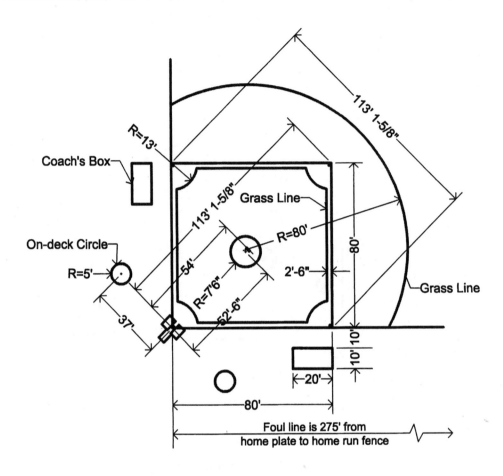

Baseball—90-ft Base Lines

This field is appropriate for ages 15 and up.

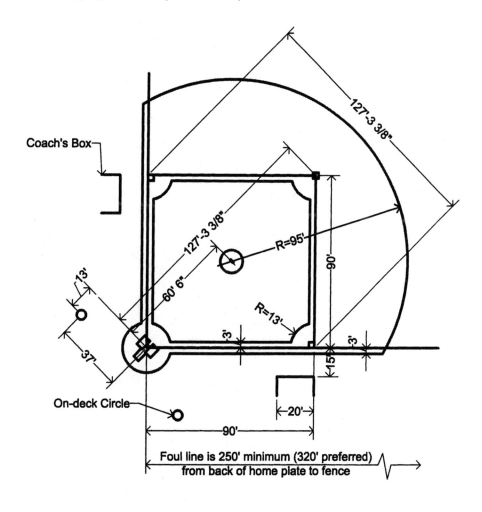

Coach's Box

127'-3 3/8"

127'-3 3/8"

R=95'

60' 6"

13'

R=13'

90'

3'

3'

15'

37'

On-deck Circle

20'

90'

Foul line is 250' minimum (320' preferred)
from back of home plate to fence

Basketball

For younger children, lower goals (8 to 9 ft high) and shorter free throw distances are desirable.

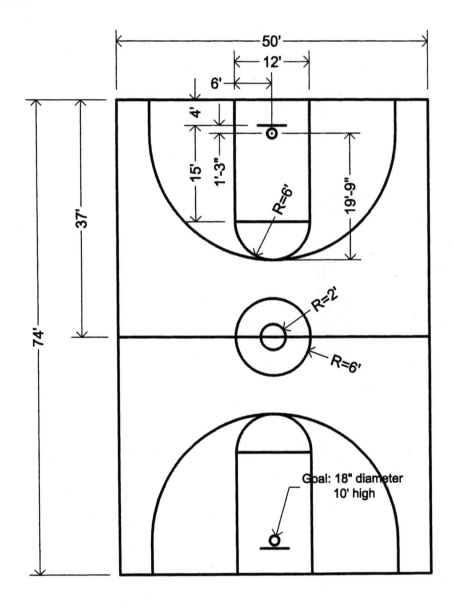

Billiards (Pool)

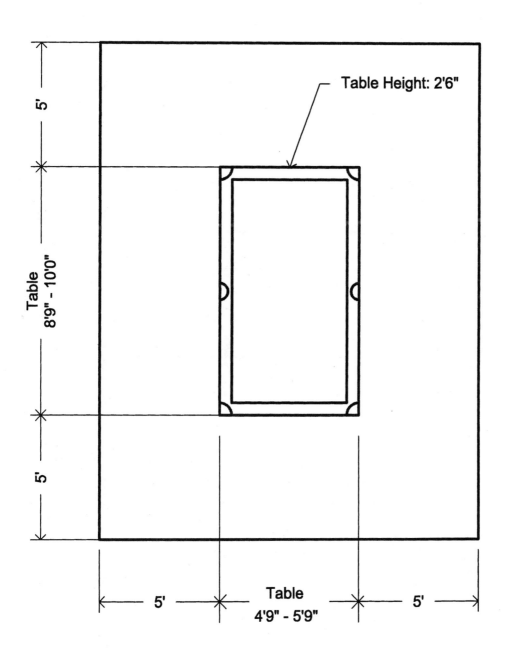

Croquet

See Lawn Croquet.

Field Hockey

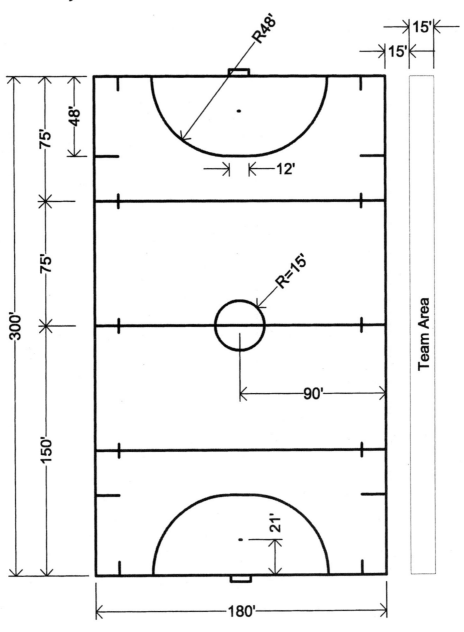

Flag Football

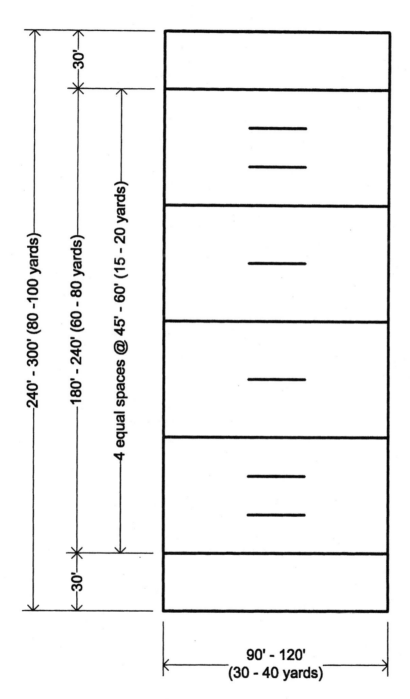

240' - 300' (80 -100 yards)

30'

180' - 240' (60 - 80 yards)

4 equal spaces @ 45' - 60' (15 - 20 yards)

30'

90' - 120'
(30 - 40 yards)

Football

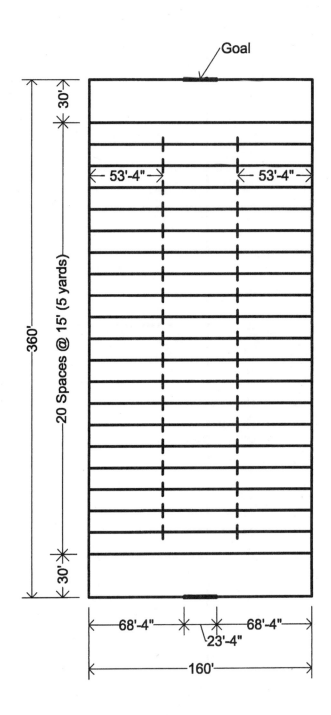

Four Square

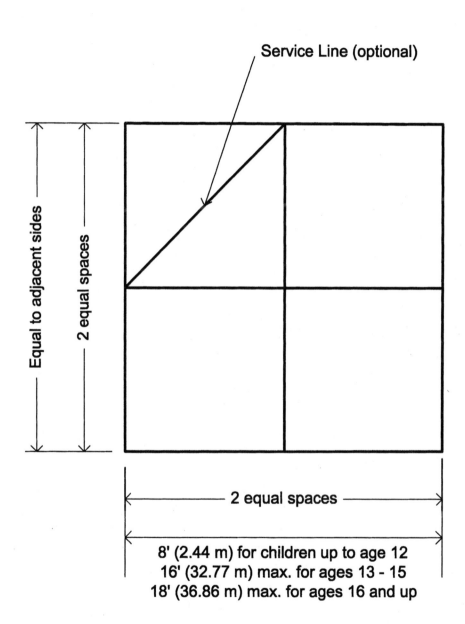

Service Line (optional)

Equal to adjacent sides

2 equal spaces

2 equal spaces

8' (2.44 m) for children up to age 12
16' (32.77 m) max. for ages 13 - 15
18' (36.86 m) max. for ages 16 and up

Handball and Racquetball—Four Wall

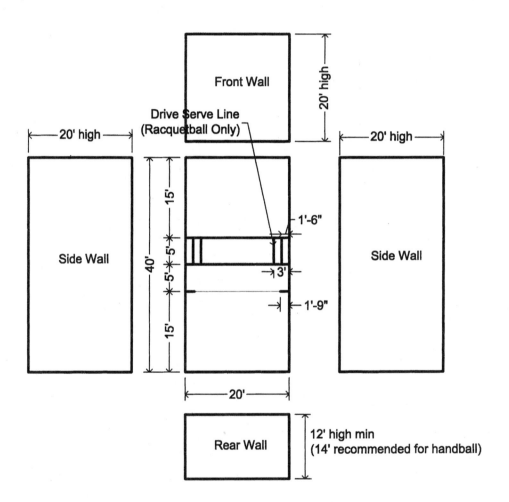

Hockey

See Field Hockey.

Hopscotch

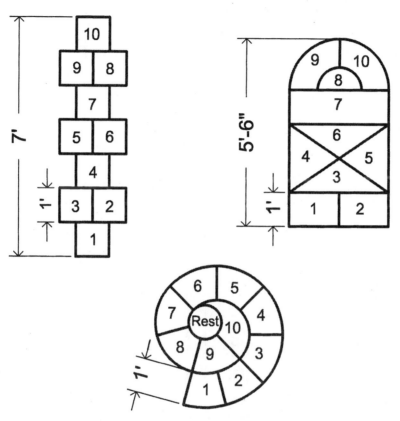

Countless variations of theme and configurations are possible. Two variations are shown below.

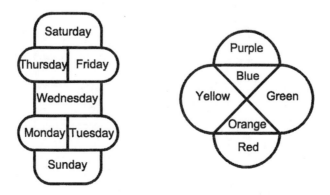

Horseshoes

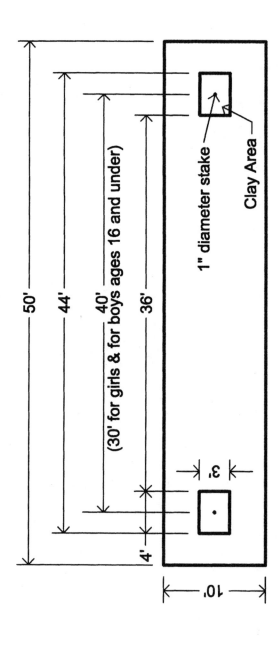

Lacrosse

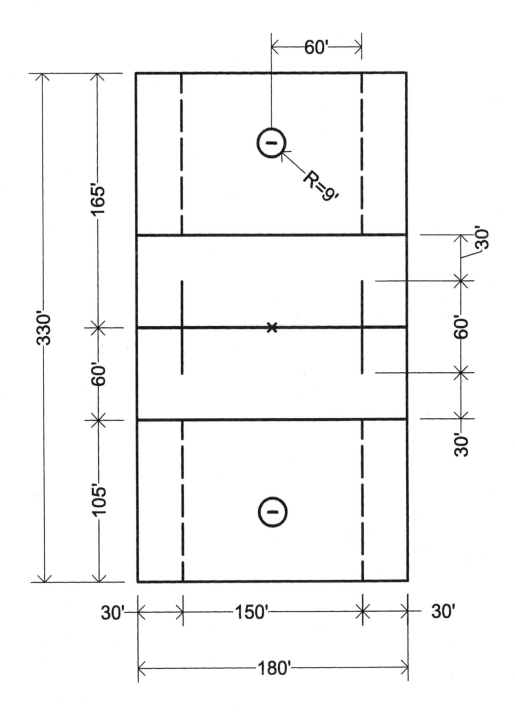

Lawn Croquet

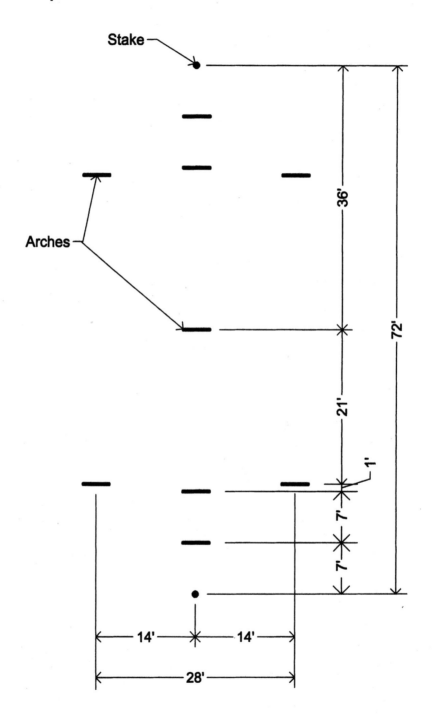

Ping-Pong

See Tennis, Table.

Pool

See Billiards.

Racquetball

See Handball.

Shuffleboard

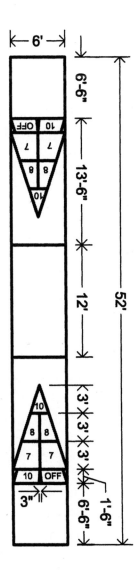

Soccer

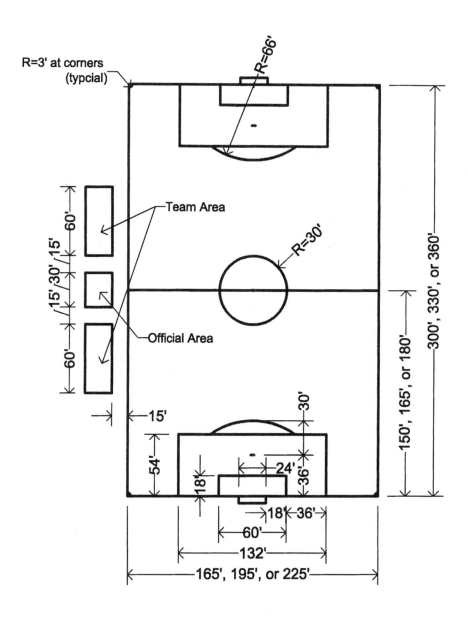

Soccer, Indoor

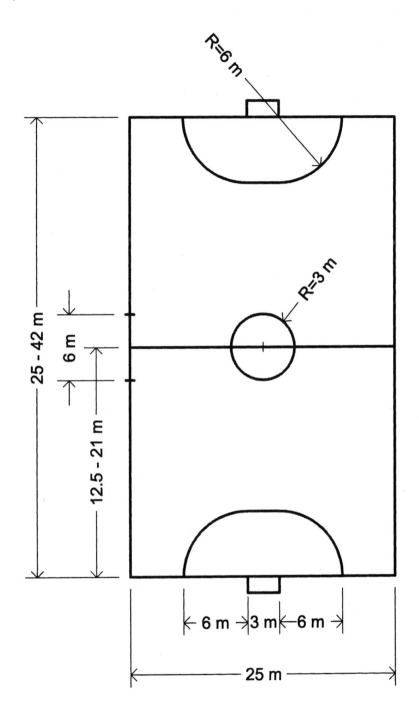

Softball

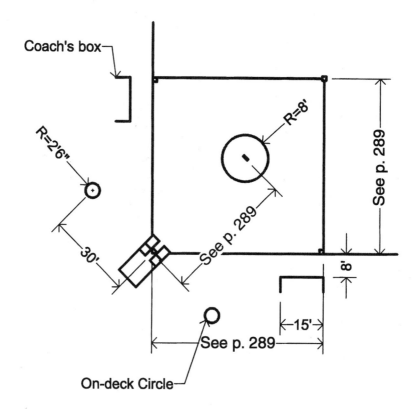

Coach's box

R=8'

R=2'6"

See p. 289

See p. 289

30'

See p. 289

8'

15'

On-deck Circle

Pitching Distances

Fast Pitch		
	Distance Between Bases	**Pitching Distance**
Girls		
Ages 10 and under	55 ft	35 ft
Ages 12 and under	60 ft	35 ft
Ages 18 and under	60 ft	40 ft
Boys		
Ages 10 and under	55 ft	35 ft
Ages 12 and under	60 ft	40 ft
Ages 18 and under	60 ft	46 ft
Slow Pitch		
Girls		
Ages 10 and under	55 ft	35 ft
Ages 12 and under	60 ft	40 ft
Ages 14 and under	65 ft	46 ft
Ages 18 and under	65 ft	50 ft
Boys		
Ages 10 and under	55 ft	35 ft
Ages 12 and under	60 ft	40 ft
Ages 14 and under	65 ft	46 ft
Ages 18 and under	65 ft	50 ft

Tennis

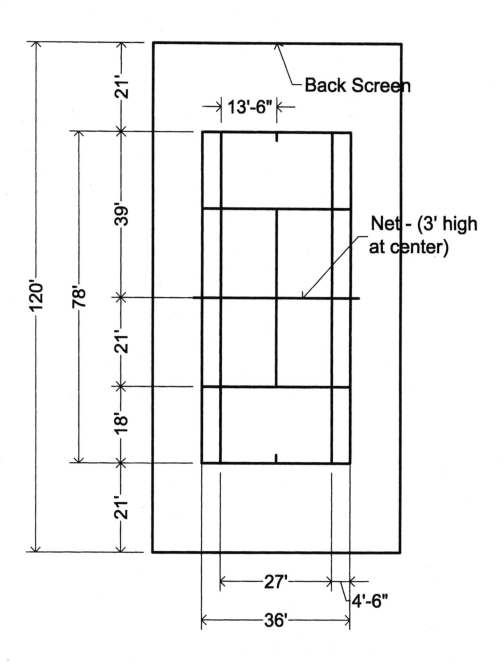

Tennis, Paddle

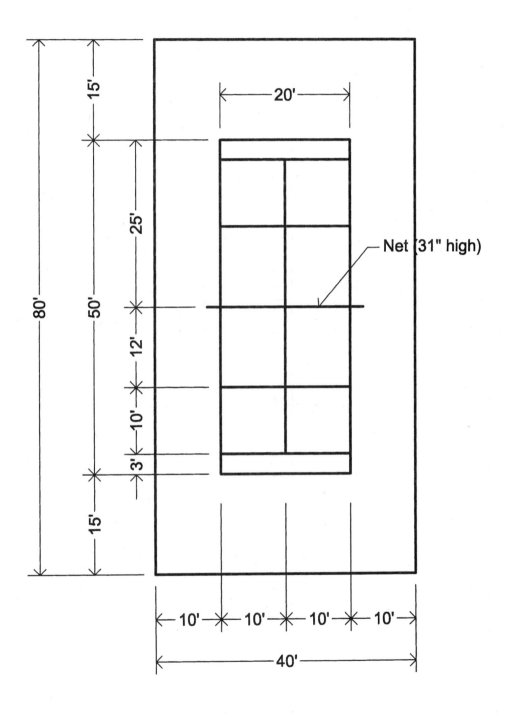

Net (31" high)

Tennis, Platform

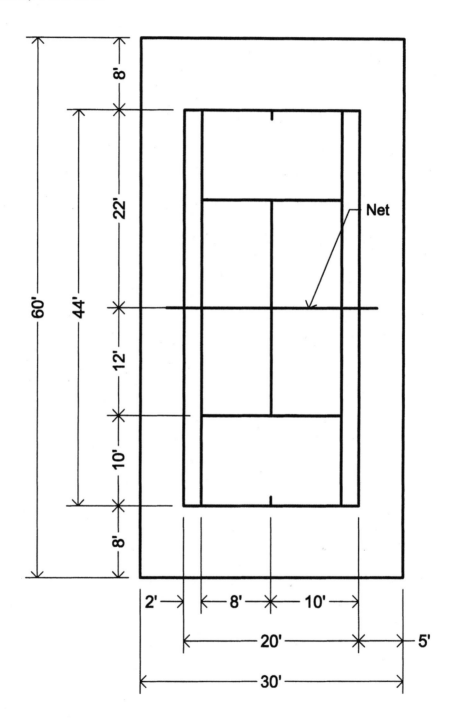

Tennis, Table (Ping-Pong)

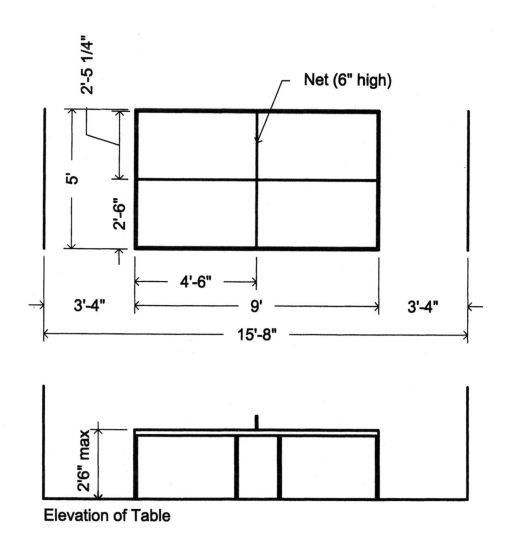

Net (6" high)

2'-5 1/4"

5'

2'-6"

4'-6"

3'-4"

9'

3'-4"

15'-8"

2'6" max

Elevation of Table

Track

The dimensions given are to the measuring line of the inside lane of a regulation track. Allowances should be made for the desired width of the track. Regulation lane width is 1.067 m (42 in). The distance of one lap is approximately ¼ mile (.249 mile), making four laps equal to approximately 1 mile (.996 mile).

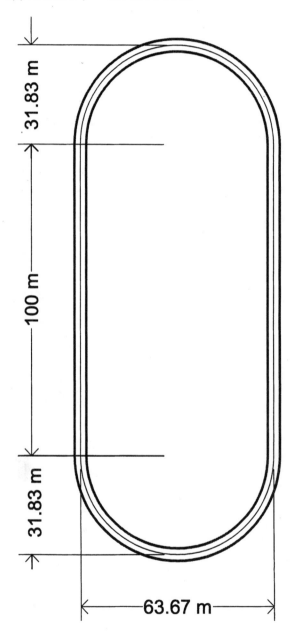

Volleyball

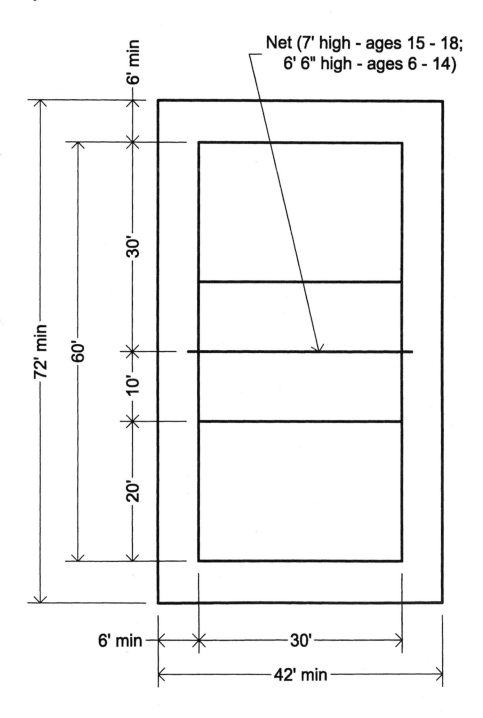

Net (7' high - ages 15 - 18;
6' 6" high - ages 6 - 14)

6' min

72' min

60'

30'

10'

20'

6' min

30'

42' min

Index

Linda Cain Ruth, AIA, is an architect specializing in the design of children's environments. The author of several articles on the subject for periodicals, she was inspired to compile this book by her own difficulties in obtaining practical design information for children's environments. In addition to her architectural degree from the University of Tennessee, Linda holds a master's in child development from Auburn University. She lives in Auburn, Alabama, with her husband, DK, and her two sons.